Unbuilt Victoria

UNBUILT VICTORIA

Dorothy Mindenhall

DUNDURN
TORONTO

Copyright © Dorothy Mindenhall, 2012

All rights reserved. No part of this publication may be reproduced, stored in a retrieval system, or transmitted in any form or by any means, electronic, mechanical, photocopying, recording, or otherwise (except for brief passages for purposes of review) without the prior permission of Dundurn Press. Permission to photocopy should be requested from Access Copyright.

Editor: Jennifer McKnight
Design: Jesse Hooper
Printer: Friesens

Library and Archives Canada Cataloguing in Publication

Mindenhall, Dorothy
    Unbuilt Victoria / Dorothy Mindenhall.

Includes bibliographical references and index.
Issued also in electronic formats.
ISBN 978-1-4597-0174-8

    1. Victoria (B.C.)--History. 2. Victoria (B.C.)--Buildings, structures, etc.--History. 3. City planning--British Columbia--Victoria--History. I. Title.

FC3846.3.M56 2012   971.1'28   C2012-900081-7

1 2 3 4 5   16 15 14 13 12

We acknowledge the support of the **Canada Council for the Arts** and the **Ontario Arts Council** for our publishing program. We also acknowledge the financial support of the **Government of Canada** through the **Canada Book Fund** and **Livres Canada Books**, and the **Government of Ontario** through the **Ontario Book Publishing Tax Credit** and the **Ontario Media Development Corporation**.

Care has been taken to trace the ownership of copyright material used in this book. The author and the publisher welcome any information enabling them to rectify any references or credits in subsequent editions.

J. Kirk Howard, President

www.dundurn.com

Dundurn	Gazelle Book Services Limited	Dundurn
3 Church Street, Suite 500	White Cross Mills	2250 Military Road
Toronto, Ontario, Canada	High Town, Lancaster, England	Tonawanda, NY
M5E 1M2	LA1 4XS	U.S.A. 14150

Contents

Acknowledgements 9

Introduction 11

Government

Chapter 1 City Hall 15

Chapter 2 Centennial Square 24

Chapter 3 Cathedral Hill 30

Chapter 4 Legislative Precinct 34

Chapter 5 Convention Centres 40

Chapter 6 City Beautification 51

Leisure, Learning, and Culture

Chapter 7 Beacon Hill Park 61

Chapter 8 The Gorge Waterway 67

Chapter 9	Universities	73
	The University of Victoria	73
	Royal Roads University	81
Chapter 10	The Art Gallery of Greater Victoria	83
Chapter 11	Theatres	94
	The Globe Theatre and the Bankside Elizabethan Village	94
	The City Lights Theatre	97

Harbours

Chapter 12	Victoria Harbour	101
Chapter 13	Wharf Street Waterfront	113
Chapter 14	Old Songhees Reserve	124
Chapter 15	Belleville Street Waterfront	132
Chapter 16	Oak Bay and Sidney Harbours	142

Transportation Schemes

Chapter 17	CPR Terminal	149
Chapter 18	Freeways	152
Chapter 19	Gordon Head Memorial Air Park	158
Chapter 20	Gorge Inland Waterway	161

Religious Institutions

Chapter 21	St. Ann's Academy	167
Chapter 22	Christ Church Cathedral	176
Chapter 23	The Ukrainian Church of St. Nicholas the Wonderworker	186

Commercial and Residential Projects

Chapter 24	Tourist Attractions	195
Chapter 25	Shopping Centres	200
Chapter 26	Hotels	205
Chapter 27	Business Buildings	209
	Mozart House	209
	Old Imperial Oil Station: *Le Club Balisage*	214
	The Pagoda Restaurant	215
	The Mystery Building	216

Afterword	219
Sources	221
Index	235

Acknowledgements

My first debt of gratitude must go to Carey Pallister. It was the exhibition "Adventurous Architecture and Daring Designs," which she mounted in the corridor of City Hall, that gave me the confidence to take on this project. Since getting me started, Carey has been a constant source of encouragement, inspiration, and help. I could not have done it without her.

Many have been generous with their research material, images, knowledge, and advice. My grateful thanks go to John Adams, Jessamine K. Barron, John Bryant, Conrad Boyce, Ronald Greene, Michael Layland, Donald Luxton, Dennis Minaker, Janis Ringuette, Les Spearing, and Greg Windwick. Architects too have been generous with their time and particularly with images of un-realized designs: Jim Aalders, Philip Chang, James KM Cheng, Franc D'Ambrosio, Chris Gower, David Hambleton, Norman Hotson, Bill Lipsey, Alan Lowe, Paul Merrick, John Neilson, CJ Rupp, Alexander Teliszewsky, Bing Thom, Terry Williams, and the family and former colleagues of John Wade. For their diligence in finding suitable images, I thank Elmerayta Baterina, Megan Culham, Weison Ha, Melissa Sanderson, and Ly Tang.

A number of people have kindly given me their time, and hospitality, to tell me about failed projects with which they were involved. Father Brian, Mary Kelty, and Alexander Teliszewsky spent many hours with me at the rectory, where the coffee pot was always on, talking about the dream of building the Ukrainian Catholic Church of St. Nicholas the Wonderworker. Patricia Bovey, former director of the Art Gallery of Greater Victoria, had many stories to tell, and Bruce Day, Jon Tupper, and Janyce Ronson at the gallery, as well as John and Jane (Gehring) Neilson, who had spent so much time in preparing the gallery program, were unstinting with their time. David and Mary Barlow were founts of knowledge about the saga of Christ Church Cathedral; Sister Frieda Raab and other members of the congregation of the Sisters of St. Ann were similarly generous; as were Richard Faulks, and Simon and Mariev Wade.

Much time has been spent lurking in archives where, as ever, the archivists have gone out of their way to track down requested material, and, in some cases, have offered suggestions based on their knowledge of the holdings: Trevor Livelton, Sarah Rahtjen, and Valda Stefani at the City of Victoria Archives; Caroline Duncan, Sonia Nicholson, Kathleen Trayner, and Evelyn Wolfe at Saanich Archives; Kelly-Ann Turkington, and Caroline Webber at the British Columbia Archives; Jacquie Nevins at the Anglican Diocese of British Columbia Archives; Jean Sparks at the Oak Bay Archives; Lara Wilson and Martin Segger at the University of Victoria Archives and Special Collections; Helen Gillespie at the Library and Archives Canada; and Brad Morrison at the Sidney Museum and Archives. In the private archive of the Victoria Conference Centre, Drew Waveryn and Jocelyn Jenkyns allowed me free run of the boxes. And the staff of the Legislative Library were ever helpful.

City planner Steve Barber, former downtown coordinator Elizabeth Low, and Councillor Pamela Madoff were generous with their time and information about the city's various schemes. And I am grateful to Calvin Woelke of the Land Title and Survey Authority of British Columbia; Dave Obee of the *Times Colonist*; Linda Fraser of the Canadian Architectural Archives; Jonathan Makepeace, Assistant Curator, Photographs Collection at the Royal Institute of British Architects; and Grant Keddie of the Royal BC Museum.

Images from the *Daily Colonist* (*Colonist*), and the *Victoria Daily Times* (*Times*) are published with kind permission of the *Times Colonist*.

Introduction

To build, or not to build? What circumstances and conditions influence the decisions of individuals and organizations? A number of factors — politics, public opinion, personal rivalries, legal opinions, the history of the place, and, of course, economics — play a role in the decision to build or leave the plans on the drawing board. The schemes that stayed on the drawing board are the subject of this book, and whether the decisions are a cause for regret or jubilation is for the reader to decide.

Until the end of the nineteenth century Victoria was a proud, confident, self-satisfied city. For over fifty years it had been the most important city in British North America west of the Rockies. First as a trading post of the Hudson's Bay Company, then colonial capital, and finally as capital of the province of British Columbia; it was the centre of trade and commerce, and the entrepôt for the entire North West, second only to San Francisco. Despite its shaky boom-and-bust economy, progress was the watchword; to be sure, some projected buildings were not built, and several transport schemes remained unrealized, but, in general there was a laissez-faire attitude where people built whatever they wanted.

As the nineteenth century drew to a close, the city's status began to fade as the new City of Vancouver — site of the terminus of the transcontinental railway — prospered and grew, gradually assuming the supremacy that once was Victoria's. Already recognized as a place of great scenic beauty, excellent fishing and hunting, a balmy climate, and healthy fresh air, promoting tourism seemed to be the answer to the city's economic woes. And so it was that tourism became the city's most important source of income, a statistic that held true until 2007. But reliance on one industry did not make the city rich, and when, in the 1960s, much of the rest of North America was razing old buildings to make space for new ones, Victoria, in general, just spruced up the old.

For those who cared about the built environment, this was cause for some rejoicing. The old Victorian and Edwardian buildings may have been dirty and dilapidated, but they were still standing. In 1968, noted architectural historian Alan Gowans, at the University of Victoria, instigated an inventory of the city's heritage buildings, the Hallmark Heritage Society was formed in 1973, and the city established the Victoria Heritage Foundation in 1983. Preservation of the city's built environment and, by extension, the entirety of its physical environment, is the guiding principle both for the city government and a good proportion of its citizens.

Predominantly, these two themes — tourism and preservation — have been both the motivation for the proposal, and reason for rejection of the building and transportation schemes discussed here.

GOVERNMENT

Chapter 1

CITY HALL

VICTORIA WAS INCORPORATED IN AUGUST 1862 and the early meetings of the council were held in the police barracks, located in a building that stood on the site of what is now the Maritime Museum, in Bastion Square. This arrangement did not suit the mayor, partly because the name "police barracks" was a euphemism; the building was in fact the town jail, in which the barracks happened to be situated. The following January, meetings were moved to rented rooms on Broad Street at Trounce Alley. Over the years there were rumblings about the shabby impermanence of this arrangement. Matters came to a head when Councillor Gosnell moved that they advertise for "designs for a hall," saying that "it was high time they were out of the rickety old shed they had to meet in now." Two weeks later the council advertised to architects and builders for designs for a city hall and city market. The city fathers, many of them merchants, did not really want a market attached to the hall; they wanted shoppers to patronize their Yates Street stores, rather than the local farmers who would set up stalls in the market. But they had to sugar-coat the pill: the citizens were adamantly opposed to the expense of a city hall, but they did want a public market.

The winner of the competition was John Teague with a Second Empire design that was published in the *Canadian Illustrated News* (Montreal) and was described by the *Colonist* as an "elaborate, expensive and altogether in-advance-of-the-times structure" (Fig. 1-1). The councillors may have thought that one of the merits of this plan was the almost-concealed location of the unwanted market facilities. These were confined to the basement along with workshops, tool rooms, and the police cells — the proximity of which would have made a visit a somewhat unpleasant experience. To avoid asking the citizens to vote on the expenditure, which the council was confident would fail, they decided to build in stages, using revenue from taxes and licences to pay for construction. By the time council was ready to start on the first phase, the south wing, the market hall had been reduced to "sheds suitable for a market." By the time the building was completed in 1891, there was no market component at all. A result of the step-by-step approach to the building program meant that the winning design was significantly compromised. But the *Colonist*, which all along had championed the wishes of the citizens in opposing the building, did concede that it was a "handsome structure well adapted to the requirements of city business."

Having got a new city hall, albeit not the one they had chosen, the councillors failed to maintain it, and by 1907 the signs of this lack of care were evident. On one occasion a cornice in the council chamber fell, taking with it a large piece of plaster. City inspector Northcott reported that the problem was water damage from the leaky roof — although some aldermen speculated that "Ald. Hanna's reverberating eloquence had something to do with the trouble," and the mayor believed it was "the general debility of the city hall" and an indication that it was time for improvements. The following year city hall, with its wood-burning stoves and narrow "crooked" staircases, was described as "the most dangerous building in case of panic of any kind in the city of Victoria," and there were calls for something to be done about this "indefensible" state of affairs. The *Colonist* was not specific about what should be done to this "fire trap," but when new mayor Alfred J. Morley took office in 1910, he had plans for a new civic centre and city hall.

Morley unveiled his ambitious scheme in October: he wanted to purchase two blocks of land on either side of Yates Street between Blanshard and Quadra Streets to make a civic centre bounded by Johnson, Blanshard, View, and Quadra Streets. This new civic centre would be, Morley hoped, large enough for imposing buildings and landscaping, which would provide for the "future growth and importance of Victoria ... and add materially to her architectural beauty." The new city hall would be in the centre of Yates Street in the middle of this double block, and Morley hoped that the provincial government would contribute to the scheme by erecting government buildings such as law courts and the land registry. He had even gone so far as to have local architect J.C.M. Keith — waiting for his designs for Christ Church Cathedral to be started — draw up a plan showing the general idea of the building. Morley had even devised an alternative plan in case the city could not afford to buy both blocks. The plan was that the city would buy one block on which the new city hall would be built, and then hope to persuade the provincial government to buy the other, then the two levels of government could be linked by a colonnade across Yates Street to make a "magnificent governmental centre."

The scheme was not rejected outright. After a lengthy discussion, during which councillors asked about alternative locations, the possibility of renovating the present hall, and the cost, it was decided that further consideration was needed. Eventually the plan was shelved until the ratepayers showed some interest, which they seem not to have done.

Over the next few years there were sporadic discussions about a civic centre scheme including city hall, the last one occurring in late 1913 before the matter was shelved for some three decades. This time two sites were under consideration: the Pandora Avenue gore, the triangle of land between Cook and Chambers Streets, now known as Harris Green Park; and the existing hall with the market building (1891, demolished), that stood on what is now Centennial Square. This scheme, again one

Fig. 1-1. John Teague's winning design, 1875. Engraved by Eugene Haberer from a photograph by Noah Shakespeare. [Courtesy Royal BC Museum, BC Archives, PDP01778, archive's stamp removed from the original.]

of Mayor Morley's, would have built a new civic centre on the site of the market hall, city hall would have been demolished, and land to the west of city hall would be purchased to create open space all along the north side of Pandora Avenue from Broad to Douglas Streets, providing an attractive setting for the new civic structure. But the financial commitment of such an extensive plan — it also included road widening and modifications to the Johnson Street Bridge — gave the councillors pause, and they decided not to make a decision but leave it to the next council.

Economic depression and two world wars intervened, and it was not until 1946 that the subject of a new city hall again came before the council. Mayor Percy George said that "the crowded conditions of the present antiquated city hall is inimical to general well-being and efficiency of city hall staff and very trying and tiring to members of the public." So the building went up for sale "as is." Within a matter of days there was an offer of $176,000 from unnamed local interests, reputedly Woodward's department store, which proposed to demolish the hall and build a modern department store. In comparison to the proceedings earlier in the century things moved speedily. If city hall was to be sold, then the councillors would have to find some land on which to build a new one. Numerous sites for the replacement hall were considered, including: land behind the Memorial Arena, which had the advantage of being owned by the city; the old cathedral site on the north side of Burdett Avenue between Blanshard and Quadra Streets, in a block known as Cathedral Hill; and the market hall.

All but one of the councillors was in favour of the scheme to sell the hall and build a new one, the lone voice belonging to B.J. Gadsen, who thought it "foolish" and "our least important project." To justify the plan the councillors wanted to know the cost of the alternative — what would it take to bring the old hall up to an acceptable condition? City inspector J.W. Oosterink expressed the opinion that "early and serious attention" should be given to repairs, as brickwork on the north side was crumbling and the plaster was loose in a number of places. This prompted the mayor to wonder whether it was worth spending any money at all on an obsolete building. The mayor also wanted the committee examining the options to consider the "the utilitarian, aesthetic and economic potentialities of the building," bearing in mind its age and location.

Selecting a site for a new hall was a key and thorny issue, not least because the prospect of sharing a hall with the municipality of Saanich seems to have been a distinct possibility, and until it was decided whether to buy land or build on land that the city already owned, there was no possibility of determining the cost. A drawing of the proposed new hall shows a rather pedestrian building, harking back to styles of the 1930s, and not set in an urban environment. There is no indication

Fig. 1-2. A speculative design for new city hall. Published in the *Colonist*, June 10, 1947.

of the designer's name or location (Fig. 1-2). As always, money was at the heart of the issue, and the ratepayers decided that it was not the right time to spend on a new city hall, even though they were offered assurances that the proceeds of the sale of the old one would be sufficient to fund the new building, and then they could look forward to a substantial boost to the city's coffers when the new department store began to pay taxes. So, with the sale off, there remained the problem of funding repairs to the hall, which Oosterink estimated would be $50,000.

Rejection of the plan was not based on any attachment to the old building, just the finances, so the councillors had no qualms about entertaining another plan that would involve its demolition, but this time one with fewer financial risks. The new plan was to lease the land on which the hall stood — plus some land to the west that the city would buy to increase the area of leased land — to a company that would build a $3 million hotel. While plans for the hotel were being prepared in Vancouver, the search for a site for the new city hall was on again. Discussions and negotiations dragged on for a year, until, in July 1948, this plan, too, was dead. It seems that the company backed out of the deal when it found it would not be allowed to use American materials.

And there the matter rested for another year, but when staff found themselves working in offices with water streaming down the walls and having to negotiate bucket-strewn floors to the constant accompaniment of "drip, drip, drip," yet another committee was formed to discuss

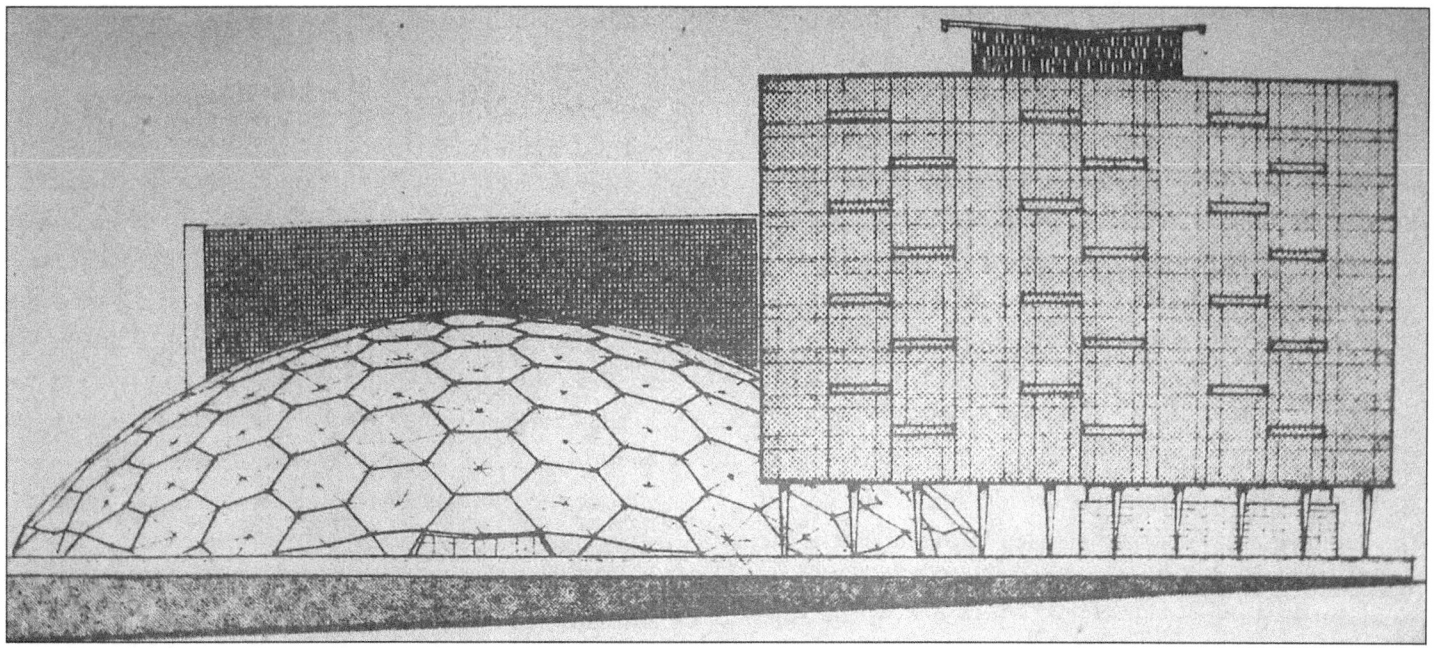

Fig. 1-3. Proposed design for a new city hall and auditorium on Cathedral Hill, drawn by city planner Rod Clack. Published in the *Colonist*, April 25, 1959.

whether to repair the old or a build new one. Eventually it was decided to modernize city hall.

In 1957 the provincial Capital Region Planning Board was proposing to build a new courthouse and land registry in Victoria, and suggested that these could be part of a civic precinct that could include a new city hall and other buildings for the city. But the city would have to pay its way. Mayor Percy Scurrah was enthusiastic about the idea, saying that the "replacement of city hall in the near future is a necessity in view of the obsolescence of the present building, and the growing need for more room." While the province proceeded with its building plans, the mayor instructed city planner, architect Roderick Clack, to prepare a plan for a civic auditorium and a new city hall on the Cathedral Hill site (Fig. 1-3).

Clack's plan recommended an auditorium in the shape of a geodesic dome with a diameter of sixty metres and seating for 3,000, at a cost of $1.75 million, and a second dome for use as a meeting hall, diameter thirty metres, seating 600, at a cost of $220,000. The new city hall, with a price-tag of $1.8 million, would have city offices on the lower floors, a council chamber at the top, and the offices in between could be used for such purposes as the Victoria School Board, then housed in Craigdarroch Castle, and for income-generating rent. The design put the building on stilts above a pedestrian plaza that would link the entire site. Provincial planners were impressed with the striking design and agreed to modify their plans for the site to produce complementary buildings. The mayor hoped that neighbouring municipalities would share the cost of the auditorium, as it would be used by everybody in the region. Their representatives, however, did not view the project with the same enthusiasm, and wanted more definite facts before making any commitment. Premier W.A.C. Bennett was enthusiastic and agreed that the provincial government would put up one third of the cost if the federal government would do the same, leaving the municipalities of Greater Victoria to come up with the rest of the funds. Cap in hand, the mayor went to Ottawa and came back empty handed. The premier advised him to "go back to Ottawa, ask again and refuse to take 'no' for an answer."

And then Marwell Construction Company of Vancouver offered the city what it considered a sweet deal: it would buy city hall for $135,000, demolish it, and build an "eight-storey, high-quality reinforced concrete building." The building, designed by R.W. Siddall, was to have shops and city departments that needed public access on the ground floor and office space above, and the council chamber would be in the penthouse "with magnificent views of the city" (Fig. 1-4). The company proposed that the city lease the entire building "at a very low rental rate, about $165,000," and then sublet space not required for city uses. Taking into consideration such items as the income from the sublet units and interest on the price paid for the property, the annual cost to the city would be "less than $30,000 a year." Hugh Martin, president of Marwell, outlined the many benefits of his scheme. For example: the city could charge its tenants more than the lease cost; the general improvements in the physical properties, and therefore in tax revenue, that could be expected in the area once such a prestigious building was in place; and the security of knowing that in the "inconceivable" event that Marwell defaulted on its mortgage, the city would become the owner — and assume the mortgage. Martin considered it a "very, very safe gamble."

While the city fathers were mulling over this deal, another developer entered the ring. Dominion Construction had already prepared a plan for city hall on the civic centre site, proposed in 1957, just west of the cathedral on Cathedral Hill, and now it revived this scheme. The company's 1959 proposal, which had been turned down by the city, was for an eight-storey, $1.8 million building, which it offered to the city on a lease-to-purchase basis for thirty years, with right to buy after seventeen years at portion of original cost. Dominion Construction vice president, G. Bentall, alarmed at what he considered an undignified marriage of commerce and civic government, decided to repeat his company's offer after hearing of the special committee that was considering the Marwell proposal.

In its editorial of October 15, 1960, the *Times* articulated the city's quandary concerning these two offers. On one hand, the Marwell scheme had architectural plans and detailed budgets; on the other hand, the Dominion scheme had no specific details and it was not clear where the building would be sited, as it had originally been designed for Cathedral Hill. On the face of it, the Marwell plan had a number of benefits: it would give the capital "a modern office and professional building of substantial attraction that would help to rehabilitate a section of the downtown area," and it had the advantage of offering protection by providing for a "release of the city from its tenancy commitments," which, the *Times* speculated, might be needed in the not too distant future. Such a need might arise if a city hall for Greater Victoria became a requirement as a result of amalgamation. The editorial was, however, not unreservedly in favour of the Marwell plan: it would force the city to be a landlord and place it in competition with private leasing firms. The *Times* wondered if this might place it in an invidious position, as these firms "pay taxes to the city," and no city with "a capital's pride" should consider sharing an office building indefinitely. It counselled "no hasty decision" and encouraged Victorians to wait for the right development.

The *Colonist* warned that the city should be wary about the financial arrangements proposed by Marwell, and suggested that the city should think twice about taking on another organization's mortgage, which it would have been required to do had the company defaulted. It advised that the Dominion plan should be given full consideration. As ever, the *Colonist*, which had, since even before the hall was erected, not been in favour of the building, had some arch remarks to make about the credit position of the city if it needed to rely on private investors for a necessary public building.

As 1960 drew to a close, the city fathers had a lot to think about, not least of which was how the city should celebrate its centennial, which was only a year away. Many councillors felt confident that they would

Fig. 1-4. Design for an office building and city hall for Marwell Construction Company by architect R. W. Siddall. Published in the *Colonist*, October 14, 1960.

Fig. 1-5. A Sid Barron cartoon satirizing the city's planning process. [Published in *2nd Annual Barron's Victoria*, with permission of the estate of Sid Barron.]

celebrate this event in a new city hall, or with the prospect of moving into a one soon. In December they adopted the advisory committee's recommendation to work with the province on the development of Cathedral Hill as a civic precinct that would house city hall and an auditorium. The province had already built the law courts on the block, and had originally proposed that it become a civic centre in 1957. Now the proposal was revived with the "council's blessing."

None of these dreams came to anything, and cartoonist Sid Barron took the opportunity to lampoon the city's endless planning (Fig. 1-5). In 1960 Victoria "resembled a port city of 1912 sealed in glass." But things were about to change. In the booming and prosperous 1960s, city planners and politicians all across North America were motivated by progress and modernization. Victoria was not immune, but not fully committed. The city's attitude was tempered, if somewhat gradually, by an understanding that the collection of Victorian and Edwardian buildings in the old town was a rarity, as well as a tourist attraction — and tourism was the city's economic engine.

The installation of a new mayor in 1962, the year of the city's one hundredth anniversary, was a seminal event in the city's progress. Prosperous businessman Richard Biggerstaff Wilson was a third generation Victorian; his grandfather, William, had arrived in the colony in 1862, and, with his brother Joseph, opened W&J Wilson — still in business on Government Street. All three generations were successful in business and active in politics at both the civic and provincial levels. Imbued with a strong sense of pride in his community and an understanding that public service was expected of a man in his position, Wilson also had boundless energy and enthusiasm. It was he who spearheaded the preservation and revitalization of the old town with the retention of the old city hall and creation of a vibrant and modern urban space — Centennial Square — and he instigated a "paint-up" program to smarten up the dull business buildings. It was on his watch that the "Overall Plan for Victoria (1965)" was devised, and although some aspects of this — for example the freeways and the shopping mall on the Market Square site — were not built, this plan "established the terms and language of the debate which would carry forward some 30 years."

Chapter 2
CENTENNIAL SQUARE

RICHARD BIGGERSTAFF WILSON WAS elected mayor in late 1962, the eve of the centennial of the city's incorporation. A man of drive, enthusiasm, and commitment to his native city, he spearheaded the revitalization of the old town, as well as the creation of the University of Victoria. Probably his most ambitious scheme was the creation of Centennial Square out of the western end of Cormorant Street. City planner Roderick Clack prepared the award-winning design and the work of demolition and reconstruction began with uncommon speed. Opened with due ceremony, the square was initially a popular place for young and old alike, but the hippies found it particularly inviting (love-ins were popular), and they were frequently seen, and heard, strumming and singing around the fountain — an activity the city attempted to stop by the application of pebble-laden stucco to the scooped coronet-like surround.

One senior provincial politician railed at the "lazy long haired louts," and city alderman Robert Baird branded them as "anti-social, anti-Christian, free-sex advocates." It may have been the presence of the hippies that made Centennial Square far less popular than the revitalized Bastion Square, but it did have a certain bleakness, enclosed by the rear walls of the McPherson Theatre, the old police station (until the CRD office building was completed), and the door-less side wall of City Hall. Even the row of shops under the parkade was shrouded under the heavy masonry canopy. By the mid-1990s the square was barely used at all, the annual folkfest drawing more visitors than at any other time of the year, and the city began to consider how to bring "some excitement and vitality to the square and make it more of a people place."

A design competition for the entire block was in preparation, and negotiations were underway with the Capital Region District (CRD) for the sale of the old police station for its new office building, which the city hoped would include retail outlets facing into the square on its ground floor. A staggering eighty-nine respondents submitted entries, and Roger Hughes Architects of Vancouver was the winner. In announcing the winning entry, Mayor Alan Lowe explained that the project would be implemented in three phases: the first being the CRD headquarters that would be bolted onto the facade of the old police station; the second phase would be changes to the McPherson Theatre and the square itself; and the third would see a new mixed-use building on the north side, and the completion of the square including the relocation of the fountain. The editor of the *Times Colonist* wondered where the mayor was going to get the money.

With the new building on the north side, Hughes's design turned the square "inside out" (Fig. 2-1). Although there was no decision on its exact use, suggested uses were the public library, with a reading plaza at street level; the art gallery; a hotel; residences; and at ground level a public arcade fronting retail shops (Fig. 2-2). All these new facilities would be accessed from within the square, giving people a reason to go into it rather than around it (Fig. 2-3). Plans for changes to the square itself reversed the present arrangement by paving the area at the eastern end, alongside Douglas Street, making it continuous with the sidewalk and an invitation to go into the square. Under this would be parking, for which the pedestrian entrance was directly onto the grassy area that would replace the present paved area within the square (Fig. 2-4). From the raised plaza, a waterfall flowing into a reflecting pool at the eastern end of the grassy area would both deaden the noise of Douglas Street and create a calming ambiance in the much more intimate square. Removal of the McPherson restaurant would open up the area and help to alleviate the claustrophobia of massed brick walls. A radical change was the removal of the fountain to the new street-level plaza, where it would be housed in a rectangular pool and not the current circular arrangement.

Of this grand scheme only the new CRD building has been built, although the shops and public arcade at its ground level were not included, and the McPherson Theatre restaurant has been demolished. It was very knowing of the *Colonist* editor to question the funding for such an ambitious project, as it soon became apparent that a revenue-generating building would be needed to pay for all the proposed changes. The city wasted no time in proposing such a building at the square's north-west corner, and models of options — nine storeys, thirteen, and even sixteen — were shown to the public at city hall. The comment boxes were overflowing. The taller the building the more vehement the objection, the consensus being that tall buildings did not belong in the old town, and certainly not in such close proximity to Chinatown, a national historic district. For many, the words of Prince Charles, "a giant carbuncle," seemed entirely appropriate. But city manager Don Roughley noted that the city's design panel thought there should be a "signature building" at the north-west corner — whether for economic or aesthetic reason seems open to question.

Council accepted that anything over nine storeys was unacceptable, and although some councillors were strongly opposed, it was decided that a proposal document for potential developers should be prepared. Then the city decided it had other uses for the development budget, and no more was heard of high-rises at the corner of Government and Fisgard Streets.

Second place in the competition to re-design Centennial Square was awarded to de Hoog D'Ambrosio Rowe with a much less formal arrangement of the

Fig. 2-1. A model of the award-winning entry for the re-design of Centennial Square, viewed from Douglas Street. [Hughes Condon Marler Architects (formerly Roger Hughes Architects).]

Fig. 2-2. A model of the proposed building on the north side of the new square. This was to house the art gallery and the library. [Hughes Condon Marler Architects (formerly Roger Hughes Architects).]

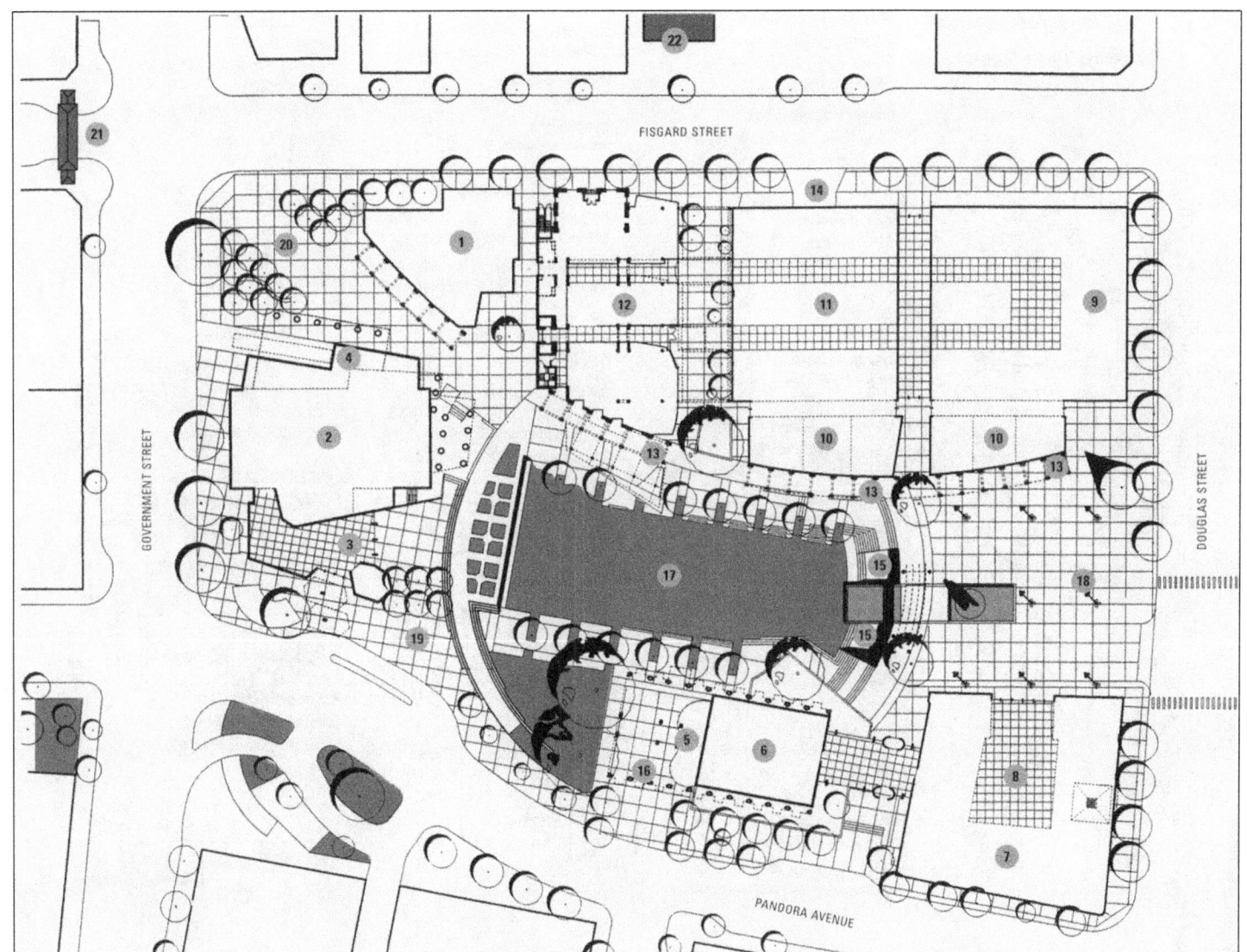

Fig. 2-3. A plan of the proposed new square. [Hughes Condon Marler Architects (formerly Roger Hughes Architects).]

Fig. 2-4. A rendering showing the lively public arcade. [Hughes Condon Marler Architects (formerly Roger Hughes Architects).]

square itself that was almost fully grassed and had angled pathways to add interest. The fountain is gone, as is the McPherson restaurant, adding to the openness and accessibility, and each of the surrounding streets has a crosswalk enhancing connections to the square, which this firm considered an important aspect of its proposal (Fig. 2-5).

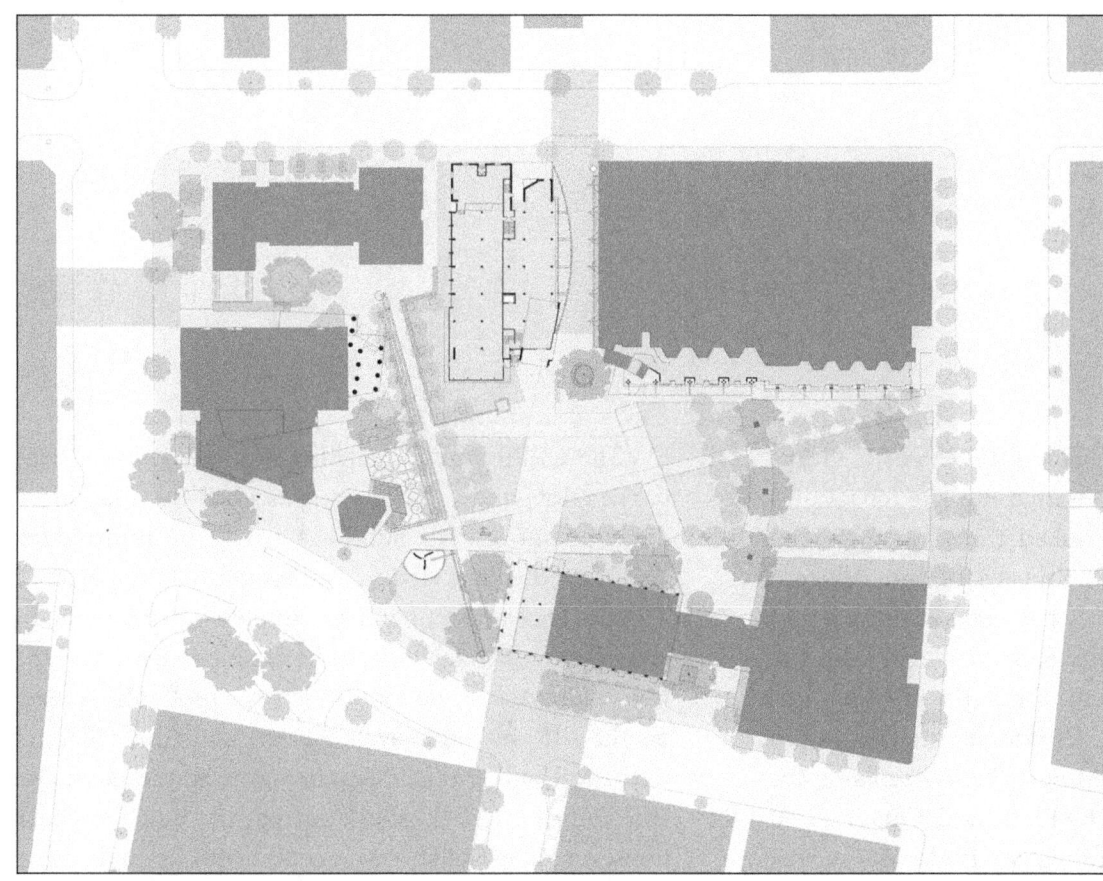

Fig. 2-5. A plan from the competition entry of de Hoog D'Ambrosio Rowe, architects, honourable mention. [de Hoog D'Ambrosio Rowe, architects.]

Chapter 3

CATHEDRAL HILL

WHEN, IN 1957, THE PROVINCIAL GOVernment was looking for a site for its new courthouse, it tasked the Capital Region Planning Board (CRPB) to find a site and devise a scheme. Knowing that the city had been wanting a new city hall since the end of the Second World War, the board proposed a joint scheme for all the public buildings of the Capital Region. Of course, the city would have to pay for its own buildings. The chosen site was the block of land bounded by Blanshard, Quadra, and Burdett Streets, and extending north almost to Fort Street, and on it was to be a new civic centre for both levels of government. The board had grand plans for this large, nearly three hectare site, and couched its report in equally grand prose suggesting that Victoria should follow "the great capitals of the world" in creating a civic centre with imaginative design and an appropriate site.

The CRPB argued that this site, then covered with parking lots and old houses, was ideal for a landmark development, as tall buildings would be immediately visible on the city's skyline and establish its importance. The site was large enough for ample landscaping and a civic square, it was close to the business district, and it was readily accessible for all the city's residents. Already on the site was the Royal Theatre, and Christ Church Cathedral and Pioneer Square were at the edge. The addition of city hall, the land registry, and the courthouse would establish a civic centre with a grandeur that could not be duplicated if these facilities were scattered throughout the city. And no other site could be obtained at a lower cost (Fig. 3-1).

On the highest part of the site, Christ Church Cathedral would close the vista from Blanshard Street, Courtney Street was to be closed, and the civic buildings sited so as to frame the cathedral. Most of Broughton

Fig. 3-1. Model of the proposed site. 1) Royal Theatre, 2) City Hall, 3) Pioneer Square, 4) suggested site for the museum, 5) courthouse, 6) land registry office, 7) cathedral. Published in the *Times*, October 29, 1957.

Fig. 3-2. A speculative architectural scheme for Cathedral Hill. View looking west from the cathedral. [CVA, CD 9.]

Fig. 3-3. A speculative architectural scheme for Cathedral Hill. View looking east from Broughton and Blanshard Streets. [CVA, CD 9.]

Street was to be closed as well, allowing services like the parking lot to be relatively obscured at the edge of the site. The civic square would be spacious enough for pageants and large gatherings, and the suggested plan for the arrangement of the buildings allowed ample space for movement throughout the complex. Although some speculative architectural designs were prepared, the CRPB recognized that the fine details would require more study (Figs. 3-2, 3-3).

The plan and report met with general approval from both the city and the province, but there were grumblings that the site was too central for a city hall of amalgamated municipalities, should that ever happen — then, as now, a contentious issue. The Minister of Public Works, A. N. Chant, struck a gloomy note with his comment that "Ottawa's tight money policy puts a crimp in a lot of things." The province found funding for its land registry and courthouse, but the city could not afford its hall. It tried again in 1959 with plans to build a new city hall and auditorium on the site, but these did not get funded either (see Fig. 1-3).

Chapter 4

LEGISLATIVE PRECINCT

WHEN THE PARLIAMENT BUILDINGS were opened in February 1898, it was to great acclaim. The correspondent in the *Victoria Daily Times* went so far as to consider them "the finest provincial parliament buildings in Canada, and second only to the federal buildings in Ottawa." Inevitably, there were grumblings about the cost, which had exceeded the budget by 50 percent. The architect, Francis Mawson Rattenbury, was a twenty-five-year-old Englishman who had arrived in British Columbia only a few months before the announcement of the competition to design the Provincial Government Buildings. Although few drawings of the sixty-five entries survive, it is intriguing to see what might have graced the southern border of the Inner Harbour.

The design of local architect Thomas Sorby, placed second in the competition (Fig. 4-1), is reminiscent of the style of the customs house on Wharf Street, built in 1873 to plans by the chief architect in Ottawa, Thomas Seaton Scott, who promoted the Second Empire architectural style for federal buildings. By the early 1890s, the federal architectural style was high Victorian eclecticism, introduced by the new chief architect, Thomas Fuller. Another unsuccessful design by a local architect, Edward Mallandaine, Jr., bears a strong resemblance to the British houses of parliament (Fig. 4-2). The entry by Dick & Wickson of Toronto (Fig. 4-3) is a truly eclectic tour-de-force, more whimsical than imposing.

Eighteen years after Rattenbury's ensemble had been completed, the library and new east and west wings were added, although Rattenbury's plans for the new library to be located on the south side of the building were not accepted (Fig. 4-4). Having become so enamoured of the Chateau style, which he was using for his CPR hotels, he tried to graft this onto the free classic Romanesque of the parliament buildings, with

Fig. 4-1. The competition entry of Thomas Sorby. Published in *The Canadian Architect and Builder*, Volume 6, Issue 6 (1893), plates 3a and 3b. [Blackader-Lauterman Library of Architecture and Art, McGill University.]

Fig. 4-2. The competition entry of Edward Mallandaine. Published in *British Columbia Pictorial Biographical*, Volume II (1914), p. 765. [Courtesy of Royal BC Museum, BC Archives, CM/14991B.]

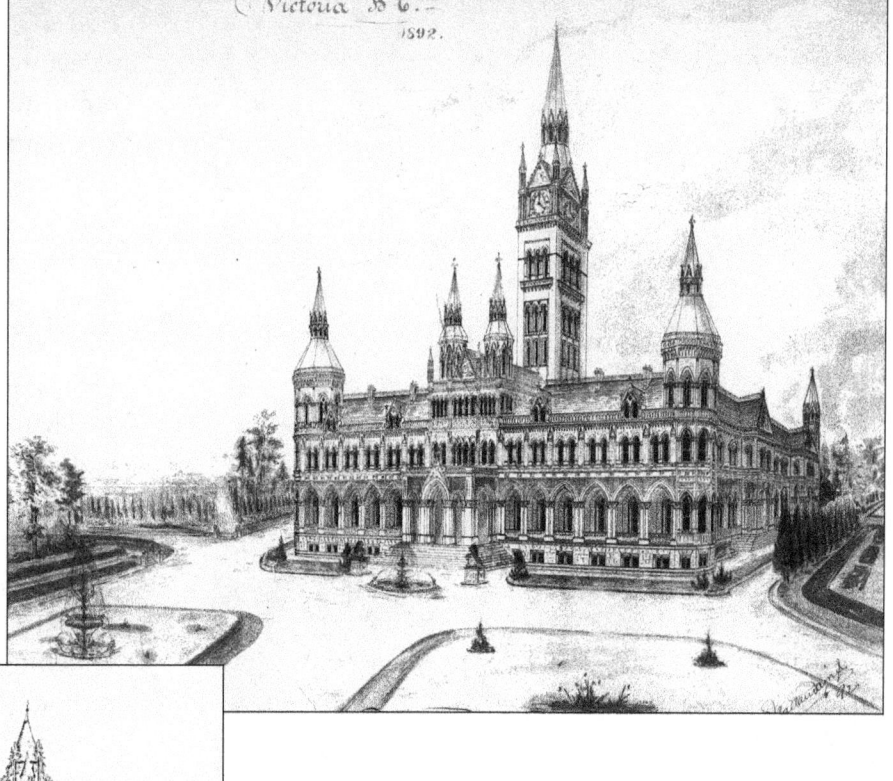

Fig. 4-3. The competition entry of Dick & Wickson, Toronto. Published in *The Canadian Architect and Builder*, Volume 6, Issue 7 (1893), plates 2a and 2b. [Blackader-Lauterman Library of Architecture and Art, McGill University.]

unacceptable results. After this major work, little was done for over fifty years, by which time the buildings were in desperately in need of repair — the lower parts rotting and the roof leaking — and the Department of Public Works undertook a major renovation.

The department also prepared a report recommending that the setting of the parliament buildings could be improved by extending the green space of Beacon Hill Park through the grounds of St. Ann's Academy, along Belleville Street (which would be closed from Blanshard to Douglas Streets), to end on the lawns of the parliament buildings. To make this greensward continuous, Blanshard Street would be elevated from Humboldt Street to Academy Close. At the rear of the building, the south entrance would be re-established, and a public square — "Legislative Square" — created in front of it. Another public square — "Douglas Square" — would be created at the junction of Douglas and Humboldt Streets, and Douglas Street would be closed south of that square. These recommendations were not followed, but the concept of a Legislative Precinct began to gain currency.

Concerns that space in the legislative chamber, which could not be enlarged, would soon be inadequate for the anticipated increase in the number of members, prompted the preparation of another report — the Legislative Precinct Design Concept and Development Plan. As well as suggesting a solution for the space problems, this report specifically outlined the blocks that were to be considered for the Legislative Precinct: Belleville, Blanshard, Michigan, and Menzies Streets. The report proposed that a new chamber be built at the south-west corner of Menzies and Superior Streets, and a new legislative library on the south-east (Fig. 4-5). Outlining a four-year program, the report also called for the demolition of the armouries on Menzies Street; the construction of government offices, with underground parking, on the entire block south of Superior Street between Menzies and Government Streets; the extension of Michigan Street through the north-west corner of Beacon Hill Park; and the relocation of good heritage homes — and demolition of the rest — within the precinct. Little of this report was acted upon, apart from the creation of some surface parking lots.

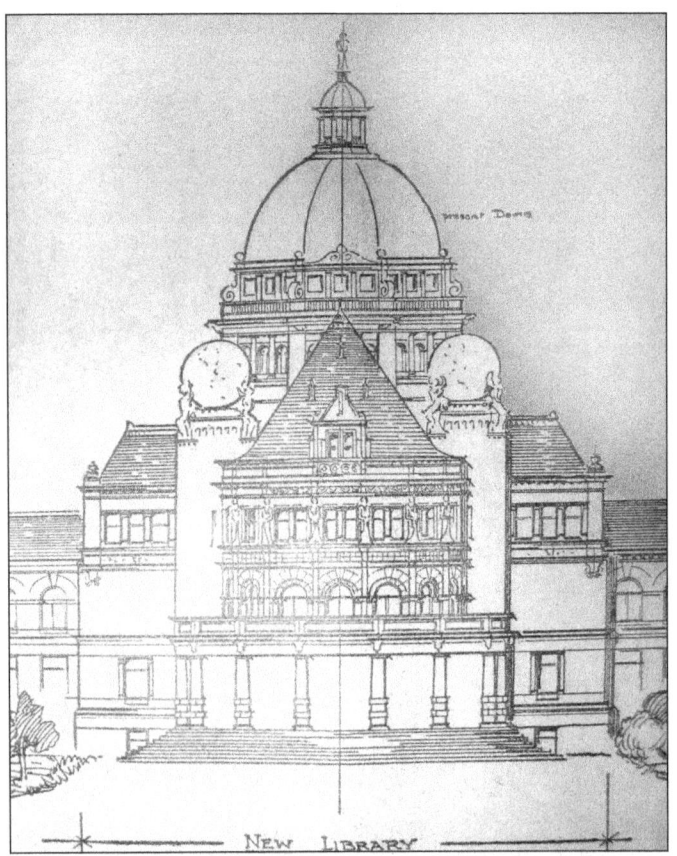

Fig. 4-4. Proposed library addition, with château-style roof, by architect Francis Rattenbury. Published in the *Colonist*, April 2, 1911.

LEGISLATIVE PRECINCT [37]

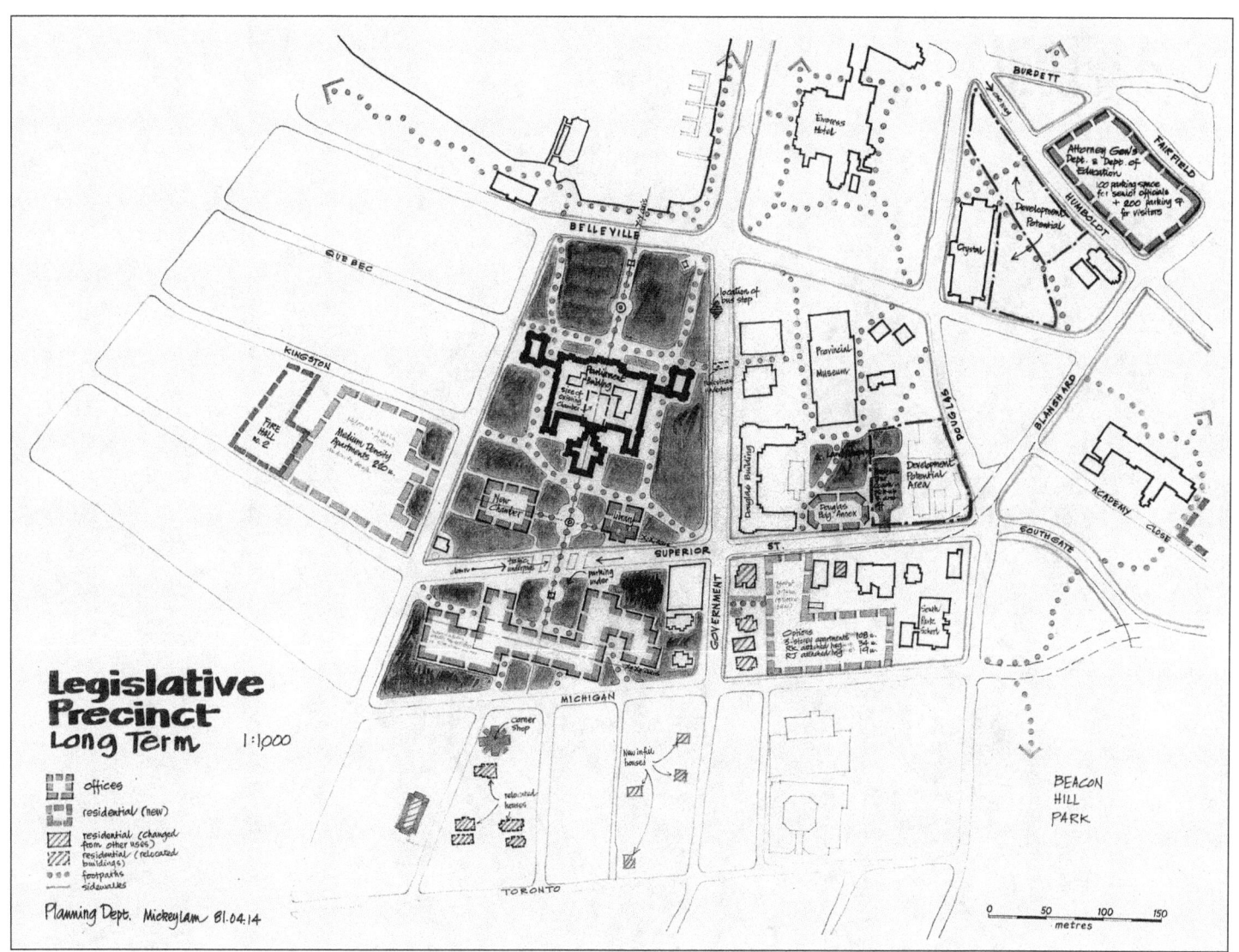

Fig. 4-5. Long-term plans for the Legislative Precinct, 1981, showing the proposed new chamber and legislative library. Note the proposed extension of Michigan Street cutting off the north-east corner of Beacon Hill Park. ["Legislative Precinct Design Concept and Development Plan" City of Victoria, July 1981. CVA, CD 73.]

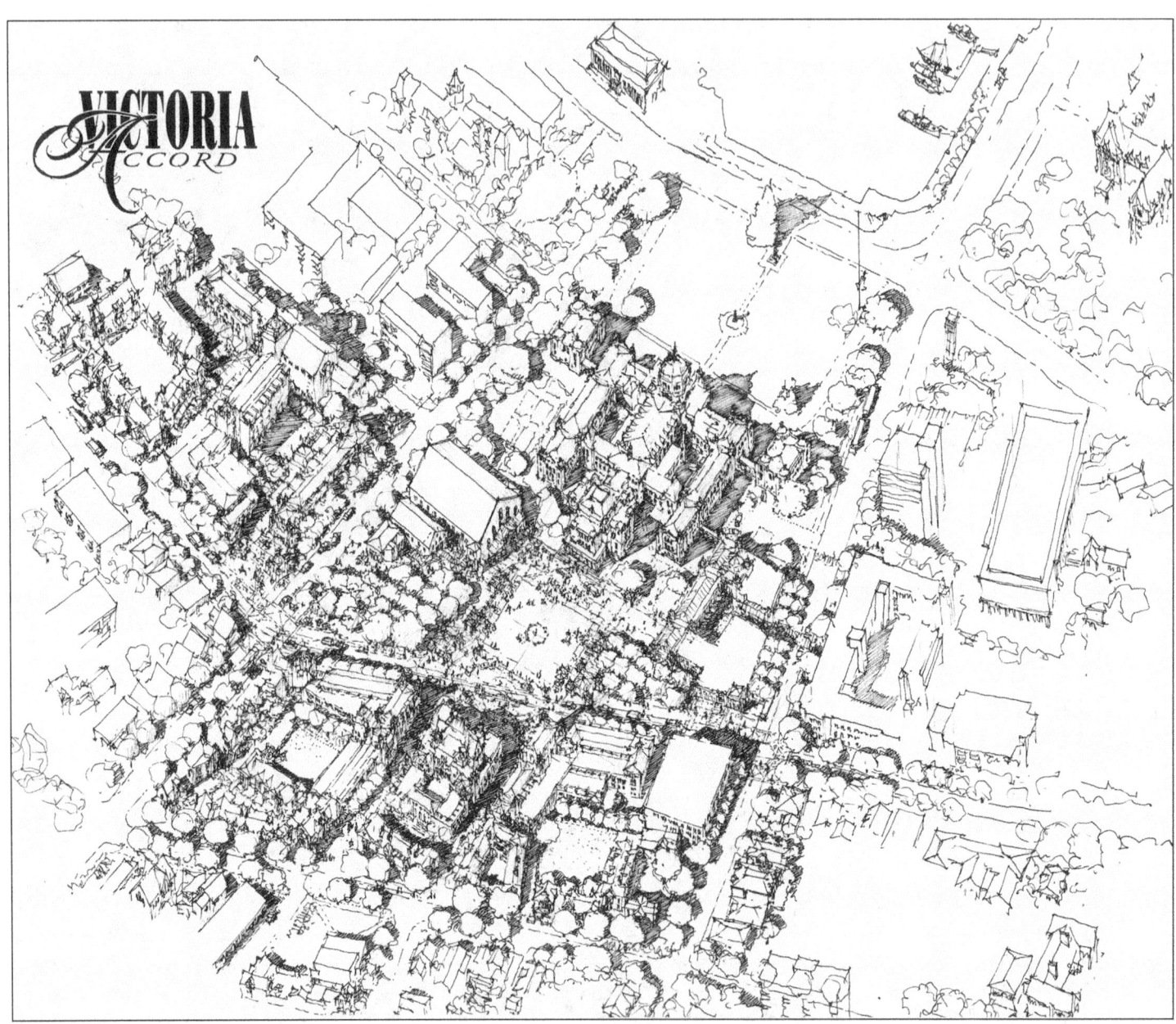

Fig. 4-6. Ground plan of the proposed Legislative Precinct. The CPR steamship terminal is at centre top, and the block bounded by Michigan, Menzies, Government, and Superior Streets is filled with new government buildings, as is the east side of Menzies Street. [Paul Merrick Architects.]

In the summer of 1993, Victoria mayor David Turner and provincial premier Mike Harcourt devised a program, which they called the Victoria Accord. It was to provide for cooperation between the city — as both a city in its own right and the city as the capital of the province — and the province by planning and funding improvement projects of mutual benefit. The Legislative Precinct was one such project, and a comprehensive two-volume planning and design document was prepared by Paul Merrick Architects. It was a massive scheme covering nearly nine hectares over some three blocks of land and including offices, retail stores, restaurants, underground parking, affordable housing, and the relocation of some heritage homes (Fig. 4-6). Over the planned ten-year implementation, the south block — bounded by Government, Superior, Menzies, and Michigan Streets — would have three buildings containing offices and some residential units, and various ensembles of relocated heritage buildings. The Q lot — bounded by Superior, Menzies, and Kingston Streets — would have four buildings containing offices, shops, and a townhouse complex with childcare facilities (Fig. 4-7). Both areas were to have landscaped walks and courtyards.

According to one James Bay neighbourhood resident, there was a "real sense of fear" in the community: the buildings were too large, the prospect of traffic chaos resulting from the increased number of employees commuting in to the offices was alarming, and equally alarming was the prediction that the building work might well take thirty years to complete, instead of the ten that the design document suggested. They need not have worried. A little over a year later, Mayor Alan Lowe admitted that the Victoria Accord was dead, although provincial politicians insisted that it was still alive, but they did not have any money — at the moment. They did, however, find the cash for a multi-billion-dollar light rail link for Vancouver. Once again, Vancouver got the railway!

The only element of the Victoria Accord plan for the Legislative Precinct that was implemented was the townhouse complex at the western end of the Q lot and a bus shelter on Government Street.

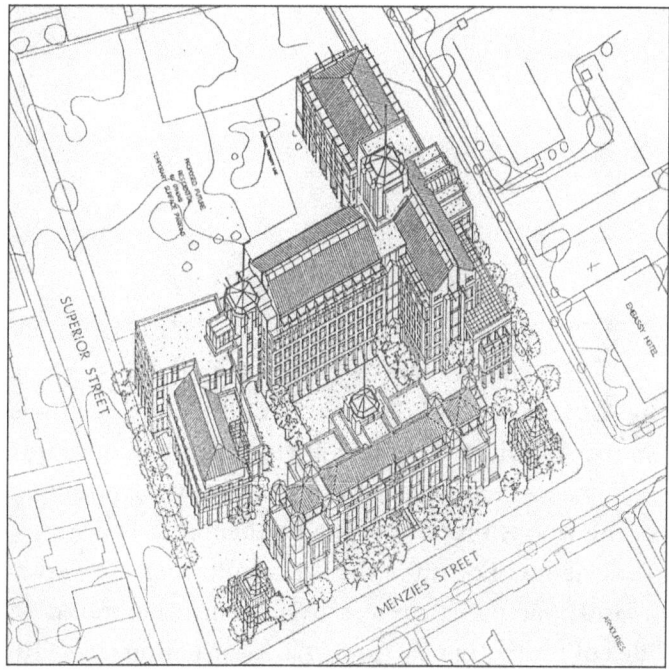

Fig. 4-7. An axonometric projection of the proposed Menzies Building on the west side of Menzies Street between Superior and Kingston Streets. [Paul Merrick Architects.]

Chapter 5

Convention Centres

The opening of the Victoria Conference Centre in 1989 marked the culmination of over thirty years of fine words and false starts. Although the possibility of having a convention hall had been mooted as early as 1909 by the promoters of the wooden replica of the Parthenon in Beacon Hill Park, it was not until the years following the Second World War that the city's businessmen embraced the idea of promoting Victoria as a "Convention City." This enthusiasm may have had something to do with the statistic, cited in 1956, that convention delegates usually spent three times more than other visitors.

Initially there seems to have been no initiative to provide purpose-built facilities. Conventions were held in halls like the Memorial Arena and the Esquimalt Sports Hall, or at the University. In the economic good times of the 1960s, the popularity of business conventions boomed and, in 1966, Mayor Alfred Toone struck a committee to investigate the city's options of a site for a convention centre. The Convention Centre Report, presented in 1967, contained and analyzed five potential locations: a site adjacent to the Memorial Arena; the blocks west of Centennial Square, bounded by Fisgard, Wharf, Government, Johnson Streets; the Crystal Garden site, with and without the land to its north, fronting onto Humboldt Street; and the Ocean Cement site to the west of Wharf Street between Fort Street and the Visitor Centre. Each proposal was accompanied by a list of pros and cons, plans, and some sketches of architectural suggestions. There was no overall recommendation, although the *Colonist* did report that the Crystal Garden site was "highly recommended."

At the same time as the city was mulling over its options, one private developer was coming up with plans of its own. A convention centre, hotel, offices, and retail complex was proposed for the block bounded by Douglas,

Cormorant, and Blanshard Streets and Pandora Avenue (Fig. 5-1). The smaller tower, at the Douglas Street end, was to be offices, and the larger, at the Blanshard end, a hotel with revolving restaurant at the top, and in between was the convention centre, with a roof garden and underground parking for two hundred cars.

By April 1968 the city had whittled it down to two contenders: the Crystal Garden with the Empress Hotel and the Wharf Street scheme, the latter having the advantage as a major urban renewal scheme, for the site was under consideration and funding might be available. Although, as the city had recently voted to the pull down the Crystal Garden and build a swimming pool in a more residential part of town, that site, too, had its merits. Particularly important to the city was the financial benefit of "plugging in" to the hotel's facilities, such as catering, and thus saving the cost of incorporating these facilities in any new building.

Getting wind that the city was considering its site, the CPR, always looking for ways of generating revenue from its land, made a pre-emptive strike and hired the architectural firm of B. G. Marr and Associates of Vancouver to design a scheme. Delighted that the CPR was offering such an apparently sweet deal, the city councillors acted with alarming, and uncharacteristic, haste. In just one day the plan was approved in principle by the city's convention committee, the committee of the whole, and the full council. This speedy acceptance of the CPR's plans concerned Alderman Ian Stewart, who proposed during the morning session that the convention committee take another look at the terms — a move that was accepted. Unfortunately for Alderman Stewart's concerns, he was

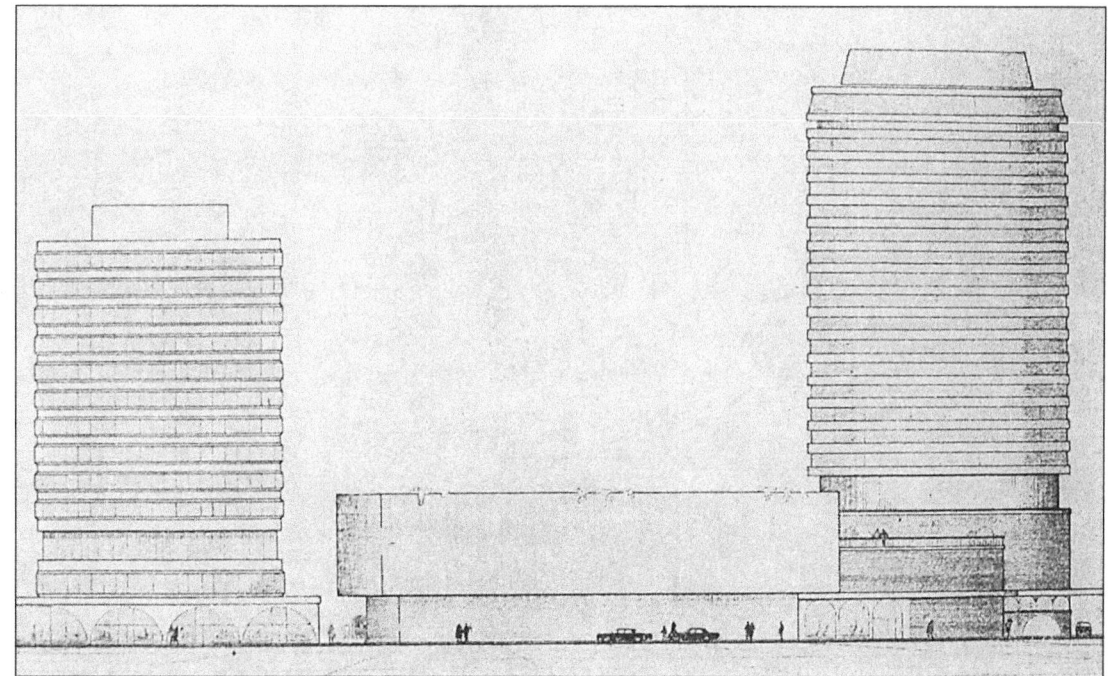

Fig. 5-1. A proposal for the block bounded by Pandora, Douglas, Cormorant, and Blanshard Streets. Published in the *Times*, July 28, 1967.

unable to attend the afternoon session, and his proposal was deleted. Keen to get on with the project, the councillors feared that a more detailed examination of the terms might delay the project for a year.

The proposal called for the CPR to lease the parking lot at the rear of the Empress — where the conference centre stands now — to the city for a period of thirty years, for $1 per annum, and on this the city would

Fig. 5-2. Three proposed tower blocks on the east side of Douglas Street, replacing the Crystal Garden. [Victoria Conference Centre Collection.]

build the convention centre and parking facilities at a cost of $2.5 million. Of course, tax concessions would be required, as they had been when the hotel was first built. In tandem with the arrangements for the convention centre, the CPR wanted to develop a complex of three fourteen-storey apartment blocks, with shops at street level, all along the east side of Douglas Street from Belleville to Humboldt Streets (Fig. 5-2). A second part of the council's approval-in-principle was approval of the sale of the Crystal Garden, paving the way for its demolition, and redevelopment by the CPR.

Municipal elections were looming in November, and the council was treading very warily. Unwilling to go to the electorate for approval of the $2.5 million expenditure, city officials were devising a financial plan based partly on using the money from the sale of the Garden. At the same time there was a concerted effort to persuade the citizens that the convention centre would be a tremendous benefit for the community, and money to build it would be money well-spent. High-school graduation ceremonies, dances, symphony concerts, banquets, and bingo could all be held there. Jack Morgan, head of the advisory committee, went so far as to suggest that the new centre would be just as much use to "local interests" as to "visiting conventioneers."

All this had a hollow ring for *Times* columnist Jim Hume, who drew the attention of his readers to a vote from December 1923, when citizens enthusiastically endorsed the Amusement Centre Bylaw, enabling the construction of the Crystal Garden as a convention centre. Then the publicity claimed that it would be "a great factor in making Victoria the leading convention centre and make a big addition to Victoria's payroll." But Hume suggested that what the people were really voting for was "dancing floors bigger than the Empress ballroom, carnivals, spectacles, grand concerts and all at popular prices." Now, forty-five years later, the "pushers" of the convention centre were using the same tactics — promoting the community benefit — in an attempt to persuade the citizens that a convention centre was a good thing for them. But while forty-five years earlier the citizens had been given the opportunity to vote for the Garden's construction, then, "if the city father's [could] manage it," there was no intention of asking the people for an opinion as to whether it should be demolished.

As election day drew nearer, a local realtor, Eric Charman, threw his hat into the ring, seeking "a heavy vote 'to demonstrate in no uncertain terms to the mayor and council what taxpayers think of this $2 million giveaway to the CPR.'" Mayor Stephen and two aldermen, all three up for re-election, decided that, although previously unwilling to back a plebiscite, they now thought it was a good idea.

In the early months of 1969, the CPR issued a press release extolling the virtues of its scheme and the great benefits that Victoria could expect. A model was unveiled at City Hall, Mayor Hugh Stephen and the CPR's architect, Bing Marr, were photographed inspecting it, and a perspective was published in the *Colonist* (Fig. 5-3). But, as the year progressed, public enthusiasm for funding a convention centre waned. In June, *Colonist* columnist Pat Murphy wondered if the plan was "dead as a dodo," as a growing number of Victorians were coming to realize that the city was prepared to spend public money to build a facility that would be of limited benefit to them but of considerable benefit to the CPR. After nearly six months of indecision, a frustrated CPR announced that it was looking for alternative uses for the land behind its hotel.

There was, however, no shortage of private developers wanting to build convention centres that wouldn't cost the taxpayer a penny, but all they needed was just a few concessions on the part of the city. A company called Imaginaction unveiled new plans for the block to the west of City Hall. Managing director N.J.R. McKinnon explained that this plan was for something similar to Place Ville Marie in Montreal, with two or three towers for offices, a hotel, apartments, a bank on each corner, and specialty shops lining the streets, and, of course, parking for at least six or seven hundred vehicles. He stressed that the company did not want public money or tax incentives — all that would be needed from the city was cooperation in re-zoning the land. A year later McKinnon announced that the project was dead; increasing interest rates had jeopardized the financing.

A few months after Imaginaction's initial announcement, yet another private proposal was being floated — in more ways than one. Morris Greene, president of Capital Iron and Metals Ltd., and Harold Elworthy,

Fig. 5-3. A perspective of the proposed convention hall attached to the Empress Hotel. Published in the *Colonist*, August 23, 1968.

president of Island Tug and Barge, had purchased the SS *Canora*, the double-decker CNR ferry that had been used to bring freight cars to the island. They proposed to moor the vessel somewhere in the Inner Harbour and place two barges on each side; the two on the landward side would be the reception area, and the other two the kitchen facilities. The cavernous cargo decks, much like the car decks of today's BC Ferries's vessels, would be used for meeting rooms, boutiques, and other facilities, and the bar in the engine room, with its huge triple-expansion steam engine, would have reinforced the nautical theme, as would the application of paddle wheels to the exterior (Fig. 5-4).

Mayor Stephen supported this plan and sent it to the planners. Although he still insisted that the deal with the CPR was not dead, he admitted that "after our capital budget referendum was turned down … we must be realistic and realize that the taxpayers will turn down a convention centre." By the end of the year, the planners had rejected the floating convention centre plan anyway, citing concerns such as the unsuitability of the boat's long, narrow main room, and the lack of both a mooring proposal and plans for parking. They were also concerned that placing the vessel anywhere in the Inner Harbour would cause traffic congestion.

By now councillors had lost all appetite for funding a convention centre or even having anything to do with one. So when J.A. Mace of Mace Homes and Investment Ltd. offered to invest $400,000 in refurbishing the Bay Street Substation, at the corner of Government and Bay Streets, as a convention centre if the city would agree to a take a ten-year lease at $70,000 a year, the plan was rejected. It was called "uneconomical, unsound and unacceptable" by Alderman Harold Olafson, who was firmly of the opinion that if there was money to be made from conventions then "private capital will smell it and invest the necessary money."

Undeterred, Mace commissioned a local architect to prepare plans (Fig. 5-5) that he intended to submit to the city. The plan shows the substation flanked by two circular eighteen-storey towers, one containing a 260-room hotel and the other 130 apartments. Nearly twenty-eight thousand square metres of retail space and parking for six hundred cars would be included in the development, and the old substation would contain convention facilities for five hundred people.

By this time the city had a new mayor, Peter Pollen, who had strong views on appropriate buildings for the city, and was not afraid to make his opinions known. Comparing the next convention centre proposal to the Mad Hatter's tea party, he called it the "height of lunacy," and told those involved to "get the top off the teapot and come before city council with a decent proposal." This plan was to build a $5 million convention centre on the site of the Royal London Wax Museum on Belleville

Fig. 5-4. The proposed floating convention centre. Published in the *Times*, October 25, 1969.

Street. The complex would contain hotel rooms, an auditorium seating 2,200, an art gallery, and satellite facilities. Although the spokesman for the developer was unwilling to discuss important issues such as the investors involved and the proposed height, he was happy to announce that there would be underground parking. The building was the old CPR steamship terminal, designed by architects P.L. James and Francis Mawson Rattenbury, now on the Canadian Register of Historic Places. It has recently undergone a major seismic and structural upgrade at a cost of $3 million. Fortunately, this convention centre complex remained unbuilt, and there was a building left standing to rehabilitate.

Back in 1967, the Convention Centre Report, commissioned by the city council, had offered four site options. The front runners were the site to the west of Wharf Street and the Crystal Garden/Empress Hotel site. The protracted negotiations with the CPR had focused attention on the Empress site, but after the failure of the Reid Centre schemes on the Wharf Street waterfront, that site was back in the running. The chamber of commerce, which had always been keen for the city to have a convention centre, launched a campaign to build one on the land to the west of Wharf Street. "Victoria cannot afford to have that valuable location become just a park that people look at but never use … we are proposing a convention centre that need not be above street level" was the opinion of Alan Emery, chairman of the chamber's harbour committee.

In November 1979, Premier Bill Bennett donned a hard hat and, and armed with a jack hammer, broke the tarmac of the Reid Centre property in preparation for construction of the convention centre, which Provincial Secretary Hugh Curtis said would "definitely start next spring." With the ground breaking ceremony over, the dignitaries retired to the Crystal Ballroom at the Empress where they were invited to view the architectural drawings by Paul Merrick (Figs. 5-6, 5-7). But everyone at the event was "shy about mentioning money," and Defence Minister Allan McKinnon was "noncommittal" when the subject of federal funding for the $7 million project was broached by the premier. The province owned the land, purchased in order to kill the Reid Centre plan, and was managing the new construction through the Provincial Capital Commission. It had agreed to contribute the land and $2.5 million, the city had agreed to put in $1.5 million, but that left a $3 million shortfall. Mel Cooper of the chamber of commerce wondered about the $10 million recently promised for a Vancouver convention centre, some of which he thought was destined for Victoria, but was told that the minister of the environment in Ottawa had other ideas.

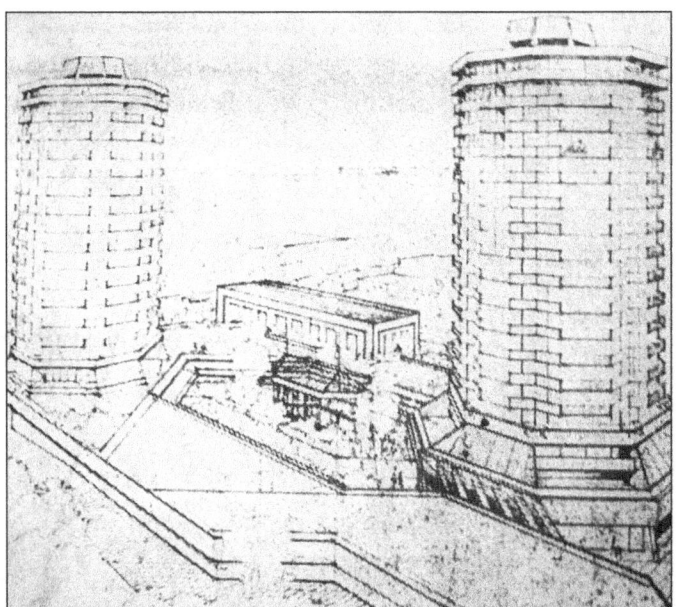

Fig. 5-5. The proposed convention centre in the Bay Street substation, with residential towers, by developer J.A. Mace. Published in the *Colonist*, October 17, 1972.

Fig. 5-6. A model of the proposed convention centre on the Reid site. [Paul Merrick Architects.]

Fig. 5-7. A rendering of the proposed convention centre on the Reid site. [Paul Merrick Architects, Bob Montgomery.]

In the end, broken ground was all the city got. There was no money from Ottawa, and in December 1981 the premier announced that the promised provincial funding was no longer available, blaming the current economic circumstances, although the rising tide of public opposition to the project may have played a role in this decision. The Victoria Waterfront Enhancement Society, formed in August 1980, was against what it saw as a private use of the waterfront, particularly as this would be funded from the public purse. Peter Pollen, who had played such an active role in killing the Reid project and was a co-founder of the society, was elected mayor in 1981, and most of the council sided with him in his antagonism to the waterfront convention centre, as did the B.C. Supreme Court, which ruled against it.

One member of Pollen's council, Frank Carson, was determined to see a convention centre in Victoria, and over the following five years he worked tirelessly to make

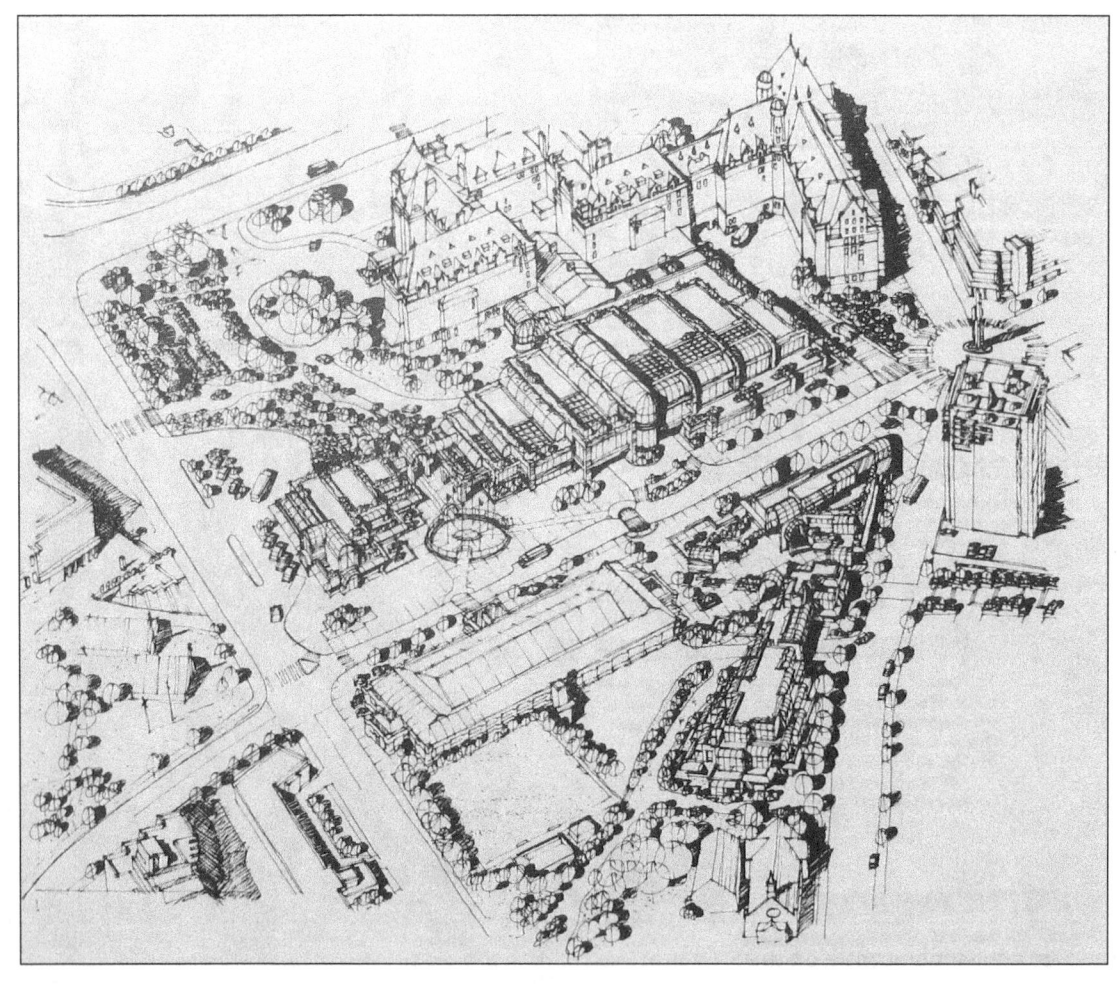

Fig. 5-8. A perspective drawing, competition entry, 1982. [Wagg & Hambleton.]

Fig. 5-9. A perspective drawing, competition entry, 1982. [Associated Architects, Bill Lipsey, Stanley Cox, Philip Chang, John Gauld.]

Fig. 5-10. A perspective drawing of the winning entry, but the curving bus station at the corner of Douglas and Belleville Streets was not done. [Bawlf Cooper Associates, Nick Bawlf.]

it happen. Hugh Curtis, a cabinet minister at the time and involved in negotiations with Carson for provincial funding, said that without Frank "we would not have the conference centre" — his "drive and perseverance" made it happen. In October 1982 the city asked Vancouver Island architects to submit "design ideas" for the Victoria Conference Centre to be built on land behind the Empress Hotel. There were twenty-two submissions. After assessing these entries, three firms were chosen to refine and develop their ideas in a formal competition. The chosen firms were Associated Architects, Wagg & Hambleton, and Bawlf Cooper Associates, with an honourable mention to John A. Neilson & Associates.

The design brief required, as well as the large conference centre building, a transit facility, an open plaza, and parking for three to four hundred vehicles. And the design had to acknowledge the significance of the surrounding buildings — the parliament buildings, the Royal British Columbia Museum, and the Crystal Garden. Wagg & Hambleton proposed a massive scheme involving the redevelopment of the east side of Douglas Street, creating a plaza running the full length from Belleville to Humboldt (Fig. 5-8). This would incorporate the Crystal Garden in a pedestrian precinct with both covered and open air markets, exhibition space, and retail and residential components for "year round vitality." At Douglas and Humboldt Streets a traffic circle with a "vertical sculptural feature" would mark the approach to the conference centre area. Douglas Street would be reduced to one lane to impede pedestrian flow as little as possible. The bus depot would be moved round to Belleville Street.

Associated Architects proposed to create a plaza to the south of the conference centre, with a covered bus station underneath. Opposite the entrance to Crystal Garden, a fountain and flame would mark the entrance to the public plaza, and a rank for horse-drawn carriages would be on the southern perimeter (Fig.5-9). After the second round of judging, Bawlf Cooper Associates was declared the winner and went on to supervise construction. Although the conference centre we see today is essentially that which this firm submitted, not all elements of their award-winning design survived the refining process, notably the planned curved bus station and the closure of Humboldt from Douglas to Penwell Streets (Fig. 5-10).

Chapter 6

CITY BEAUTIFICATION

UNLIKE MANY OTHER TOWNS AND cities in the colonies of British North America, Victoria was not planned — no military engineers laid out the town in accordance with British military order as they had in, for example, Halifax, Nova Scotia, or New Westminster, British Columbia. The southern tip of Vancouver Island was chosen in 1842 by James Douglas, a chief factor with the Hudson's Bay Company (HBC), to be the site of the company's new trading establishment. The main criteria for his choice were the existence of a safe harbour with flat land behind it for the site of the fort, fresh water, timber for building, and agricultural land. The creation of a town and provision of facilities for settlers were the last thing on James Douglas's mind.

This lack of a plan was directly linked to the sequence of events that brought the city into being. In a reversal of the customary sequence of colonization — explorers "discover" the place, missionaries and the military tame it, and then the settlers and businesses move in — in Victoria it was businessmen — traders of the HBC — that "discovered," tamed, organized, and governed.

Douglas's mission was to create the administrative centre of a trading empire that stretched from the border with the United States north to latitude 54°40' — the southern boundary of Russian territory, and from the eastern foothills of the Rockies to the Hawaiian Islands. In 1849, the colony of Vancouver's Island came into being, with HBC as proprietors at a rent of seven shillings a year. The company was required to establish, within five years, "a settlement of resident colonists, emigrants from the United Kingdom of Great Britain and Ireland, or from other Our dominions." If the HBC failed to establish a satisfactory settlement it would forfeit the island.

Settlement was anathema to the HBC — it would disturb the habitat of the fur-bearing mammals that were its trading staple as well as bring some who were not sympathetic to the company's single-minded pursuit of monopoly trade. One such man was Walter Colquhoun Grant, a Scot and a military man, which were qualifications that the company thought fitted him for the task of surveying. He was to prepare plans to be sent to London as evidence that the company was ready for settlers. Having only completed the baselines for the town, he handed in his resignation in March 1850 and headed for the gold fields of California. The company then hired Joseph Despard Pemberton, who was a professional surveyor. He arrived on Vancouver Island in June and by January 1852 had produced the first town plan. This was taken to London and exhibited as an enticement to settlers, but few came (Fig. 6-1).

Pemberton's plan "of the town of Victoria showing proposed improvements" shows the fort and 332 town lots laid out from Rock Bay to James Bay. The lots measured 18 x 37 metres and hugged the shoreline, thus optimizing the number of commercially valuable water lots although a substantial portion of water access in

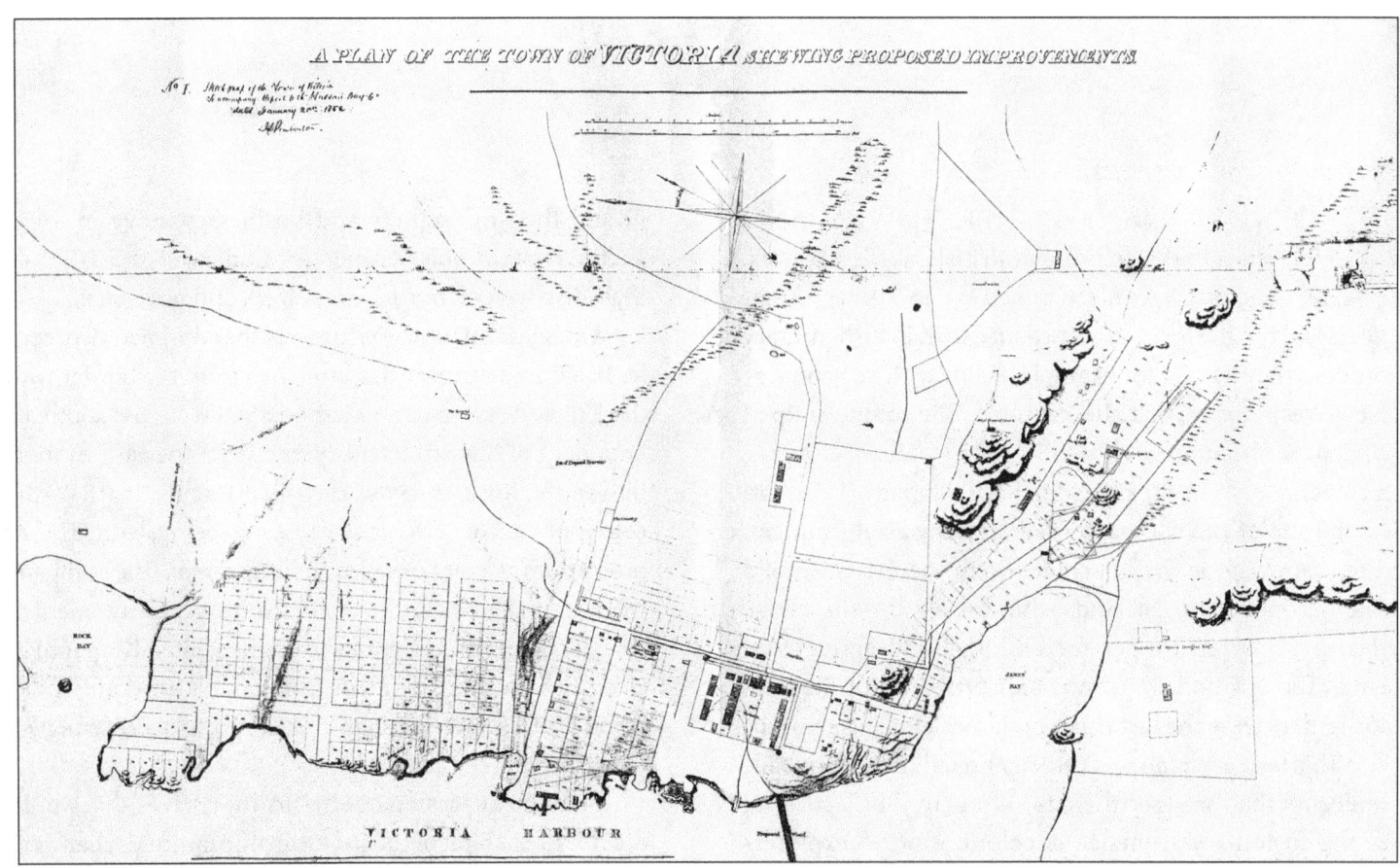

Fig. 6-1. The 1852 town plan, prepared by Joseph D. Pemberton, for the Hudson's Bay Company. [Private collection.]

front of the fort was left uncharted — it was company land. Behind the water lots the town was surveyed in blocks of twenty-two lots in something approaching a grid fitted in around the already existing fort and shoreline, but without any semblance of an overall design or town plan — it was just a survey of land for sale. There were no civic squares or parks, no broad avenues terminating in vistas, the streets were all the same width, with no imposing government buildings; and when the provincial government buildings were built, it was on a site well away from the planned town.

The reservoir was plotted at Blanshard and Johnson Streets. It was never built, and there wasn't one until the city developed Elk Lake in the 1880s. Land at the corner of Douglas and Johnson Streets was marked as the cemetery, and for a few years it was used for burials, although it could hardly be called a cemetery, as it was more like a convenient place to plant the dead. Contractors excavating for the building that now stands on the site discovered these burials were often without coffins. Use of that land as a cemetery stopped in 1855 with the opening of the Quadra Street burying ground, now Pioneer Park. Pemberton placed the hospital for the city on Pandora Avenue at Chambers Street, and although one was built there to plans of Wright & Sanders, it was not until 1864, and it was not the city hospital but the Female Infirmary. The HBC and the government in London had decided that the colony should be settled on the Wakefield scheme of systematic colonization, but Pemberton did not initially set aside land for a school, a church, the clergy, or a public park — all components of the system.

By 1861, Pemberton had produced an official map. The eastern limit was Cook Street, and beyond that was the school reserve; plans for a reservoir had been abandoned. The fort garden along the east side of Government Street, between Fort and Broughton Streets, was shown marked into quadrangles, but whether this was to be the required public park or a nicely organized vegetable garden is not clear, although the latter seems more likely. It is now retail outlets.

At the turn of the century, when the tourist association was determined to make the city attractive to visitors, it encouraged paving the streets with wooden blocks, making concrete sidewalks, and repaving the wooden bridge across the mouth of James Bay. All this was done, but aside from the construction of the stone causeway to replace the bridge, it was really just tidying up what was there — nothing was done to improve the city's plan and environment. Then, in 1958, visionary architect and planner Roderick Clack joined the city staff, and along with a group of enthusiastic and committed architects, planners, and engineers, he began a program of renovation and revitalization in the city's downtown. The creation of Centennial Square, an appropriate setting for city hall, the renovation of the McPherson Theatre, construction of strategically-located parkades, and street beautification schemes are all testaments to Clack's "acute appreciation of public spaces." But not all the proposals were so successful.

In 1958, Clack, along with the city's engineering staff, proposed an ambitious twenty-year plan that contained the construction of eleven parking facilities, traffic pattern changes, and street closures to create pedestrian shopping malls. The first project was deck parking for over three hundred vehicles on View between Douglas and Blanshard Streets; View Street was to be closed to west-bound traffic beyond this point, and from there to Government Street was to be a pedestrian mall, interrupted only by traffic at Douglas Street (Fig. 6-2). Planned in two phases, the first costing $2 million and the second $3 million, the scheme was to be self-financing using parking revenue, which would require an increase in charges to ten cents an hour. The business community were all in favour — any project that made it easier for customers to shop downtown was bound to have its approval — but residents were not amused by the increased parking charges, although the prospect of greenery on View Street invited some ribaldry (Fig. 6-3).

Fig. 6-2. Artist's concept of the view west along the proposed View Street Mall from the elevated parking on View between Douglas and Blanshard Streets. Published in the *Times*, November 7, 1958.

City Beautification [55]

Fig. 6-3. A cartoon responding to the proposed landscaping in the View Street Mall. [Published in *Barron's Victoria*, with permission of the estate of Sid Barron.]

Although the money by-law required to finance the View Street mall was passed, nothing was done; it seems that the Clack's office was "burdened to the gunwales with work," and other projects commanded the city's attention.

With the election of Richard B. Wilson as mayor (1961–1965), vigour and enthusiasm were injected into the city's improvement plans. The creation of Centennial Square and the revitalization of Bastion Square revived part of the 1958 plan for street beautification with pedestrian malls. Visitors to downtown would be able to promenade in a loop of Broad, Government, and View Streets, which would be beautified with trees and street furniture. Some of the proposed beautification of Government Street was done — the sidewalks were widened, trees in large planters were added, and so was seating — but it is only a partial mall allowing one-way traffic. Tenants of the smaller shops were not happy that their customers would not be able to park at the doorstep. Until recently little was done to smarten up Broad Street, and even now there is a notable absence of foliage and street furniture, although the pavement is decorative. Part of the plan was to create a mid-block alley linking Government and Broad Streets between Johnson and Yates Streets, where

Fig. 6-4. Proposed beautification of the mid-block alley between Broad and Government Streets between Johnson and Yates Streets. [CVA, CD 49.]

Fig. 6-5. A contemporary photograph of the alley. [Collection of the author.]

there was to be an intimate place with seating, tables, and planting. Instead, the alley has been blocked with a new building on Government Street, and the opening on Broad Street is the inevitable parking lot (Figs. 6-4, 6-5).

Another pedestrianization proposal was for Chinatown. The block of Fisgard Street between Government and Store Streets was to be paved over and closed to traffic. Among the many advantages would be

Fig. 6-6. A proposed new entrance to Chinatown. [Capital Region Planning Board of British Columbia, "City of Victoria Urban Renewal Study," 1961. CVA, CD 604.]

the provision of "much needed space" for the locals to congregate, sit, and chat. The need for such an urban space was a reflection of the state of Chinatown's population, which was mostly "elderly, single Chinese men who still lived in small communal groups and shared cooking and washing facilities." The elimination of thirty-one parking places on the street would result in the need for alternative spaces, and this would encourage the demolition of derelict buildings, and to house those dispossessed from these "crowded tenements," some empty buildings would be rehabilitated for low-rent housing for the elderly. Another benefit would be improved traffic flow with the elimination of the cross intersection at Government Street, and the newly tidied area would be a tourist attraction.

This proposal was met with little enthusiasm from the residents of Chinatown, which was hardly surprising as they had not been consulted. The merchants did not like it because they would no longer be able to load and unload goods in front of their stores, the restaurateurs did not like it as most of their patrons drove to Chinatown, and there was considerable doubt that the area could become a tourist attraction. The entrance to the mall (Fig. 6-6) is bland, there is nothing to indicate that this is Chinatown, nothing to invite the tourist to enter, and this artist's conception appears to have obliterated every vestige of the buildings' Victorian facades. In the end, the federal and provincial governments decided that the redevelopment of Blanshard Street was more deserving of the funding that was available for housing in urban renewal areas, and the Chinatown scheme was dropped — a decision that was partly influenced by the assessment that the aging population would decline to the point that new homes for the elderly would be irrelevant.

The consensus among politicians was that if Chinatown was to be revitalized then the Chinese should take responsibility for it themselves. Twice, in 1971 and again in 1974, they tried, with a plan to build a Chinese cultural centre on land to the rear of the Chinese school, but both attempts failed due to factional disputes between the Chinese Consolidated Benevolent Association, owner of the land, and the Victoria Chinatown Lions Club, which was to sponsor the building. And when the city applied to Ottawa for Neighbourhood Improvement Program (NIP) funding for Chinatown and it was refused, it seemed that Chinatown was doomed.

Concerned for the fate of the Victorian business buildings, constructed by wealthy Chinese and now largely uncared for, the city's Heritage Advisory Committee instigated a public consultation process in 1978. Involving both the Chinese associations as well as the Chinese community — the first time these groups had been involved in the rehabilitation and revitalization of their own environment — the process successfully coordinated the wishes and opinions of all the various factions. The result is the Chinatown we know today — a vibrant and instantly recognizable community entered through the Gate of Harmonious Interest.

LEISURE, LEARNING, AND CULTURE

Chapter 7

Beacon Hill Park

Beacon Hill Park is a treasured seventy-five hectare public park at the southern end of the city, stretching along the shore of Juan de Fuca Strait. It has some of the usual park amenities: a children's play area, a band-shell where concerts are free, an interpretive kiosk in one of the former bandstands. But, despite twelve applications made since 1946, there is no restaurant or tearoom, and some twenty-three other proposals for structures large and small have been turned down.

Although the land had been declared a park reserve in 1859, its management see-sawed between the city and the colonial legislature, and the terms and conditions of its use were unclear. But, in February 1882, the land was conveyed to the city in trust. It was to "be maintained and preserved by the Corporation and their successors for the use, recreation and enjoyment of the public." As soon as the city obtained the land, twenty acres were transferred to the B.C. Agricultural Society for the construction of a hall for agricultural fairs. This action set in motion legal proceedings to test the terms of what is generally referred to as the Trust — proceedings that culminated in a landmark ruling by the Chief Justice Sir Matthew Baillie Begbie in 1884.

Begbie ruled that the agricultural building "was not an acceptable use because it did not constitute public recreational use and enjoyment, according to The Trust." He listed uses which, in his opinion, were not permitted, which included "a university, sanatorium, a barracks for soldiers a lunatic asylum, and a cemetery," and he concluded that the park was not to be used "for general purposes of profit, or utility, however great the prospect of these may be." Begbie's ruling has guided every decision about park use up to this day, and various individuals and organizations have rallied to ensure that the terms of the Trust are honoured.

When the city took control of the park it was a wild and natural place, and the city fathers thought it should be beautified, so a competition for a design to landscape and embellish the park was announced. In April 1889 Henry R. Cresswell's design was judged "decidedly the most artistic" and was accepted unanimously. It was a relatively simple plan, with many fewer roads than we see today, and leaving much of the area in its natural state, with the only exception being a flower garden in the north-eastern corner. Cresswell's emphasis was on the provision of foot paths meandering across the virgin land, retaining the forest, and not on manicured formal arrangements, although he did suggest some amenities such as drinking fountains and rustic seating and "even a pit for the pet bear."

Cresswell's plan also met with the approval of the citizens who were given an opportunity to examine a watercolour of the design that was exhibited in city hall. Then there was silence for over a month until the parks committee recommended the "adoption and purchase of Mr. Blair's plan and Landscape design for Beacon Hill Park." Four months later Cresswell's watercolour was removed from display and replaced with Blair's. John Blair is a shadowy figure about whom little can be confirmed; he claimed to have had landscaping experience in Chicago, and seems to have convinced the city fathers that Cresswell's plan was too modest, that his own design for the park was far more in keeping with their grand ideas, and should be implemented. His plan was far more elaborate, and costly, than Cresswell's and included more roads and a new, and large, lake on the eastern border — many of the roads, and the second lake were never built.

What happened between April 19, when Cresswell's win was announced, and May 27, 1889, when Blair's design was accepted, remains a mystery. Unlike Blair, Cresswell was a trained architect, and the watercolour, now in the City of Victoria Archives, has the quality of an architectural rendering, but it is not signed. The best guess is that Blair embellished Cresswell's work and passed it off as his own, but it is still unknown why a city council that could not even find the funds to complete the city hall would approve this more expensive design.

An early proposal for a building in the park was a response to the city's efforts to revitalize its economy after its demise as the trade and transportation centre for Canada's west coast. Boosting the city's economy by attracting tourists was one of the main aims of the Tourist Association, formed in 1902. These visitors were to be enticed to Victoria, not in order that they spend money enjoying themselves, as happens today, but rather so they could be made aware of the business opportunities that the city and area had to offer and be persuaded to settle and invest in the city and the island.

Inspired by the construction of forestry buildings in Portland and Seattle, the Vancouver Island Development League, a group of businessmen keen to improve the island's resource economy, came up with the idea of a forestry showcase for Victoria. The American buildings were expressly used to promote the timber and wood products of the Pacific Northwest and advertise the commercial potential of these resources. The one in Portland was dubbed the "the world's largest log cabin," and inside was a colonnade of raw logs, each capped with a block of wood, presumably in emulation of a Doric column. The Forestry Building, built in Seattle for the 1909 Alaska Yukon Pacific Exposition, had a classical exterior, with logs in place of stone columns. The Victoria building would go one better and be a scaled replica of the Parthenon.

The project was announced in the *Victoria Daily Colonist* on July 6, 1909, with the headline "Parthenon on Beacon Hill, Suggested Structure of Island Timber as

Permanent Advertisement." The monument, it was suggested, "would become one of the wonders of the world and people would be attracted from far and near to see it." This half-scale replica of the Parthenon was to stand "on an elevated part of Beacon Hill" looking out over the Juan de Fuca Strait "just as the Parthenon overlooks the Aegean Sea." It would be built of wood harvested from Vancouver Island — fir trunks on the exterior, fir and cedar inside — and of "great architectural beauty."

Although Mr. E. McGaffey, secretary of the League, touted the building as a "practical demonstration of great commercial value," he also offered some more altruistic ideas for its use — a sugar-coating to give the project appeal to the wider community. The wooden interior would give the building an "unsurpassed" acoustic, making it eminently suitable for concerts; it could be a convention centre capable of accommodating hundreds of delegates; or it could be a museum exhibiting specimens of the Island's ores, animals, birds, and fishes. The promoters also suggested that the building would have an educational use in demonstrating the value of the Island's forests and urged that the Parthenon be built "before all the big timber on the island has been cut down and manufactured" so that the building would be "a continuous reminder of an incentive to the preservation of the island timber." All that was needed for the project to proceed was for the city to donate the land and for the public to support it. "It certainly would be a great attraction and would spread the fame of the city far and wide" (Fig. 7-1). McGaffey needed to stress the many public benefits the building would offer, as only the month before the *Times* had published a letter by Dr. Helmcken in which he reiterated Begbie's ruling that "all buildings erected in the park should be built by the corporation for the use of the public at the public cost or expense, in fact that everything in the park should be for the enjoyment of the public and paid for by them."

Just five days later, a rendering of the projected replica of the Parthenon graced the front page of the *Colonist*. The plans were drawn by John Wilson, a recently arrived British architect whose main claim to fame is that he designed the House of All Sorts for renowned B.C. artist Emily Carr. Wilson proposed that the building would be thirty-five by sixteen metres, half the scale of the Parthenon in Athens, and it would hold eight hundred people. While the *Colonist* unequivocally supported the project some objectors felt that a broom-clad hill was beautiful enough without a building on top of it. The *Colonist* editorial countered that the broom and building would make a "majestic picture." But the promoters had not reckoned with the Trust and the park's defenders. Within the month all talk of a Parthenon on the highest point of Beacon Hill Park had faded from the press.

Fig. 7-1. A sketch of the Parthenon proposed for the top of Beacon Hill, by architect John Wilson. Published in the *Colonist*, July 11, 1909.

Another scheme that was consigned to the reject pile was Henry Whittaker's proposal in 1933 to construct a replica of an Indian village in concrete, which would be "a permanent memorial to the Indian dwellers of the land, and also a work of museum value and tourist attraction." According to Whittaker, this "tableau in concrete of the Indians, their homes and mode of life would give a realistic impression to visitors of the older forms of civilization on this continent, and would certainly be a unique exhibit" and would be "so realistic that the materials of construction would deceive anyone at a casual glance." Whittaker was, at the time, the province's chief architect and was keenly interested in "Indian" art and architecture and concerned with the increasing loss of these skills

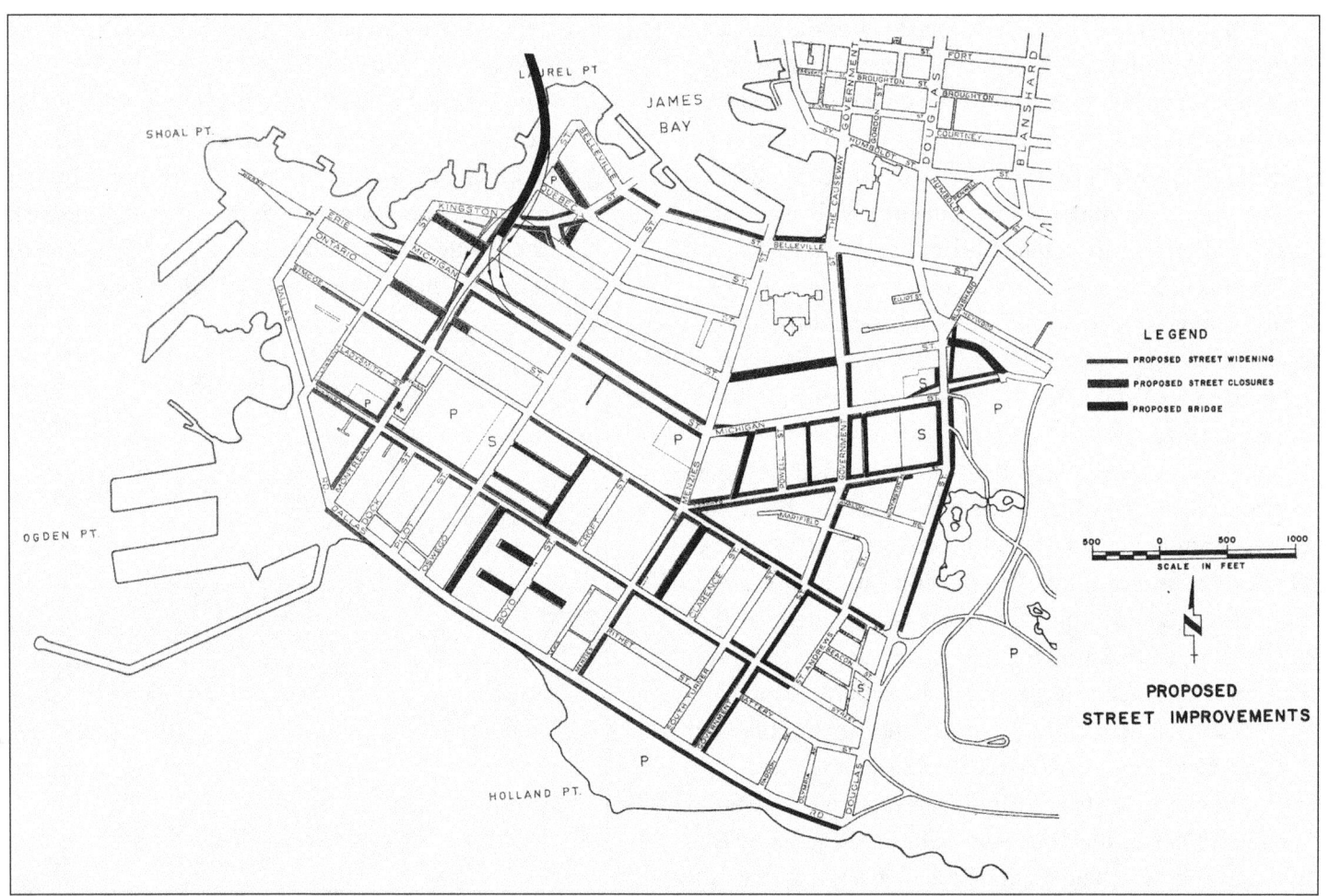

Fig. 7-2. A map of the proposed street improvements in James Bay neighbourhood showing the Michigan Street extension. ["James Bay Land Use & Transportation Plan," City of Victoria, 1967. CVA, CD 68.]

under the influence of the "white man's ways." However, it is hard to imagine how this astonishing plan would have been of any benefit to the culture of the First Peoples.

In 1966 a Vancouver company whose representative was Milton Tisdale, who had been spokesperson for the Sherwood Forest Playland in the Gorge four years earlier, proposed a space-age tree house for the top of Beacon Hill. The proposal was for a twenty-five metre tower with a series of four decks on the top and resembling, according to the *Times*, the Bastion at Nanaimo. The base of the structure would be the office of the Victoria Visitors Bureau, the provincial government tourist and trade promotion bureau would be at the eleven-metre level, at the fifteen-metre level would be the federal tourist agency, and above these, at eighteen metres, there would be a display telling the story of reforestation and viewing deck. On top, visible for miles, would be a beacon. And with this nod to all three levels of government and the forest industry, Tisdale proposed that the venture might be funded by a consortium of all four.

Another unacceptable suggestion for "improving" the park came from Clare Brynjolfson. In a letter to the *Colonist* he proposed that a convention centre be built in the south of the park, overlooking the strait. Not only would this be a spectacular and inviting location, but tidying up the uncultivated "jungles" and getting rid of those wild and natural characteristics that most citizens value would, in his opinion, civilize the place. In response, a letter from David R. Williams reminded readers of Begbie's ruling, and nothing more was heard of the idea.

In her comprehensive history of Beacon Hill Park, Janis Ringuette catalogues all thirty-four rejected proposals, including twelve for a restaurant/tearoom. Most of them were either mentioned in the newspapers or the park records and then heard of no more. But one plan was so dear to the city that it was discussed for nearly a decade before finally being voted down, and that was the Michigan Street Extension (Fig. 7-2).

In 1965 the city commissioned an "Overall Plan for Victoria," and one of its proposals was the construction of a freeway looping through the James Bay neighbourhood and slicing off the north-west corner of the park. The rationale was Michigan Street would be extended from its junction with Government Street through the park and then link up with Quadra Street at Southgate. Surprisingly, both the major newspapers — the *Victoria Daily Times* and the *Daily Colonist* — opposed the project. This was a testament to the extent of antipathy to the plan, as each prided itself on taking an opposing view (Fig. 7-3). In the *Times*, writer Art Stott raised the spectre of Begbie's ruling, now some eighty years old,

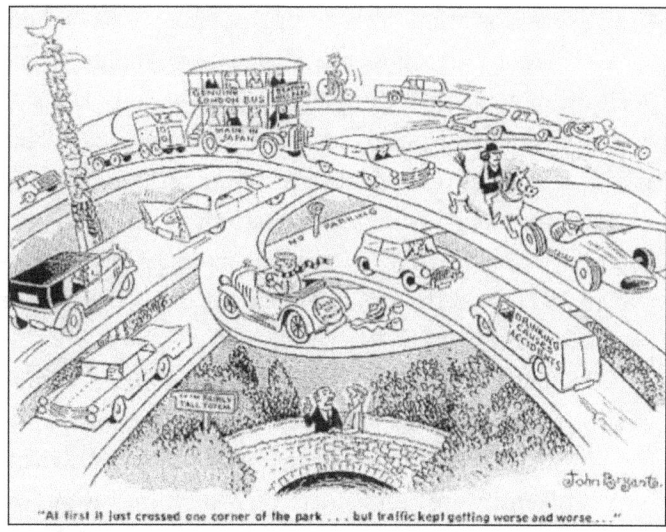

Fig. 7-3. A cartoon published in response to the traffic woes anticipated by the city's traffic plans. Published in the *Colonist* in 1965. [John Bryant.]

that the council seems to have hoped was long forgotten, but the general public remembered it. The strength of public opposition persuaded the council to abandon its intentions — for the time being.

Two years later, the "James Bay Transportation Land Use and Transportation Plan" recommended that Michigan Street, from its western end at St. Lawrence Street through Beacon Hill Park to Heywood Avenue, be designated as an arterial road. The population of the James Bay neighbourhood was increasing rapidly, and the narrow streets, many of them planned over a century before, were inadequate for the increased traffic. The Michigan Street extension was considered the most important element in this land-use plan, and the city council approved it in 1968, along with the widening of Dallas Road, Heywood Avenue, and Government Street, all at the expense of park land.

This betrayal of the Trust galvanized interested parties into action. Most active among them was the Beacon Hill Park Association, formed in December 1970. It kept up a constant barrage of press releases, pamphlets, and position papers. In a campaign to persuade citizens to "become a Greenspace Guardian," it publicized such alarming facts as the extent to which the original area of the park reserve had already been diminished, from over eighty hectares in 1862, to seventy-six in 1940, to sixty-two in 1971, and the unknown extent of the loss if the council's plans went ahead.

The battle raged on. The influential international environmental organization, the Sierra Club, joined the fray. More and more politicians, journalists, and ordinary citizens were persuaded that nibbling away yet more green space was unacceptable. Finally, Malcolm Anderson was elected to the council on a platform that included opposition to the Michigan Street extension.

He became chairman of the Parks Committee, and in late October 1974 announced that the city would not use any part of Beacon Hill Park for future road building. Since that time, no work that did not comply with the terms of the Trust has taken place in the park, and today its value to the citizens and visitors is such that any inappropriate proposals will meet with the same determination as that for the Michigan Street extension.

Chapter 8

THE GORGE WATERWAY

ON A SUNNY SUMMER'S DAY, A VISIT to the Gorge Waterway is a gentle, tranquil, and fragrant experience. Well-manicured parks line its banks, and the quiet is broken only by the squawks of gulls wheeling over head, and, from time to time, the *phut-phut* of the small harbour ferry boat. But until the eve of the Second World War, "the Gorge of summers gone" was Victoria's playground. There was a Japanese Tea Garden, an outdoor theatre, stalls selling every necessity for a day out on the water, picnic sites, camp grounds, and a diving tower. The waters teemed with swimmers and boaters, some for pleasure, others in serious competition, and the banks swarmed with young and old. On public holidays, such as Queen Victoria's birthday and Dominion Day, regattas brought virtually the entire population, as well as the navy round from Esquimalt, to the Gorge Waterway, or The Arm, as it was sometimes called.

In the early years of settlement, the Gorge was considered to have commercial potential. When James Douglas was surveying the area in 1842 for the new Hudson's Bay Company post, he noted that the Gorge was an ideal site where "flour or sawmills may be erected." He based this assessment on the tidal rush at its narrowest point, which he considered "of a force and velocity capable of driving the most powerful machinery." Industrial development never happened, and the Gorge became the hub of recreation — water sports in summer and skating in the winter — but its popularity was its downfall. Stretching from the Selkirk trestle west to Portage Inlet, the Gorge is tidal, and shallow in its upper reaches — conditions that limit the ability of the tides to flush the waterway. When the banks were lined with pristine forest, this mattered little, but as the popularity of the place grew, houses began to line the banks, and these flushed their sewage directly into the water.

As early as 1906 the city council discussed the need for septic tanks on properties alongside the waterway. It was concerned that the water's continued use for leisure activities would soon be impossible since the water was so polluted, the stench at low tide so unbearable, and an outbreak of disease a distinct possibility. And yet the popularity of the Gorge continued until the early 1930s.

Undaunted by the quality of the water, in 1926 the James Bay Athletic Association — "formed in 1886 and the oldest Canadian sports organization west of Montreal" — planned to move its clubhouse from the waterfront at Belleville Street to the Gorge. The celebrated architect Francis Mawson Rattenbury, designer of the parliament buildings and the Empress Hotel, prepared drawings of a new boathouse and a landscaped four-acre lot (Fig. 8-1).

In June, the association voted to float stock of $14,000 to finance the building and landscaping of its new clubhouse and grounds. Unfortunately, the members' enthusiasm and ability to cope with the financial commitment was seriously affected by the economic depression of the late 1920s. Many were unable even to afford the journey out to this more isolated location, and membership declined. In the end, the property had to be sold, and the architect-designed boat house was never built.

These financial constraints also saw a general decline in the Gorge's popularity. Swimmers particularly were lured away by the downtown convenience of the all-year indoor pool at the Crystal Garden. In 1938, sanitary engineer John Day devised a plan to revitalize the waterway as a playground for the locals and as a tourist attraction.

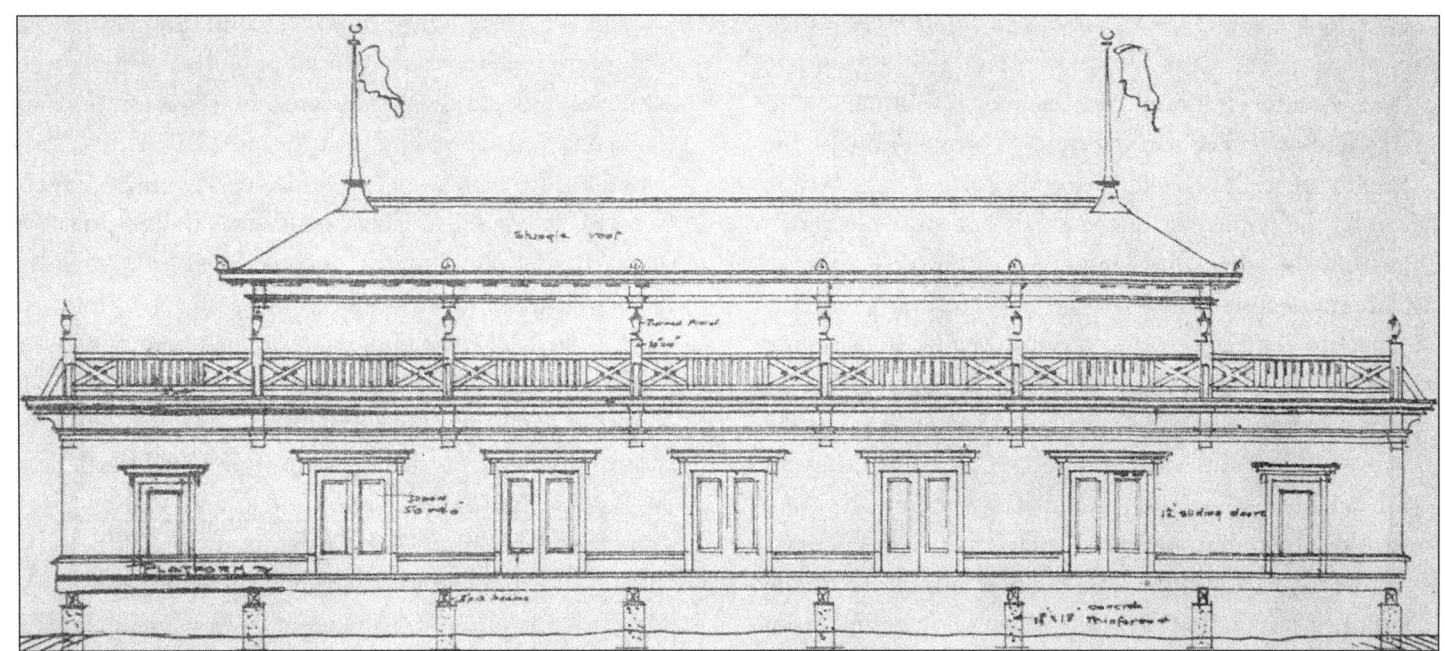

Fig. 8-1. A proposed new boat house for the James Bay Athletic Association, by architect Francis Rattenbury. Published in the *Times*, May 14, 1927.

His scheme required a pair of lock and sluice combinations, and a canal from Portage Inlet to Thetis Cove — the same location as had been suggested eighty years earlier for the movement of goods from Esquimalt Harbour to the Inner Harbour. Only this time, the goal was to clean and beautify the waterway and maintain the level of the water at four feet above the low tide level. One lock and sluice pair was to be where the waterway narrows at the western end of Selkirk Water, and the other at the end of a canal that would be dug between Portage Inlet and Thetis Cove in Esquimalt Harbour. The plan was that between the locks the water would be maintained at a level four feet above low tide. At high tide the sluice at the Esquimalt end would be opened to allow "clean and fresh" water to rush in, filling the Gorge to the required level. As the tide turned, that sluice would be closed to prevent the water from rushing back into Esquimalt Harbour, and the one at the Selkirk end would be opened to allow the water to rush out, taking with it the waterway's debris, and then carrying on with its cleansing sweep along the industrial waterfront of Victoria West and the Old Songhees Reserve.

The tourist-attraction element of this plan was, Day thought, the possibility of cruising around Esquimalt, which would, in effect, be an island. Passengers would board eleven-metre-long launches at the causeway in front of the Empress Hotel, cruise through the upper harbour, and then be lifted by the lock into the Gorge. Here they would pass "bathing beaches at which some hundreds of merry children and adults are diving and bathing in the calm and clear salt water." After sampling the delights of the Japanese Gardens, the tourist could stop for a meal, a swim, or even a game of golf, and see the beautiful homes on Portage Inlet. From the inlet the launch would pass under the railway and the Island Highway and enter the canal leading to the lock, then into Esquimalt Harbour, and back to the Empress. The *Colonist* was enthusiastic, exclaiming "What an attraction for the tourist!" and speculating that it would be a great advertisement for the city and encourage construction of new homes in the area. The timing of this proposal was unfortunate, as before the year was out the country was embroiled in the Second World War.

By the end of the war the Gorge was a deserted place. "No Swimming" signs were posted, the bottom was covered with thirty centimetres of filthy, slimy sediment, and the waterway was choked with weeds. The Gorge Waterway Improvement Association decided to take advantage of the $10 million improvement fund that had been earmarked by the Capital Improvement District Commission, a provincial body founded in 1956 to advise and encourage municipalities in the capital area on beautification and enhancement projects. The association asked the Vancouver engineering firm of R. Gordon Knight and Associates to prepare a plan for cleaning up the Gorge. Once again the proposal to cut a canal to connect Portage Inlet and Thetis Cove was proposed; the water would be controlled with a lock and dam at both the Thetis Cove and Selkirk ends. This arrangement was not in order to raise the level in the waterway, but to allow it to be isolated for dredging; and with Esquimalt effectively an island, around which the tides could wash, the Gorge would be purged.

Despite the determination of Saanich councillor and member of the association Geoffrey Edgelow, who was determined to give Victoria back its playground, the project died when it was found that the waters of Thetis Cove were themselves polluted and a cleanup of Esquimalt Harbour would be required before its waters were in any condition to flush the Gorge. The expense of the harbour cleanup killed the project. By the mid 1950s, the need to be able to continually flush the Gorge had become less urgent as water conditions improved with the introduction of a sewer system, so the failure of the projects to clean up the water did not doom the Gorge forever. While there was general enthusiasm for bringing the waterway back to its former glory as a place of recreation, it was recognized that funding was going to have to come from private enterprise. So when a Vancouver syndicate made a proposal to build a medieval theme park in 1962, it was met with approval by the City Parks Committee, which recommended to council that it approve the plan in principle.

Sherwood Forest Playland Ltd. wanted a twenty-year renewable lease on four-and-a-half hectares of woodland near the Gorge Bridge in order to build what it called a medieval encampment. The list of facilities and amusements was comprehensive: a concrete block castle, a torture chamber, a museum containing artifacts from the middle ages, a realistic dungeon displaying old instruments of torture, a medieval village of stores selling souvenirs and handicrafts, a children's playlot, parking for four hundred vehicles, barbecue pits, a refreshment centre designed as an authentic "mill house" complete with a steam-driven mill, well-known Robin Hood figures scattered throughout the woodland, two Viking longboats to transport tourists to the Gorge playland from the Inner Harbour, and a drawbridge gate and moat at the Gorge Road entrance. On paying the admission fee, visitors would exchange their dollars for medieval coins, which would be required for purchases within the amusement park.

With successive presentations, Martin Tisdale, spokesperson for Sherwood Forest Playland, improved the quality and extent of the features that his company's amusement park would offer, even going so far as to suggest that the open-air theatre would "offer exchange possibilities with Theatre Under the Stars and even Stratford."

In March the council approved the project, but there was considerable public opposition to what seemed like a give-away of public land for commercial purposes. And the Capital Region Planning Board of B.C. agreed. Its report noted that the land in question was under consideration for use as a public park, and its use for commercial purposes, which would charge admission and close it over the winter months, was not an acceptable use for public land, as it would be a tourist attraction rather than an amenity for the residents. The board recommended that the request to re-zone the land be denied, and added that council should undertake the necessary work to make it into a public park.

The University Women's Club also objected. It suggested that the woodland should be preserved and developed as a public park as part of a revitalized waterway. The club made suggestions for other amenities that would benefit the area. It proposed that an Indian village be constructed on the shore near the Songhees Reserve; that the old Japanese tea garden, which had been such a well-loved and patronized feature of the Gorge before the war, be reconstructed; and urged the preservation of a number of heritage homes on its banks. None of these proposals were acted upon.

Having been eventually denied permission to build its playland on public land, the company decided to attempt the venture on two and a half hectare of private land just to the west of the park, and publicized its intention with a drawing of the proposed castle (Fig. 8-2). But the project seems to have been abandoned; no longer an issue of the appropriate use of public land, it disappeared from the record. At the time there were at least two other theme parks in the vicinity of the city — Wooded Wonderland at Beaver Lake Park; and Fable Cottage in Cordova Bay, now moved to Denman Island

— so the prospect of having to pay for land as well as face the competition probably persuaded Sherwood Forest Playland to abandon the project.

Then, in 1965, another proposal involving a dam was prepared by Richard Faulks and Lloyd Smith. This dam was more modest that the earlier ones, but the goal of the project was massive. Only one dam would be required, and a simple hinged wooden mechanism was suggested. It would be constructed underneath the Gorge Bridge, on Tillicum Road, and during most of the year it would lay on the bottom, but once a year it would be raised for the annual cleaning. The overall project was to create a beach park at the north end of Portage Inlet, adjacent to the Trans-Canada Highway. The inlet's clay bottom would be dredged and piled up at the west end, leaving a depth of water suitable for swimming, then sand would be brought in to create a beach (Fig. 8-3). The park would contain the various facilities required for a day out at the beach, and parking lots were planned for both sides of the highway, with a pedestrian overpass. The estimated cost for this work was $425,500, but a hidden cost would have been the destruction of the fish habitat caused by such comprehensive dredging. In the end the proposal was rejected by the 1967 Centennial Committee, which was just as well — the two-lane highway just a stone's throw from the proposed beach is now one of the city's few stretches of freeway. And there is still something to fish for from the bridges across the Gorge.

Fig. 8-2. The replica castle proposed for the private Sherwood Forest Playland development. Published in the *Colonist*, October 11, 1962.

The Gorge Waterway has been revitalized in terms of clean water and nicely manicured parks. Its sheltered waters are again popular with boaters, but it has not achieved its former popularity as in the days of summers gone — it is very nearly back to the state in which Sir James Douglas found it over a century and a half ago.

Fig. 8-3. Beach Park on Portage Inlet at the Trans-Canada Highway, from the booklet *The Challenge of the Gorge*. [Richard Faulks.]

Chapter 9

UNIVERSITIES

THE UNIVERSITY OF VICTORIA
A decade after the Gordon Head Memorial Air Park scheme was roundly defeated by the ratepayers of Saanich, the land was purchased by Victoria College as part of its expansion and development program. The plan was that the main campus at Lansdowne — now Camosun College — was to remain the academic centre and the Gordon Head land would be used for such ancillary purposes as sports fields and student residences. Dealing with a split campus would require campus planning, and Richard B. Wilson, chairman of the college's Development Board, asked Robert Siddall, the college's consulting architect, to find the best campus planners he could.

After a six-day visit to the site, Wurster, Bernardi & Emmons (WBE) of California, the chosen planners, persuaded the college's council that developing only one campus was the way to proceed, and the site at Gordon Head offered the best location. The campus plan that the firm came up with is very like the campus we know today. One element of the plan was that there was to be no "flamboyant architectural statement." This meant that local architects should be asked to design individual buildings that should be compatible with each other and sensitive to the overall ensemble. "No one building must be allowed to dominate or upstage another, but each must blend into a harmonious unity." There were no competitions; architect Robert Siddall remained as the local representative of WBE and coordinated commissions for individual buildings, which were distributed among local architects.

An early study by Siddall was for a university apartment scheme, located to the east of the ring road, where the student housing is today. His plan was for five high-rise buildings graduated in height with increasing distance from the campus (Fig. 9-1). This plan was rejected after vigorous objection from the residents of Oak Bay who did not want such a high-density development in close proximity to their borders.

The Administrative Services Building was completed in 2008, the first time this non-academic function had a dedicated building, although there had been thought of constructing an administration building in the 1960s. Architect John A. Di Castri prepared a concept rendering in 1964, showing an administration building with a domed central bay and colonnade, located east of the MacLaurin Building, which is ten-storeys tall on the plan (Fig. 9-2). Later he prepared two more schemes, both more fully defined, and both unbuilt.

In his 1966 schemes, as in the 1964 concept plan, the administration building was located at the south-west corner of the quadrangle, facing the "entrance court," which would have been just inside University Drive, the proper, though virtually unused, name for the ring road at the end of the main entrance to the campus. The building would also look out over the quadrangle, and, at six-storeys tall, the proposed building would not overpower the adjacent MacLaurin Building, then nearing completion at a maximum height of five storeys. The proposed administration building would be the first that visitors would see, and it should, explained Di Castri, convey both the dignity of an administrative body and office of the president, as well as the stimulating atmosphere of an academic campus.

After preparing preliminary sketches for consultation, Di Castri formally presented his proposals. At the consultation stage his first scheme (Fig. 9-3) had been

Fig. 9-1. The University Park Apartment Study by architect R. W. Siddall, circa 1961. [University of Victoria Archives, Acc. No. 2004-003.]

criticized for looking too much like an apartment building with balconies, lacking in dignity, being too busy, too different, and, of course, too expensive. Although he roundly defended this scheme with such remarks as "conformity does not necessarily result in dignity and often tends towards mediocrity," his alternative offering was more conventional (Fig. 9-4). He was obviously less pleased with this design, as he remarked that it smacked of commerce rather than academe. Neither scheme was built.

By the mid-1960s the "harmonious unity" that was the cornerstone of the WBE campus plan was beginning to draw criticism. The feeling of restlessness among students and the general public was more than just a manifestation of the general campus discontent of

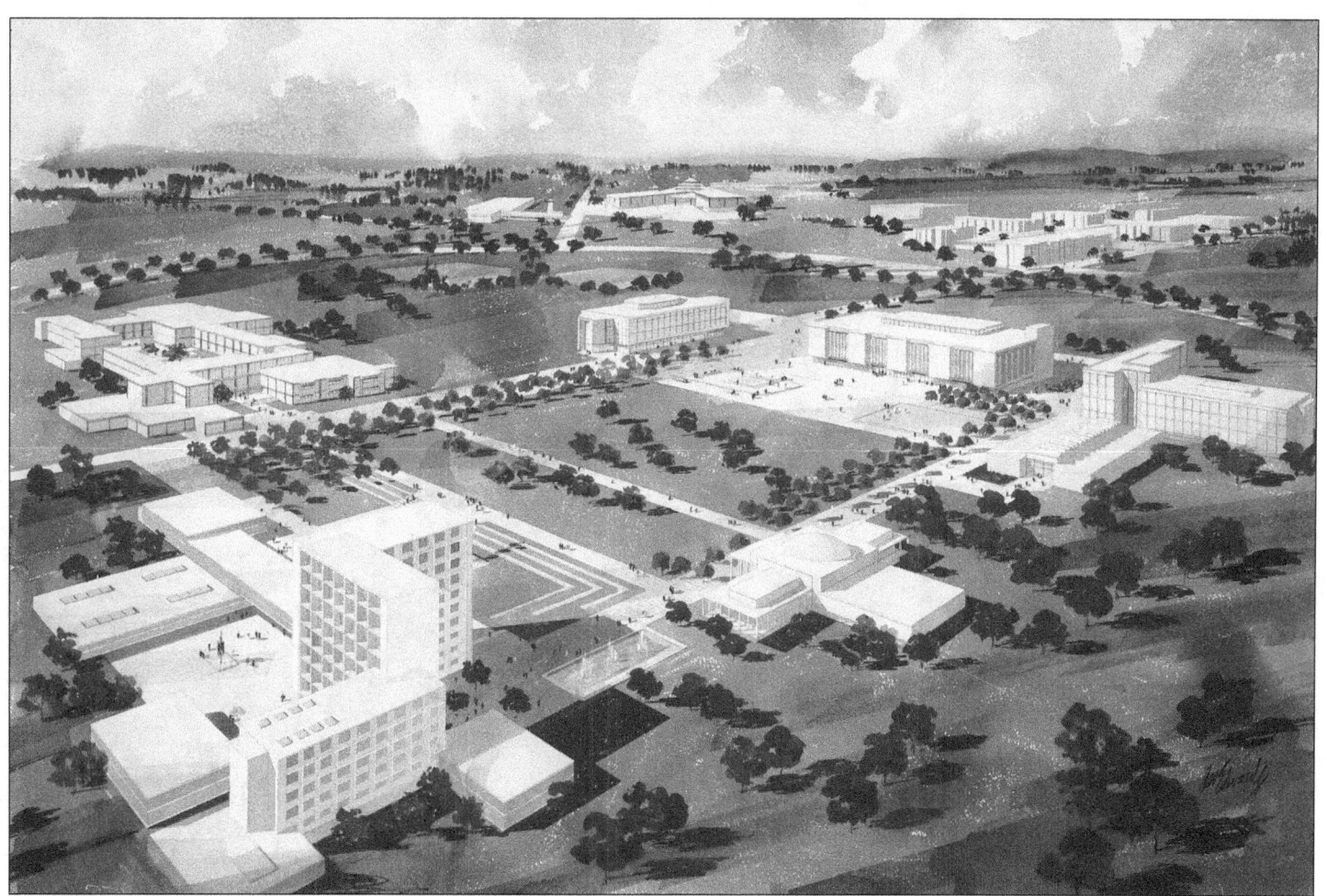

Fig. 9-2. A concept plan for the campus showing the domed administration building, 1964. In this plan by architect John Di Castri, the proposed MacLaurin building is ten-storeys tall. [University of Victoria Special Collections, John A. Di Castri, RG: SC429.]

Fig. 9-3. A rendering of first scheme for the University Administration Building, by John Di Castri, 1966. [University of Victoria Special Collections, John A. Di Castri, RG: SC429.]

Fig 9-4. The entrance detail of second scheme for the University Administration Building, John Di Castri, 1966. [University of Victoria Special Collections, John A. Di Castri, RG: SC429.]

the times, it was also a reaction to the praise, publicity, and funding that was being directed to the new Simon Fraser University in Burnaby. Its architects, Arthur Erickson and Geoffrey Massey, had earned international acclaim for the design and, in an attempt to bring the University of Victoria some of the recognition that Simon Fraser was attracting, that firm was retained as campus architects for a period of three years, beginning in 1967. Two buildings of this period, the Cadboro Commons, and the Lansdowne College Residence, both of which, in their use of exposed concrete, show evidence of the Erickson Massey influence, were not generally well received. Neither was the Cunningham Building, designed by the firm itself and built at the end of its tenure.

Erickson Massey's progress report of April 1968 was critical of the WBE plan, suggesting that the problems with the current campus plan were that the library was not in a central location, the student union building was too far out, the location of buildings had not been made with sufficient consideration of future requirements, and that there was a lack of unity in the arrangement of the buildings. The report concluded that the "existing development does not indicate any clear design objective or design criteria for the general architectural character of the campus." Some of the changes being considered were the downgrading of the ring road to service and visitor access, the creation of a four-lane outer ring road, and improved pedestrian circulation by the creation of continuous covered pedestrian ways connecting all facilities around the quadrangle.

The long-range plan that the firm delivered in June 1969 contained proposals for every corner of the campus. The main entrance along University Drive, off Cedar Hill Cross Road (Fig. 9-5), would lead to a paved public square surrounded by the theatre, art and music studios, galleries, lecture theatres, and workshops. Each of the four sides of the square would give access to groups of buildings arranged according to function; academic buildings were to be grouped around courtyards, humanities to the north, science to the south. To satisfy the newly-instituted college system — abandoned in 1972 — college complexes were to the east and the west. The west college complex, it was proposed, would be reached via an underpass, under the ring road, where a series of lakes (probably where the faculty club is now) would be lined with student residences and a commons block (Fig. 9-6). An outdoor theatre would be at the west end of the MacLaurin building. To the east of the quadrangle, the East College complex would achieve the tranquillity of the lakeside setting of the west college by the creation of berms that would shelter the residences (Fig. 9-7).

Unlike the WBE plan, the Erickson Massey plan was prescriptive: on the subject of building materials, concrete was preferred; if brick were used, it should be "buff"; if wood, it should be stained natural; stone should only to be used as a landscape element, not as a building material. All metalwork was to be "statuary bronze," which should be used for all exposed metal, including window and door frames, light standards, signs, and structural elements. Throughout the campus the street furniture was to be uniform, and all signs in the same font. A program to eliminate existing signs which did not comply should be instituted.

Even before this long range development plan was delivered to the Senate and Board of Governors, it was apparent that too many of the essential tenets of the WBE plan were being cast aside and this was not acceptable. Although the WBE plan was only partially completed, there was consensus that it should not be compromised.

UNIVERSITIES [79]

Fig. 9-5. The proposed new main entrance to the campus, from Foul Bay Road, 1969 Erickson Massey Architects. ["Long Range Development Plan," Erickson Massey Architects, June 1960. University of Victoria Archives.]

Fig. 9-6. A sketch of the west college cluster, 1969, by Erickson Massey Architects. ["Long Range Development Plan," Erickson Massey Architects, June 1960. University of Victoria Archives.]

Fig. 9-7. A model of the east college cluster showing the earth mounds, by Erickson Massey Architects, 1969. ["Long Range Development Plan," Erickson Massey Architects, June 1960. University of Victoria Archives.]

The Erickson Massey plan was not accepted, and in 1972 Donn Emmons of WBE again became the university's planning consultant. During one of his frequent visits he remarked "time, planting and a receptive climate have done wonders to the appearance of the campus. The landscaping unifies and modifies the often divergent architectural character of the many campus buildings."

Royal Roads University

Unlike the University of Victoria, which started with almost virgin land and a professionally designed plan, Royal Roads University inherited a fully-formed campus from the Royal Roads Military College. Since 1940 the college had occupied the Hatley Park estate, a three-hundred-hectare property that was once the home of one of the province's most influential and wealthy men, James Dunsmuir, elected premier in 1900 and named lieutenant governor in 1906. Over the years the college added various buildings around Hatley Castle, the Dunsmuir home. In 1995 the college closed and the provincial government created Royal Roads University. In the same year the federal government declared the property a national historic site, recognizing both the military college and the Dunsmuir family.

A campus plan was adopted in 2001 that included a commitment to sustainable development and green building principles. So, when the university needed another building in 2004, it went to the firm of Williams D'Ambrosio architects who designed a "green" building that satisfied LEED Platinum criteria. The Living Learning

Fig. 9-8. The Royal Roads University Living Learning Centre, 2004. [Williams D'Ambrosio, architects.]

Centre contained student residences on the upper floors, with lecture halls, classrooms, a cafeteria, and service facilities on the lower floors. Physical plant on the lower levels contained facilities for geo-exchange heating, water collection, storm water collection, and treatment for use. Since it was to be located on an existing parking lot, construction would not require the removal of any trees (Fig. 9-8). Funding for this "green" building was not forthcoming, and the university built a more conventional academic building on another site.

Another project was an open-air amphitheatre to be built with the mountains of the Olympic National Park in Washington State as a backdrop. The theatre would have a steel wall and wooden rail defining its circumference and enclosing 1.8-metre-wide terraces of grass and stone, which could accommodate an audience of one thousand, and an oval stage that could be covered by a retractable, tensile fabric roof. The amphitheatre was to be used as a venue for university events, including convocation, and as a potential attraction to bring community-based cultural activities and events onto the campus (Fig. 9-9). In view of other building needs, this project was postponed indefinitely as a lower priority amenity.

Fig. 9-9. The Royal Roads University Amphitheatre.
[Williams D'Ambrosio, architects.]

Chapter 10

The Art Gallery of Greater Victoria

EMILY CARR, VICTORIA'S MOST RENOWNED and celebrated artist, was probably the first in the city to attempt to open an art gallery. Called the People's Gallery, it was set up in the two lower apartments in her home, the House of All Sorts, at 646 Simcoe Street in James Bay. She wanted a "gallery that would be a warm and pleasurable place to visit on a raw winter days; and she wanted it specifically for honest working people." But there was, as Carr put it, "that pestiferous money business." The Lieutenant-Governor thought it "a fine scheme" of which he "heartily approved," but "could not think of lending his name to a little thing in a private house in a quiet district," and while he said he was sure that a number of people in Victoria would donate $500 each, Carr noted that he did not do so himself. And Carr's suggestion of associating the gallery with Beacon Hill Park, just across the road from the House of All Sorts, met with the mayor's dismissive comment that, in the park the people had a Kermode bear and the ducks, what more could they want? After just three months, Carr told Eric Brown at the National Gallery in Ottawa that the project was "dead."

In the following years local artists made a number of attempts to set up a gallery using various rented spaces, but it was not until 1951 when Miss Sara Spencer offered her family mansion for the creation of a permanent gallery that the dream became a reality. Daughter of David Spencer, one of the city's pioneer businessmen, and founder of the city's biggest department store, Miss Spencer was rattling around alone in the family mansion on Moss Street and becoming very tired of its upkeep. She told Patricia Bovey, when the latter arrived to take up the directorship of the gallery in 1980, that she had not meant that the house should be the gallery, but that it should be used to fund one — she said "I don't know why you're still here, I gave the house away because it was a liability and I wanted to get a gallery started." But the Art Gallery of Greater Victoria (AGGV) did use the Spencer mansion, and, sixty years later, it still does; although, over the years there have been numerous attempts to find another location.

Despite various additions to the property, by the 1980s the gallery board recognized that more space was needed to house and exhibit its collection of almost seventeen thousand works, but the economic recession of the late 1980s prevented any major expenditures, so it had to make do and mend. It was recognized that the current Moss Street location was "hidden" and the one mile uphill tramp from the main tourist area was a real deterrent to all but the most determined. The gallery and storage space were insufficient, and there was certainly no room for the amenities that gallery-goers have come to expect — amenities such as an auditorium, library, and restaurant — and there was no room for facilities such as a conservation laboratory. With very

Fig. 10-1. A perspective view of the suggested art gallery on the grounds of St. Ann's Academy. [Paul Merrick Architects.]

The Art Gallery of Greater Victoria [85]

Fig. 10-2. A perspective view of the speculative art gallery, government office, and performing arts centre on the Y-lot, seen from Humboldt Street. [John A. Neilson & Associates.]

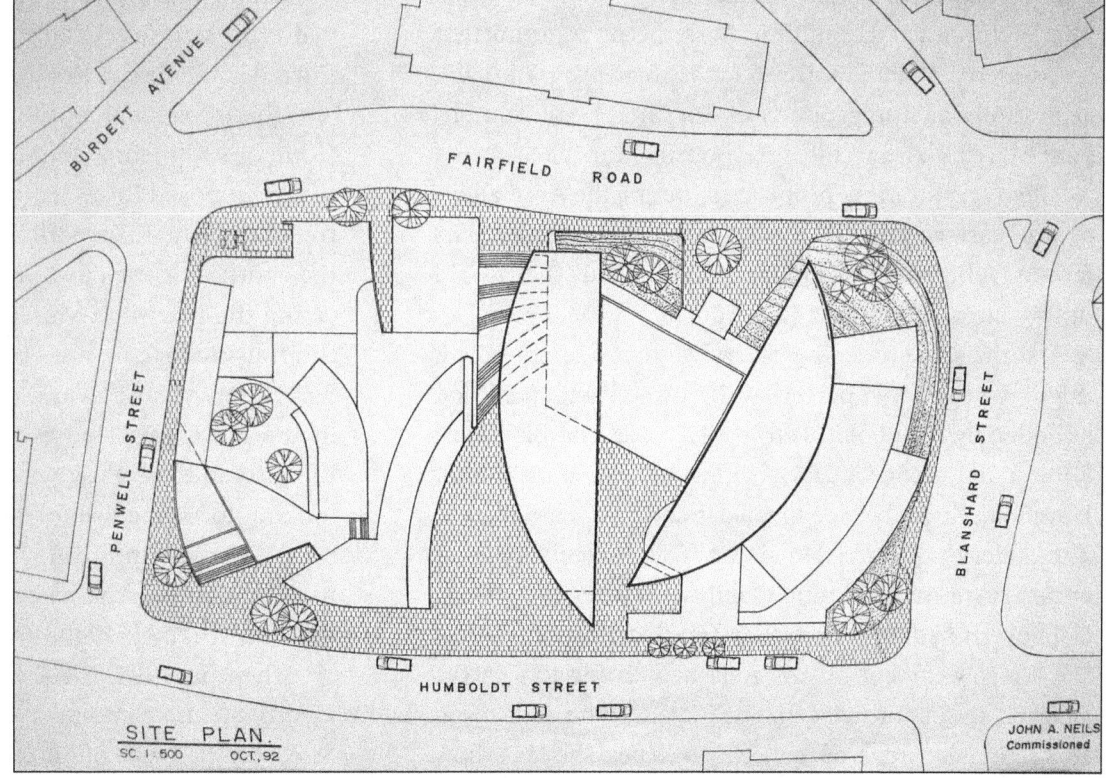

Fig. 10-3. The speculative site plan for the art gallery, government office, and performing arts centre on the Y-lot. [John A. Neilson & Associates.]

little unused land on the site and a restraining Land Use Agreement, further additions were impossible. In 1991 the board concluded that "the AGGV can serve its mandate more effectively from a new Art Gallery at a more visible location," and it made a commitment to relocate. Its options were to build a new gallery, either with or without a collaborating developer, or to purchase a suitable existing building.

At the same time that the gallery was considering its options, the province and city initiated a cooperative development agreement known as the Victoria Accord that examined possible revitalization schemes for various parts of the city, and one of these was the Humboldt Valley/St. Ann's precinct. The process involved soliciting public opinion about how the sites were valued, and how the community would like to see them used. The Victoria arts community was the only group that "expressed a strong desire to focus their programmatic aspirations on the grounds of St. Ann's." Accordingly, Paul Merrick, the architect responsible for the St. Ann's Academy restoration, proposed situating the Art Gallery on the eastern edge of the St. Ann's property, with its facade facing west to provide a public focus that would draw visitors to the area (Fig. 10-1).

At the same time, the gallery was considering how it might use two other parcels of city-owned land: the Y-lot, bounded by Humboldt, Penwell, Fairfield, and Blanshard Streets; and a consolidation of lots on the south side of Humboldt Street between Douglas and Blanshard Streets. The gallery considered that the Y-lot offered the best options in terms of size and visibility, however, the provincial government also had its eye on that lot as a possible site for government offices. As a negotiating tool in the gallery's discussions with the politicians, John A. Neilson & Associates prepared concept sketches showing how the art gallery, government offices, and a performing arts centre could co-exist on the site (Figs. 10-2, 10-3). This scheme had to be abandoned the following year when the provincial government was discussing plans to fill the entire lot with high-rise, high-density office buildings for its own use, revenue from which would provide funding for the art gallery as part of the St. Ann's revitalization.

The city then offered the gallery another option, the use of the old post office on Government Street — now the P.L. James building. To show their cooperation the gallery did evaluate its use, but it was never really a contender. Although it offered a sufficient square footage, the space was poorly arranged with numerous internal columns and insufficient ceiling height, making it unsuitable as a gallery space. The cramped rear access on narrow Langley Street posed potential difficulty in manoeuvring the large trucks delivering sizable art works, and it was in, what was considered at the time, a less than salubrious part of town.

There were land options on the Wharf Street waterfront: one to the north of the Malahat Building, the site of the proposed Reid Centre and later a convention centre, but it remains a parking lot to this day; and one to the south. But the city council had committed to relocating the Maritime Museum to the southern site, and fundraising for that was "reported to be on target." That was twenty years ago and the Maritime Museum is still in the old Court House on Bastion Square. Although the city and the Provincial Capital Commission were looking for some use for these parcels, the community pressure to retain the views and open space meant that use of the land to the west of Wharf Street for a building that was seeking a high profile would not get approval.

Then, in 1994, there was a possibility that the BC Hydro site, a promontory at the northern end of Store Street on the shore of Rock Bay, might become available, and architect John Neilson prepared a scheme for the AGGV. The concept acknowledged the industrial nature of the site's history and its role in the working harbour of the late nineteenth century and the early years of the twentieth. Three heritage buildings on the site would be rehabilitated. Two of them that had been part of the Victoria Gas Company's premises were to frame the entrance to the gallery complex, and the third, the former powerhouse of the National Electric Tramway and Lighting Company, would be used for indoor and outdoor exhibits. The ensemble would close the vista up Store Street, and have an impressive presence from the intersection of Government and Pembroke Streets (Fig. 10-4) and from the water (Fig. 10-5).

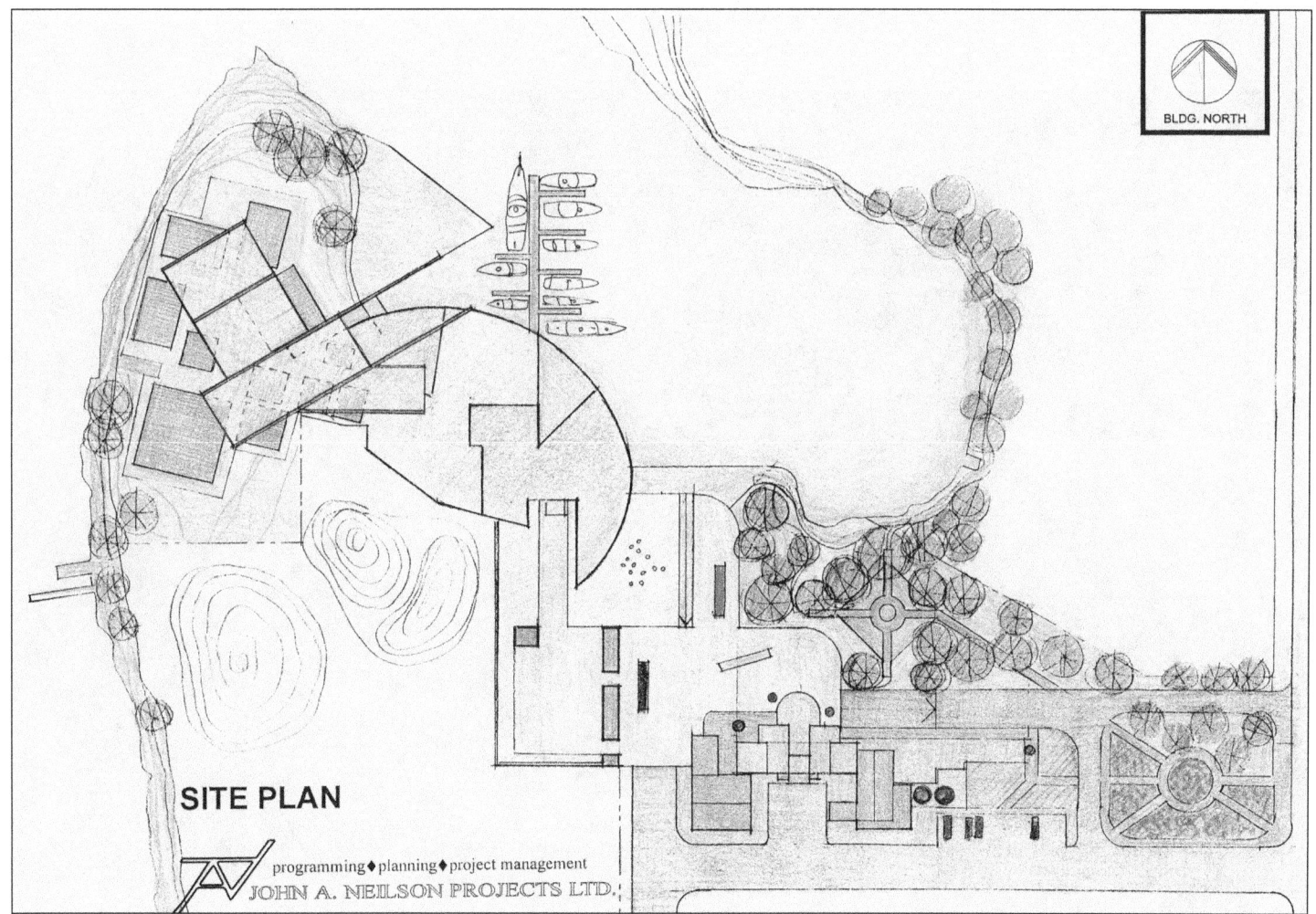

Fig. 10-4. A site plan for the Rock Bay concept, with Pembroke Street at lower right-hand side. [John A. Neilson Projects Ltd.]

[88] UNBUILT VICTORIA

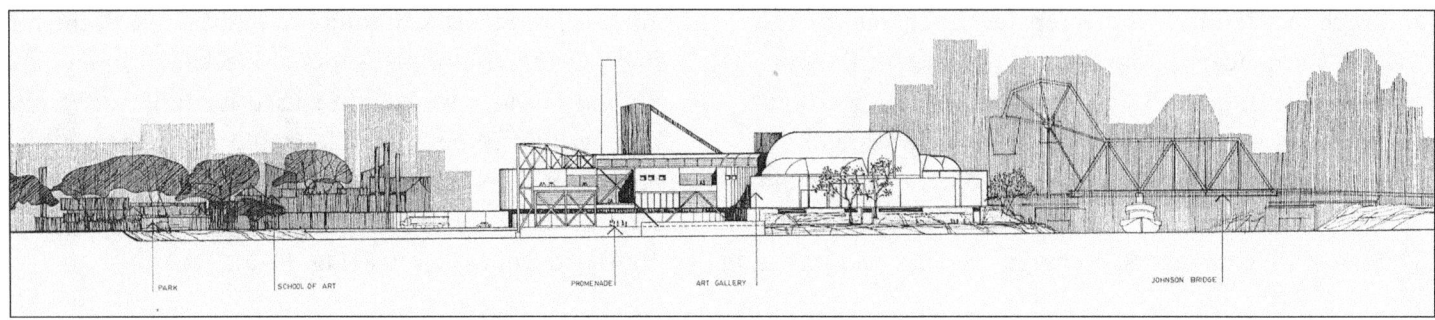

Fig. 10-5. A sketch of view of gallery ensemble from the harbour. [John A. Neilson Projects Ltd.]

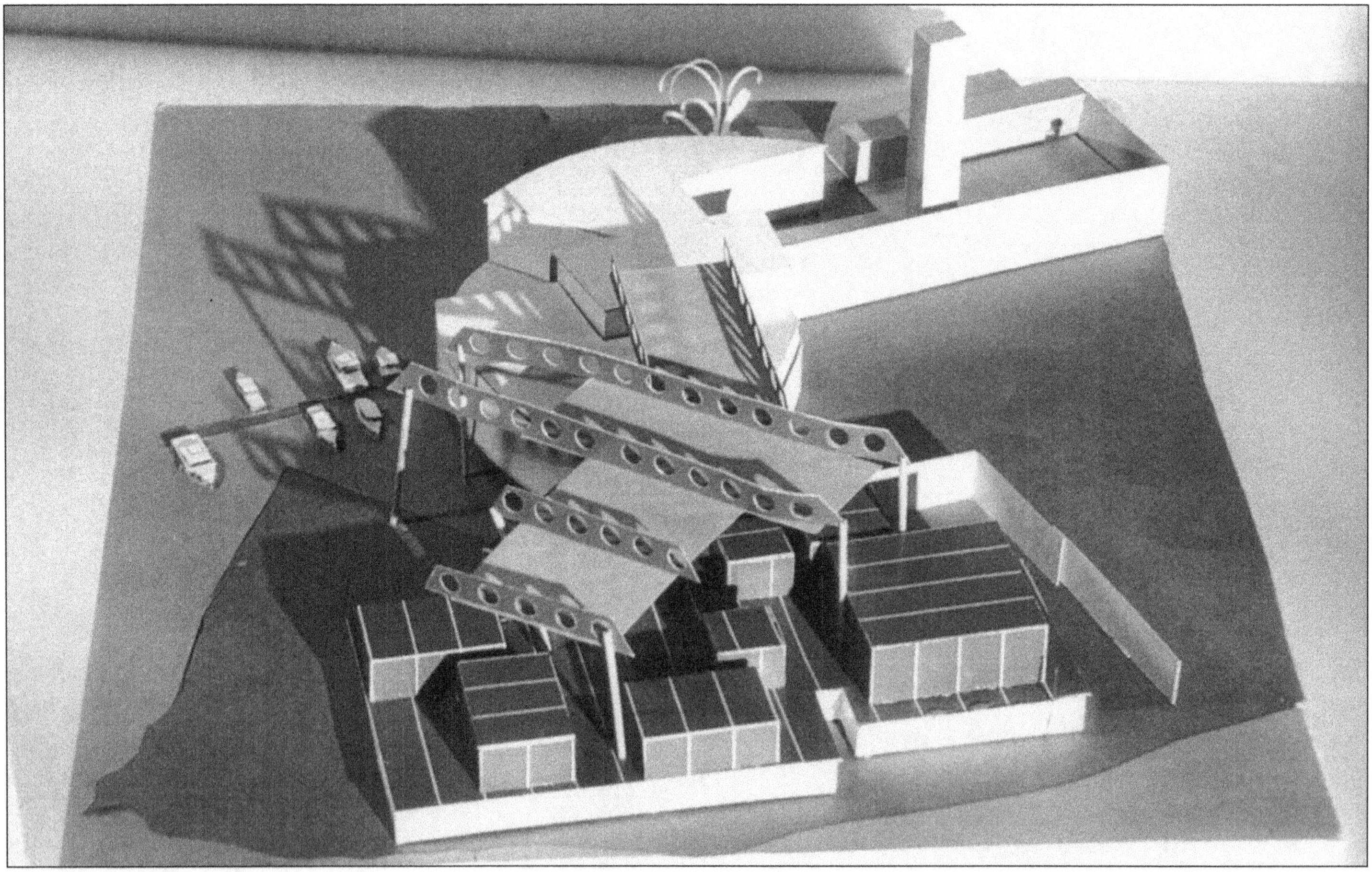

Fig. 10-6. A model of the main gallery buildings, showing the industrial design. [John A. Neilson Projects Ltd.]

The galleries were grouped at the promontory and their architectural form had the appearance of large shipping containers and warehouses to reflect the types of buildings customarily found lining a working harbour (Fig. 10-6). Other buildings were designed for complementary uses, such as artist's workshops, an auditorium, a seminar room, etc. The outdoor space was given over to such amenities as exhibition plazas and space for a sculpture gallery. On the perimeter of the property was a park-like area that extending around the bay in a "coastal promenade." The property was large enough to accommodate facilities for large groups — which was particularly important for the gallery's schools' program that then-director Patricia Bovey considered a vital component of its activities — and room for large trucks that contained valuable and sensitive travelling exhibitions to manoeuvre and unload indoors.

This scheme gave the gallery every facility required in its functional program. It had the unanimous support of the board, a public survey of Victorians indicated that 88 percent thought that the gallery should move, and local MP David Anderson was all in favour. A fundraising "guru" was confident that the money could be raised, and the gallery had even considered possible future uses for the Spencer mansion.

And then the axe fell.

The land at Rock Bay had been used for nearly a century by the Victoria Gas Company for a coal gasification plant, and it was heavily polluted with coal tar. Before the site could be used, the land would have to be re-mediated, and this, the gallery was told, would be its responsibility. While it was confident that it could raise the money to build, the burden of the cleanup was the last straw. Ten years later Transport Canada announced a joint project between the Government of Canada and BC Hydro to clean up Rock Bay; it was to cost $32.1 million, and take three years.

The bitter disappointment at the loss of the Rock Bay scheme was somewhat assuaged by another offer from the city. This time it was land, not a building. The city fathers had decided that it was time to re-vamp Centennial Square, which had been built in the early 1960s in a bold attempt to create a vibrant civic amenity, but after early enthusiasm it fell into disuse. Part of the revitalization plan was the sale of land in the northeast quadrant of Centennial Square for use by various cultural organizations. The city proposed to provide the gallery with enough land for the development of a new Art Gallery facility with floor space of up to fourteen thousand square metres — a floor area the gallery's analysis had found to be ideal. Additional buildings, like the city archives, a college of performing arts, the Civic Heritage Trust, and an interpretation centre, would also be considered for the site. The Art Gallery was to come up with a space and facilities study and a fundraising plan within eighteen months.

As the gallery started planning, Victoria entrepreneur Robert Wright put together what he called a "blue ribbon panel" of nineteen like-minded businessmen — and no politicians — to spearhead the creation of a downtown arts centre. Prompted by the proposal to spend over $20 million on refurbishing the McPherson and Royal theatres, Wright and his team proposed that a brand new purpose-built arts complex containing two theatres, one seating three hundred and the other 1,800, and the art gallery would be a much better use for arts funding. The proposed site for this new complex was the Y-lot, again, which still had not been built on as the provincial government found it could not afford its new office towers. Now part of the land had been sold, and

Concert Properties of Vancouver were in the final stages of preparations to start building a Marriott hotel. The company was alarmed at the prospect of having this project delayed, or worse, derailed. Wright was adamant that the project should occupy the entire Y-lot and resisted suggestions that his group work with Concert — which had an option to buy the remainder of the lot — on a joint venture. In a move that mayor Alan Lowe described as "fortuitous," and nothing to do with the arts complex proposal, city councillors asked for a review of land use on the Y-lot. Concert were threatening to pull the plug, and the Citizens Committee for the Performing Arts and Cultural Centre was delighted. But within a month the review was completed and a development permit issued, leaving the arts centre proponents pragmatically discussing with the developer what could be done on the remainder of the lot. But with no firm plans, no funding in place — the original plan had been to fund the arts centre with the sale of the Royal and the Art Gallery on Moss Street, with additional funds from the federal and provincial governments — and the Marriott scheduled for completion with a year, the project became more and more of a pipe dream. Enthusiasm dwindled, and in January 2001, it died.

While the majority of councillors were still in favour of an art gallery in Centennial Square, the mayor wanted to prioritize a new multiplex arena to replace the Memorial Arena, and the city could not afford both. Plus there were other infrastructure projects vying for funding. In what the *Times Colonist* called a "feeding frenzy" for infrastructure grants, the council changed its priorities and made the Gorge/Burnside community centre top of its grant-application list. Disappointed, especially as they had invested some $100,000 in preparing the study the city had asked for, the gallery board still hoped that with its own fundraising, the city's promised $3 million in 2003, and federal and provincial grant money, it could build a $25 million Art Gallery of Greater Victoria at Centennial Square … eventually. Optimism soon faded in the face of an economic downturn and cost-cutting measures by the provincial government, and the board accepted that the house on Moss Street would continue as the main gallery, but it hoped to build a satellite site adjacent to the Marriott hotel on the Y-lot.

Yet another option presented itself when Austin Hamilton purchased the Crystal Court Motel on the south side of Belleville Street and developed plans for a two-storey satellite gallery and a 51-metre-high, fourteen-storey apartment building at the corner of Belleville and Blanshard Streets. The gallery, it was proposed, would have "sweeping copper roofs," extensive windows, and a public plaza in front. But the gallery portion of this scheme was dependent on funding from Ottawa, which did not materialize. In conversation with Councillor Pamela Madoff, Hamilton asked what he should do with the motel. She told him, "I would never have bought it in the first place. It is one of the most challenging sites in the city." Hamilton turned around and sold the property to the Westbank Corporation.

Westbank also decided on an art gallery/residential building proposal. It hired architect James K.M. Cheng who devised a scheme that Westbank thought would please all interested parties — city planners, the community, and the Art Gallery (Fig. 10-7). The proposal was for two buildings on the block: a two-storey art gallery with an open-air sculpture court at the west end of the property at the corner of Government Street, and a "slender 19 or 21-storey residential condominium tower" at the east end (Fig. 10-8). This gallery would be a satellite site to its Moss Street location, and would be the gallery's property.

The quid pro quo for this generosity would be the city granting permission to build the tower. The benefits of this plan to create an "exciting cultural and residential destination" were that there would not be a "view-blocking slab" along the entire south side of Belleville Street between Government and Blanshard Streets. The Queen Victoria Hotel would be able to retain its harbour views, the sculpture park would be a "virtuoso amenity at street level," and Westbank would fund its donation to the gallery from the sale of the condominiums.

Fig. 10-7. The Vicinity Plan showing the location of the Westbank Corporation proposal. [James KM Cheng Architects.]

Fig. 10-8. A rendering of the proposed Westbank Corporation scheme for a residential tower and art gallery, looking east along Belleville Street from Douglas Street. [Gene Radvenis.]

When Westbank was told that city planners were unlikely to approve the tower height, they went back to the drawing board and came up with a pair of shorter towers, but the gallery was now integrated into one of them. After much deliberation the gallery board decided that a standalone facility was an "indispensable requisite" and declined the revised offer.

In March 2008 the city announced yet another plan to locate the art gallery in a central location, on the site of the bowling green and Cridge Park, just to the east of the Crystal Garden. The Canadian Pacific Lawn Bowling Club had leased part of this city-owned land for $1 a year for over seventy years, but now the city wanted to do something more culturally vibrant with this important piece of real estate so close to the main tourist area. Mayor Alan Lowe suggested selling part of the two-hectare site for the construction of an office building and using the remainder as the site of the art gallery and a children's museum, with two storeys of underground parking. The proposal met with a storm of protest from residents of the Humboldt valley, the Cridge Park Rescue Group, and heritage organizations, and in January 2009 the city council, and its new mayor Dean Fortin, voted to remove this land from its development portfolio.

In March 2011, gallery director Jon Tupper announced that "the gallery has no intentions of moving anywhere in the foreseeable future." After almost two decades of thwarted dreams, the gallery board decided to stay in the heritage home on Moss Street. As one board member put it, it has a "human and welcoming dimension," and while it may not have all the facilities that the board desired, it has "habitability."

Chapter 11

THEATRES

THE GLOBE THEATRE AND THE BANKSIDE ELIZABETHAN VILLAGE

In March 1980, the District of Saanich Council was treated to an oration worthy of the Shakespearean stage. The actor delivering this speech was Barry Morse, former artistic director of the Shaw Festival, Niagara-on-the-Lake, and remembered by those of a certain age as the tireless Lieutenant Philip Gerard who chased *The Fugitive* across the television screens of North America for 117 episodes from 1963 to 1967. Morse was appearing before the council in the role of founding artistic director of The Lord Chamberlain's Players — a name borrowed from a group of which the bard himself was a member — asking for support for the group's plan to build a re-creation of the Globe Playhouse that Shakespeare had known.

The proposal outlined by Morse was for the replica of the theatre to stand on the grounds of the former Maltwood estate on a two-and-a-half hectare triangle of land between the Pat Bay Highway, Royal Oak Drive, and West Saanich Road. The property already had a building that was the ideal complement to the Elizabethan theatre: a house modelled on a fourteenth century Elizabethan hall house, with a thatched roof, mock-Tudor half-timbering, and eye-brow dormers. Originally built in 1936 by a couple with grand plans to open a tea room in the English fashion where afternoon *thés dansants* could be held in the double-height great hall, the house was, by 1980, home of the Maltwood Museum of the University of Victoria, and the university was moving the museum onto the campus and selling the property.

The Lord Chamberlain's Players planned to use the house as a restaurant and build the theatre just to the east of it. These plans then "mushroomed into a full-blown tourist attraction that will envelop visitors in a 16th century London atmosphere." As Morse explained to the council, the addition of an Elizabethan village would be of "cultural, tourist and educational value," and would be a financial support for the theatre's operations. Visitors would experience the "sights and sounds of the Elizabethan era ... swordsmen duelling, a smithy shoeing horses, minstrels serenading patrons of an Elizabethan-theme restaurant." But there were concerns that the venture would be of more benefit to visitors than the local residents, that it would be an "Elizabethan Barkerville," an allusion to the former gold-rush town in the Cariboo mountains that has become a major tourist attraction where the visitor can pan for gold, meet locals in nineteenth-century costumes, take in the sort of entertainment that would have been seen in gold-rush days, and shop in replica stores.

Morse's presentation was long on rhetoric but short on figures, and the company was given sixty days to formalize its plans. It produced a comprehensive prospectus explaining that the Globe Playhouse would be surrounded by the Bankside Elizabethan Village (Fig. 11-1) in which the visitor would experience "the sights and sounds (but not the smells!) of London Town in the days of Good Queen Bess" — marketing to the perceived Englishness of Victoria, perhaps. Amongst the experiences under consideration were the Shakespeare Memorial Garden planted with all the herbs and flowers that are mentioned in the plays, each with its appropriate quotation ("a rose by any other name"); a craftsmen's corner with displays of such skills as weaving and blacksmithing, etc., with products for sale; "Elizabethan banquets with ale, sack, and

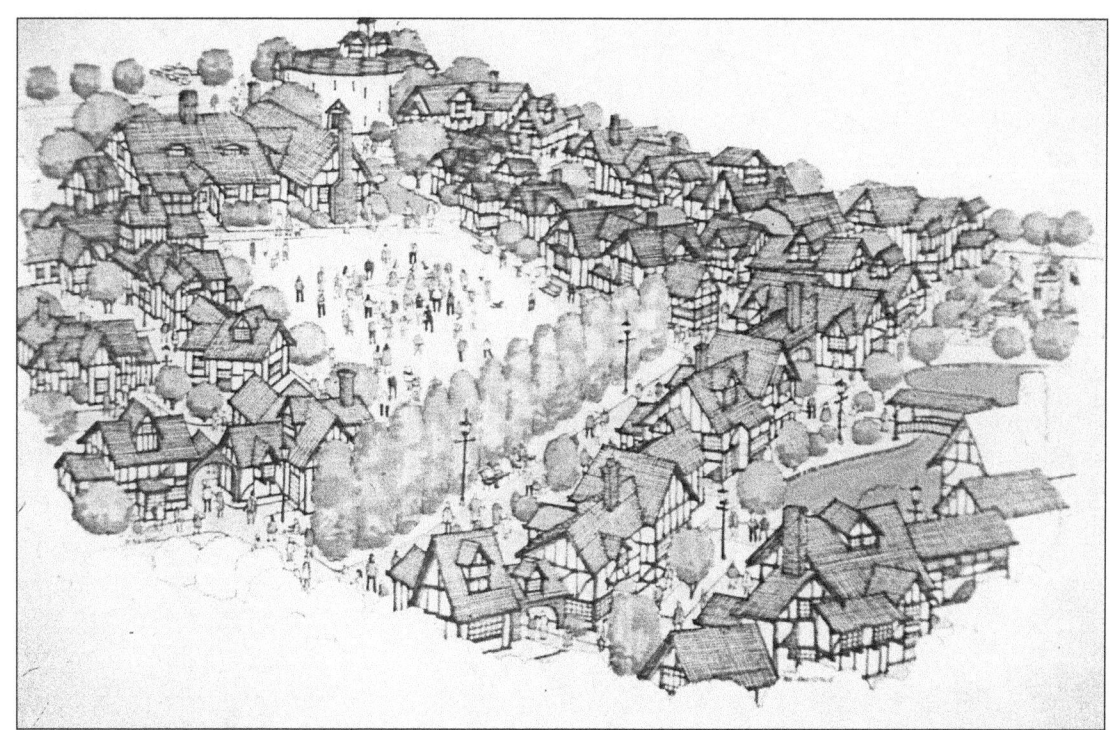

Fig. 11-1. Artist's concept of the proposed Bankside Elizabethan Village, with the replica of the Globe Theatre in the background, from a painting by Ardath Boyce. [Saanich Archives.]

mead"; and displays of sports such as duelling, archery, and jousting. All in all, it would be a festival that would provide both pleasure and profit and bring "pride to the community, to the Province, to Western Canada, and indeed to the whole country."

The original idea for the theatre came from Conrad Boyce, journalist and theatre enthusiast, who was working in the Yukon and had plenty of time on his hands to dream. Inspired by works such as *Shakespeare's Theatre* and *The Globe Restored* by noted Shakespeare scholar C. Walter Hodges, he conceived the idea of building a replica of The Globe Theatre in Victoria, where his family lived. The grounds of the Old English Inn in Esquimalt, which contain a replica of Anne Hathaway's cottage, seemed an ideal location, although he eventually realized that there was too little space. So he turned his attention to the Maltwood estate. Needing help to get the project going Boyce hired a project manager, who was successful in marshalling an impressive board of directors, including local politician Peter Pollen, University of Victoria professor of theatre Alan Hughes, Canadian diplomat Hugh Keenleyside, and Barry Morse.

Hughes instigated a graduate student project to investigate how an old playhouse could be adapted to modern building codes (Fig. 11-2), and the project seemed set to go. All it needed to get started was financing, which the

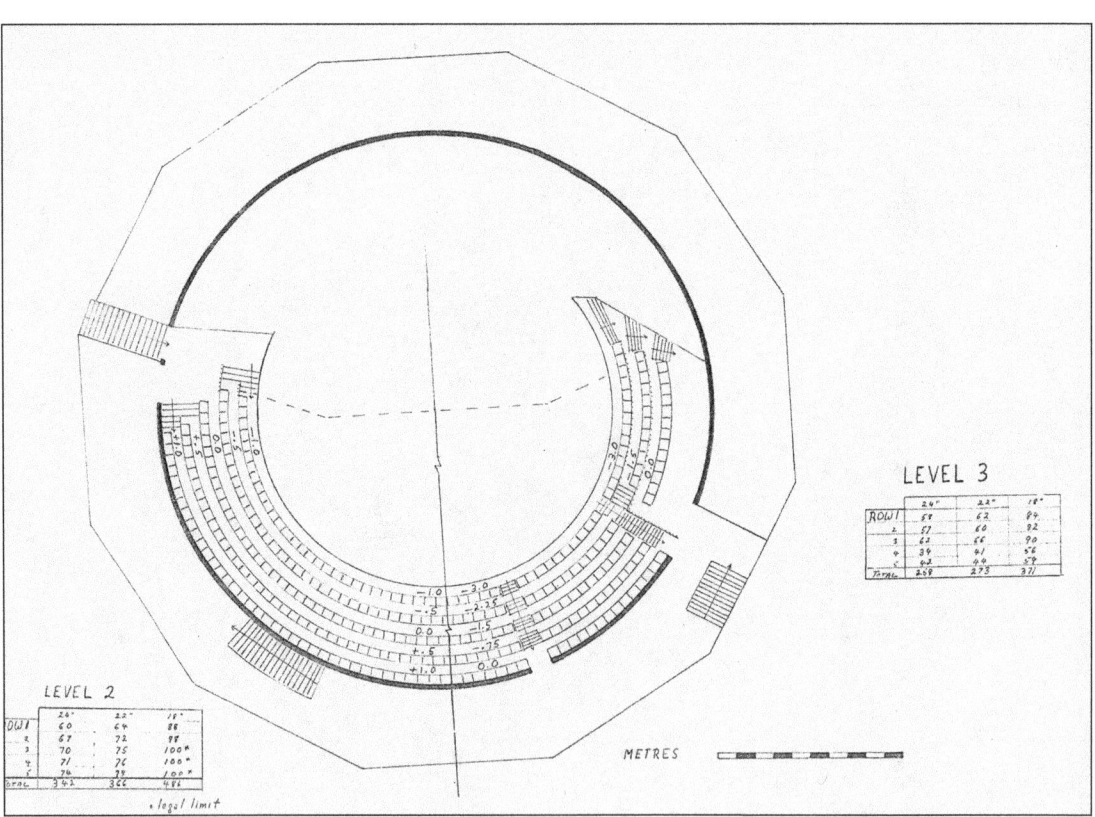

Fig. 11-2. A plan of the proposed theatre. [Saanich Archives.]

board hoped would come from all three levels of government, private and corporate donations, the banks, and the travel industry. After the initial outlay the project would, it anticipated, be self supporting. But it could only be self-supporting if the Elizabethan village theme park was included, and this was not part of Boyce's original scheme. Eventually differences about the goals of the project, coupled with financial woes, led to the departure of Morse and the collapse of the scheme.

THE CITY LIGHTS THEATRE

Designed by architect J.C.M. Keith — who was building up his practice during the long wait for a start on his designs for Christ Church Cathedral — the brick building at the foot of Swift Street was, from its construction in 1894 until 1940, the power-generating station for the Victoria Electric Railway & Lighting Company. Over the following years the building had a variety of uses, the first being as a terminus for municipal garbage barges, which would haul the city's waste out to Juan De Fuca Strait — a marginally better

Fig. 11-3. A perspective from the harbour of the plaza and amphitheatres of the proposed City Lights Theatre on the former BC Electric site, Swift Street. [The wade williams corporation, principal/architect Terence Williams with Christopher Gower.]

place than James Bay — and dump it, a practice that eventually became unacceptable. Then the city rented it to small businesses such as a welding shop and a grain warehouse.

By the 1980s it was in need of revitalization, and the city, who owned the property, called for proposals stipulating that the historic brick building would be conserved, restored, and adapted for a new public use. The Kaleidoscope Theatre, with architects the wade williams corporation, submitted this 1988 proposal to convert the building into a theatre/restaurant, to be called, appropriately, the City Lights Theatre. At the waterfront would be a public plaza with two small amphitheatres and mooring for diners and theatre-goers arriving by boat (Fig. 11-3). The proposed interior had an open stage, a gallery for casual viewing, and raked seats for the more traditional theatrical experience (Fig. 11-4). The city rejected this public-use scheme in favour of the Canoe Brew Pub.

Fig. 11-4. A perspective of the interior of the City Lights Theatre. [The wade williams corporation, principal/architect Terence Williams with Christopher Gower.]

HARBOURS

Chapter 12

Victoria Harbour

THE HARBOUR WAS ONCE THE THROBbing heart of Victoria. The settlement was, after all, founded as a trading post of the Hudson's Bay Company (HBC). Everything that the colony needed, and could not make for itself, was brought in by sea, and the abundant resources of the hinterland and ocean went to the world's markets the same way. The harbour was the city, and Wharf Street the city's main thoroughfare. Sailing vessels were moored all along the Wharf Street waterfront from Johnson Street to Ship Point, at low tide James Bay was a stinking mud flat, and to the south lay the Legislative buildings and the estate of James Douglas, HBC factor and, later, governor of the colony.

The unkind among the citizens suggested that Douglas had chosen the site of the government buildings, so conveniently close to his own house, in order to get a bridge built across the mud flats and save him the journey around the head of the bay when he wanted to go between home and the fort. A wooden trestle was built across the mouth of the bay, at a cost of £800, an expenditure that some considered excessive and indicative of the governor's autocratic ways, but it had the effect of making the condition of the flats more visible from the vantage point of the middle of the bridge. Architect and local politician Richard Lewis suggested draining the bay to make land that could be used for a public park, but the editor of the *Colonist* thought it a much better, and more profitable, idea to dredge it and build more docks. Neither solution was acted upon.

By the 1890s the condition of James Bay had deteriorated to the extent that the problem demanded serious attention. In the 1860s the bay was smelly and unattractive, this was due to stagnant shallow water — it was even possible to dig for clams there then. Thirty years later it was polluted by the effluent of the soap works on its banks and had accumulated three decades of the city's rubbish — animal, vegetable, and mineral. The trestle had become rickety and dangerous, school children marching across it were advised to break stride. The city may have lost its status as the province's commercial and trading centre, but it was not going to forfeit its position as provincial capital; the old wooden parliament buildings, colloquially known as the Birdcages, and the butt of local humour, had to go. The provincial government announced a design competition for new parliament buildings to replace them — it was time to do something about the eyesore and embarrassment of the mudflats and the hazardous bridge that led to the site (Fig. 12-1).

Civil engineer H. Badeley Smith had been working on his plans for a year when he made a public announcement that he proposed to buy the mudflats and replace the bridge with a permanent stone road linking Government Street to Superior Street. The harbour in front of the new road would be dredged and a wharf built so that vessels drawing over six metres could load and unload at the end of Government Street. The bridge was to be two storeys tall, with shops on each side and storage vaults beneath. The cost of this endeavour was $300,000, a sum that failed to attract investors.

But replacing the tottering bridge was now firmly on the council's agenda and it held a competition for plans,

Fig. 12-1. Looking north over James Bay, the rickety old bridge is on the left-hand side, William Pendray's factory is on the north bank, and St. Andrew's Presbyterian church is on the horizon to the right. The date is undetermined, but after 1890 and before 1905. [Collection of Greg Windwick.]

not only for a new bridge but also for reclamation of the harbour, which was silting up. The winner of the competition was Thomas Sorby (1836–1924), an English architect who had come to Canada at the age of forty-seven and had never really been comfortable in the unsophisticated pioneer environment. He was nearing his sixties when he drew up his comprehensive plan for the entire harbour, and promoting it became his obsession for the remainder of his life. Although his was the winning entry, the council refused to pay him the $350 award as it did not think the work could be done for the stipulated $80,000.

Sorby's ambitious scheme (Fig. 12-2) not only included the causeway across the mouth of James Bay and the reclamation of land to its west, although the mud

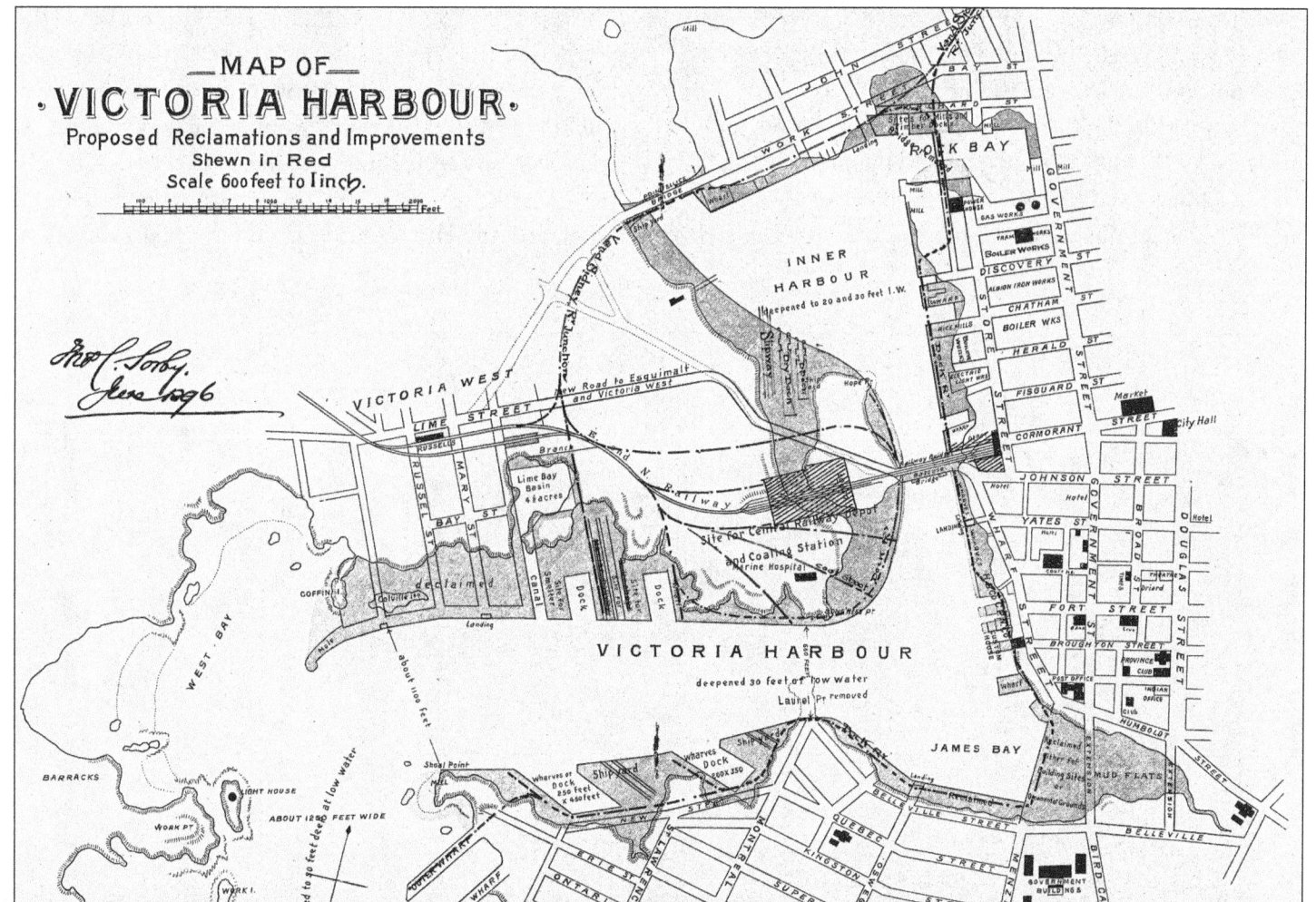

Fig. 12-2. Design for proposed reclamations and improvement in Victoria Harbour by Thomas Sorby, 1896. [CVA A0019.]

flats seemed to remain, but also called for land reclamation all around the edge of the harbour and the construction of numerous docks. Laurel Point was to be removed, various sites for industrial activity — such as a smelter, shipyards, and railway works — were earmarked, as was a new railway hugging the shore from the outer wharf all the way round to Rock Bay where it would link to the Victoria and Sidney railway. The plan essentially enlarged the harbour as a working harbour, and even though Sorby travelled to Ottawa in order to convince the government that it should assist in funding the project, the money for such a major undertaking was never forthcoming.

The mudflats did get filled in and the causeway built between 1903–1905, not as part of improving either access to the parliament buildings or the facilities of a working harbour, but in the cause of attracting tourists. Herbert Cuthbert, head of the newly formed Tourist Association, was convinced that the causeway should be built and the land behind it should be filled in to the height of the new road and be used as a pleasure ground and winter garden. The road, he suggested, should be lined with shops along its east side, and roofed with glass to create a shopping arcade. Cuthbert claimed that his plan would not cost the city a penny as the profit from rents for shops and attractions would be $25,000 a year. Unprepared to take the financial risk, Mayor Charles Hayward proposed that the reclaimed land be subdivided into sixty-one building lots — perhaps not coincidentally since Hayward was a builder — the sale of which would fund constructing the causeway and reclaiming the land.

It took two years to dam the bay and reclaim the land, and the city seemed not to have had a clear plan

Fig. 12-3. A sketch of the proposed harbour basin and CPR hotel by F.M. Rattenbury. Published in the *Colonist*, May 23, 1903.

of how the land should be used — but Francis Mawson Rattenbury did. Fresh from his success as architect of the newly completed parliament buildings, Rattenbury had persuaded the CPR that a hotel to complement his parliament buildings, designed by him, would be a sound business proposition, as indeed the Empress Hotel proved to be (Fig. 12-3).

In the modernizing and improving climate of the 1960s, the city commissioned a seemingly unending series of studies, reports, proposals, etc., examining what should be done in the harbour, but few led to any action. As the years went by, the question became more complex. The decisions of the councillors and planners about what was in the best interest of the city were

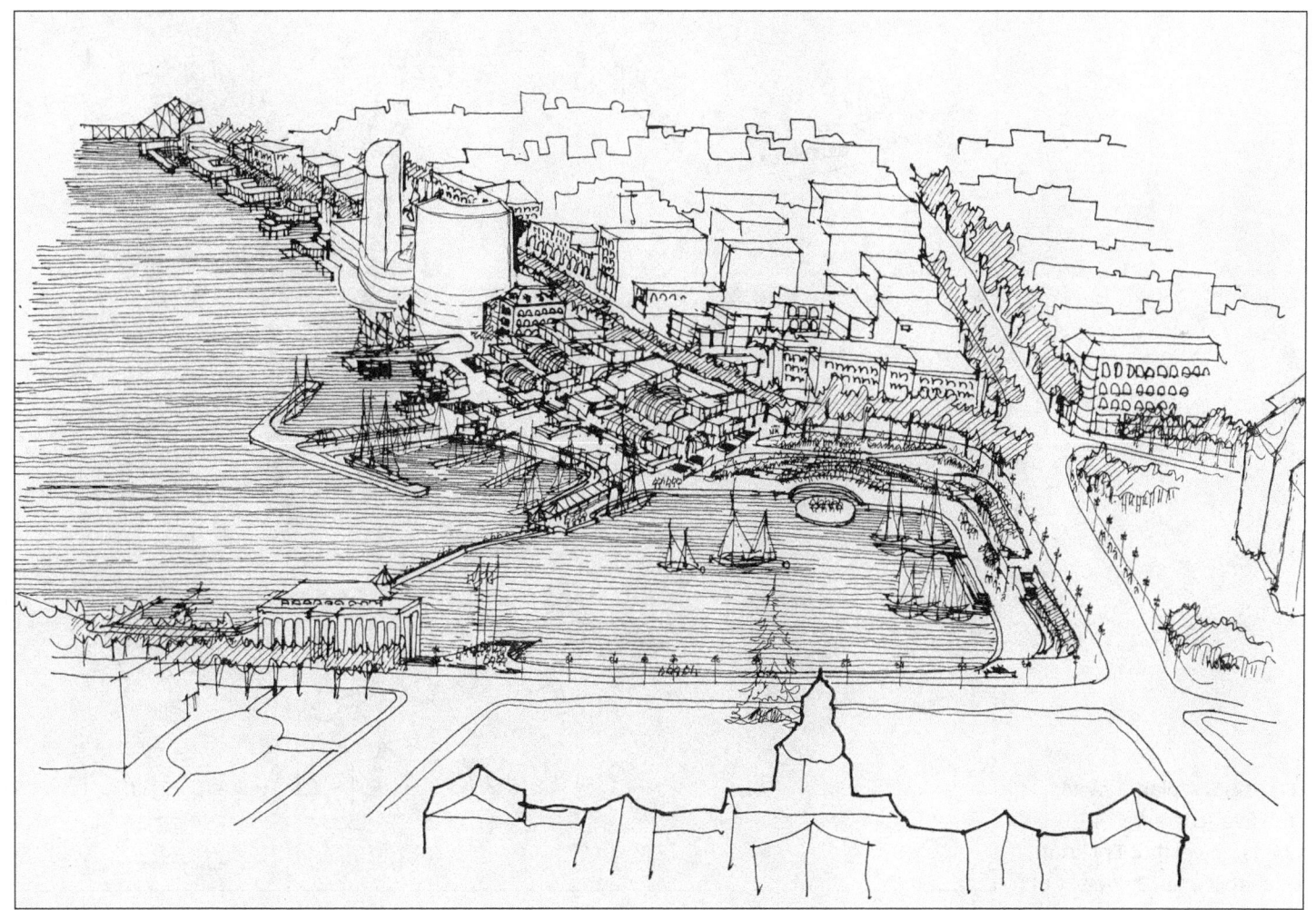

Fig. 12-4. A sketch of the recommended changes in Victoria Harbour by Arthur Erickson Architects, 1973. [CVA, CD 65.]

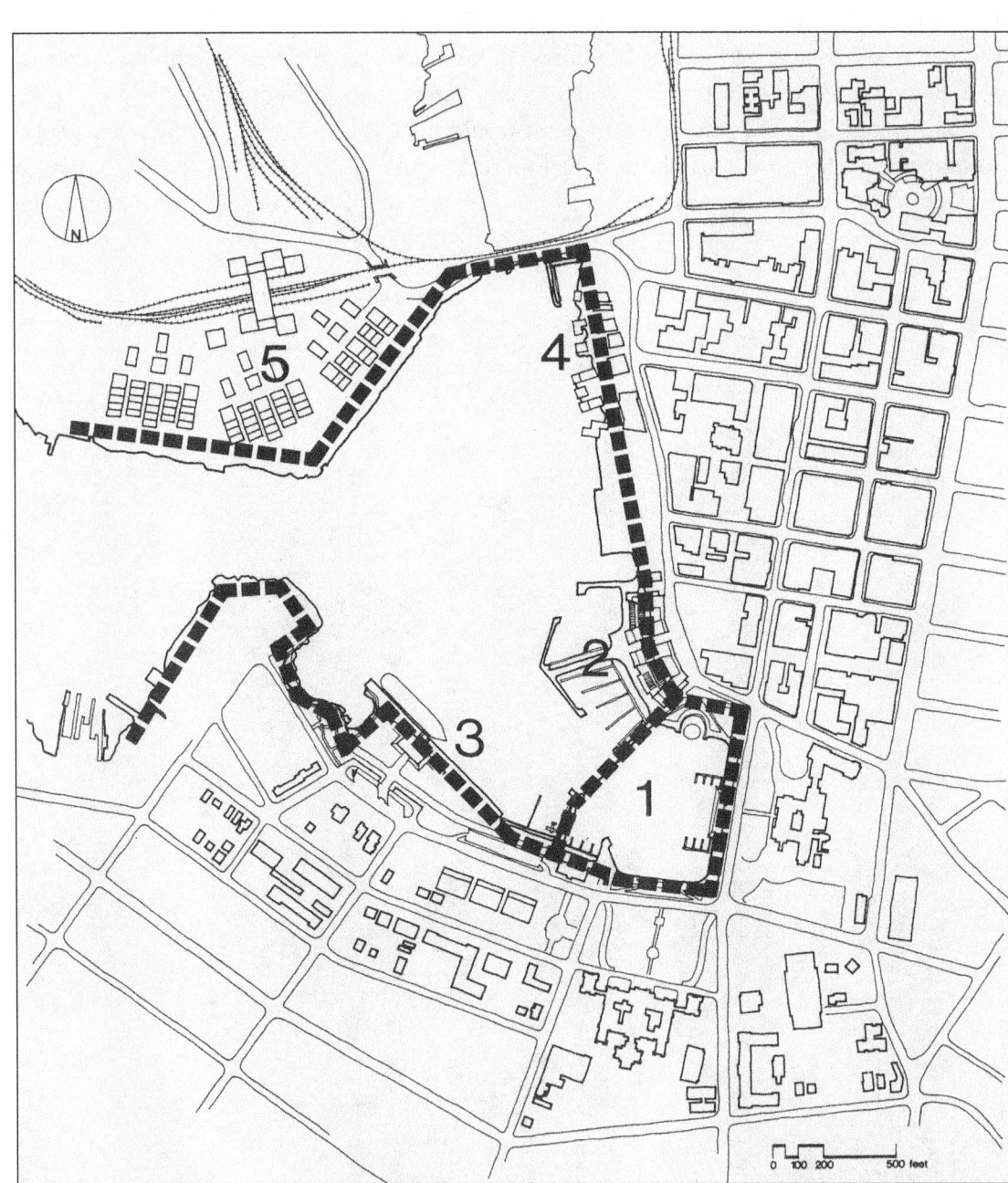

Fig. 12-5. A plan showing the five "character areas," by Arthur Erickson Architects, 1973. [CVA, CD 65.]

Fig. 12-6. A sketch of the interior of the galleria in area two by Arthur Erickson Architects, 1973. [CVA, CD 65.]

frequently at odds with popular opinion, and citizens began to demand a say in changes in their environment. Citizens' protests, financial constraints, the heritage lobby, jurisdictional disputes between the city and the province, and some political grandstanding all combined to produce inertia.

One of these studies was more influential than most, the Inner Harbour Study of 1973, by the noted architect Arthur Erickson, developed a "detailed design concept" and was the most all-encompassing plan yet produced (Fig. 12-4). Erickson divided the harbour into five "character areas." Each was to have its own style of development and the areas should all be connected by a walkway that would extend all around the harbour from Laurel Point to Songhees Point (Fig. 12-5).

The Inner Harbour basin, in front of the Empress Hotel, would become an activity basin. It would be made more pedestrian-orientated with the creation of a promenade running below the surface level of the causeway in front of the parliament buildings, and connecting to form a loop over two jetties and a pedestrian bridge. The suggestion of having an amphitheatre on the slope of Ship Point is one that reappears in later studies of the Wharf Street waterfront.

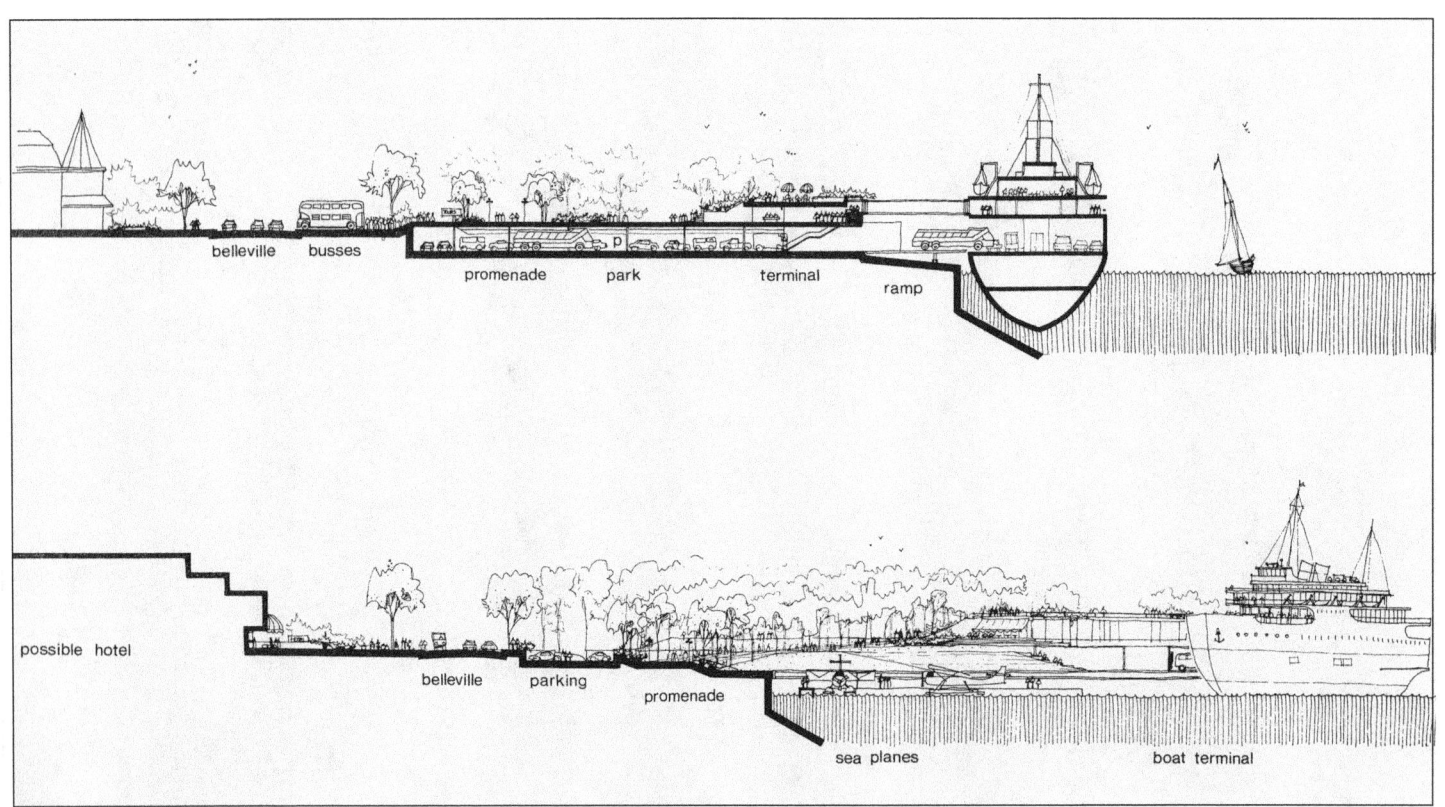

Fig. 12-7. The plan of the James Bay Waterfront by Arthur Erickson Architects, 1973 [CVA, CD 65.]

As the area closest to downtown, Erickson proposed that the land in front of the Malahat Building, area two, should be developed as a commercial area with a multiplicity of activities, which could provide a stimulus to the businesses in the old town; it should be a "social, recreational, cultural, civic market place." There should be an indoor/outdoor space, terraced towards the water and with plenty of glass for both light and openness. Suggested uses might be specialty food shops, book stores and reading rooms, and craft and theatre workshops — all activities that would not breach the public-use requirement that had been placed on the property when the city bought it with provincial and federal funding assistance. The existing wharves should be replaced by two mooring basins for pleasure craft in the summer and, perhaps, fishing boats in the winter (Fig. 12-6).

The James Bay waterfront, area three, should be the transportation hub for ferry and seaplane passengers and a recreation area for James Bay residents. Parkland, with a tree-lined promenade leading to the city core, would extend eastwards from Laurel Point, and include the landscaped roof deck of the sea-level ferry parking (Fig. 12-7). Area four, extending from the northern end of the Reid site, on the west side of Wharf Street at the foot of Bastion Square, to the Johnson Street Bridge, would preserve the collection of early brick and stone buildings and add small intimate shops at the water's edge and pedestrian walkways, giving the feeling of a mews (Fig. 12-8). And, finally, the Old Songhees Reserve should be developed as a residential area, which, Erickson recommended, should be a mix of terraced houses, apartments, and condominiums — a distinctive neighbourhood created with integrated commercial, recreational, and educational facilities, and a transport hub (Fig. 12-9).

Of this far-ranging plan, only part of the proposed promenade below the level of the causeway has been built: the Old Songhees Reserve has become a residential area, but not the integrated neighbourhood that Erickson envisaged; ferry traffic has been consolidated along the James Bay waterfront, but seaplanes have not; and the possibility of showcasing the old masonry warehouses and creating a mews-like environment north from Hartwig Court to the Johnson Street Bridge has been lost with the construction of a huge waterfront hotel. Interestingly, Erickson assumed that the twin-towered version of the Reid Centre (Fig. 12-4) would be built, and it was not.

In 1988 Victoria's bid to host the 1994 Commonwealth Games was successful, in part because it promised spectacular opening and closing ceremonies in the harbour. The initial plan was to have a stage and athletic field on barges, and the spectators seated on bleachers on Government and Belleville Streets. The wade williams corporation architects were asked to explore a range of options for utilizing the Inner Harbour basin as a setting for Games ceremonies and also for a range of athletic events. It soon became apparent that these early ideas would place the audience, and the television cameras, with their backs to city's iconic ensemble of the parliament buildings and the Empress Hotel, so the firm suggested reversing the plan.

The spectators and the media centre would be on a floating platform facing into the harbour basin and viewing the floating stage with the parliament buildings and the Empress Hotel as the stage set, as it were. Dignities, athletes, and entertainers were to enter from the arrivals plaza at Government and Belleville Streets via a tidal ramp; spectators and those connected with services and facilities on the viewing platform would enter via tidal ramps from adjacent streets (Fig. 12-10). With this arrangement, the media, placed high at the rear of the bleachers, would have the mountains of Olympic National Park in Washington State framing the buildings as a backdrop to events. It would have been a spectacular image to show the world.

Industrial barges were to be the floats on which the seating and the stage would be built, and both were to be angled at a forty-five degrees so that the parliament buildings and the Empress Hotel would flank each side of the central view of the floating field. Services such as washrooms and concessions were to be housed within

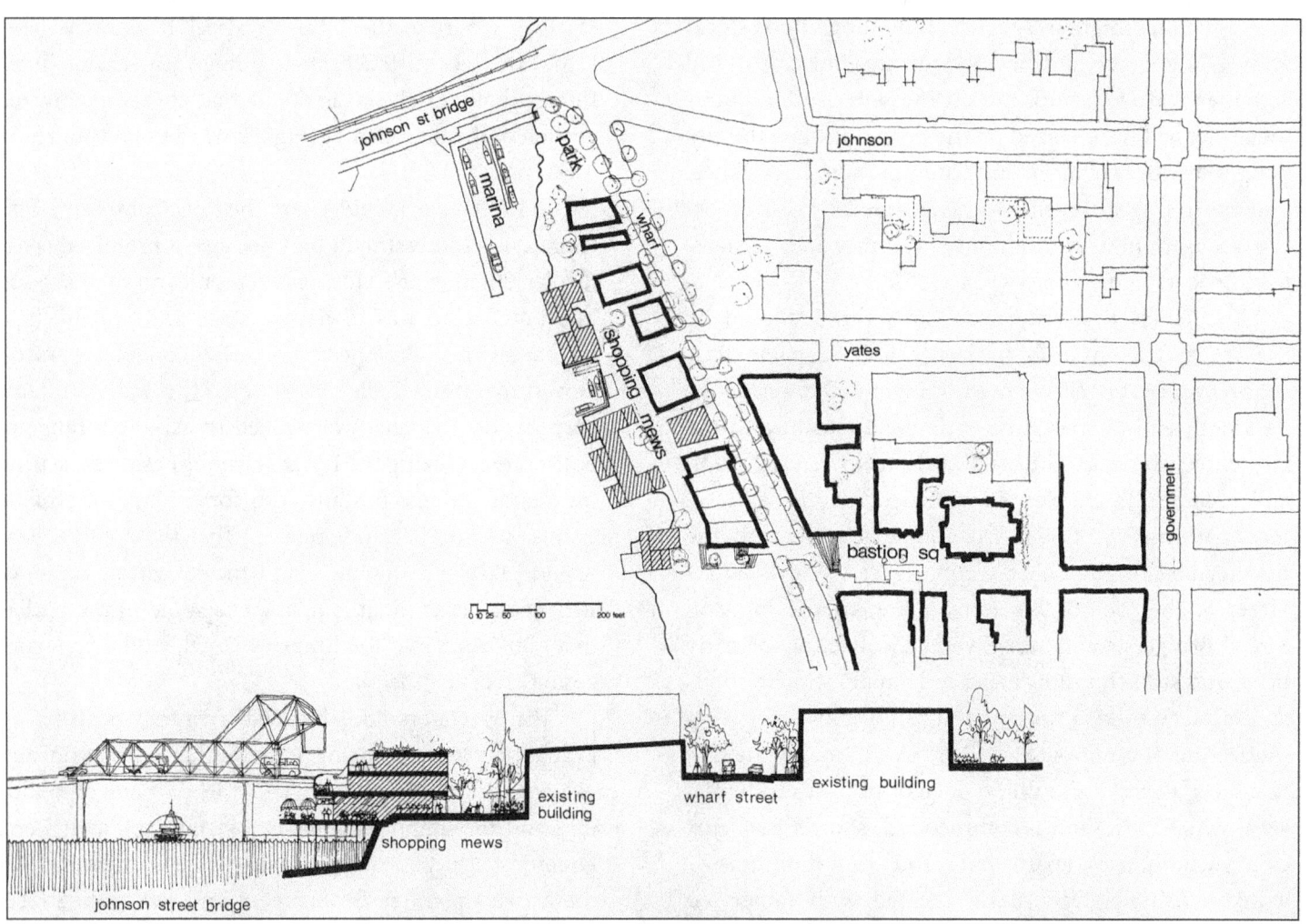

Fig. 12-8. The plan of the Wharf Street Waterfront south from the Johnson Street Bridge to the Reid site. By Arthur Erickson Architects, 1973. [CVA, CD 65.]

Fig. 12-9. A plan of residential area on the Old Songhees Reserve by Arthur Erickson Architects, 1973. [CVA, CD 65 page 44.]

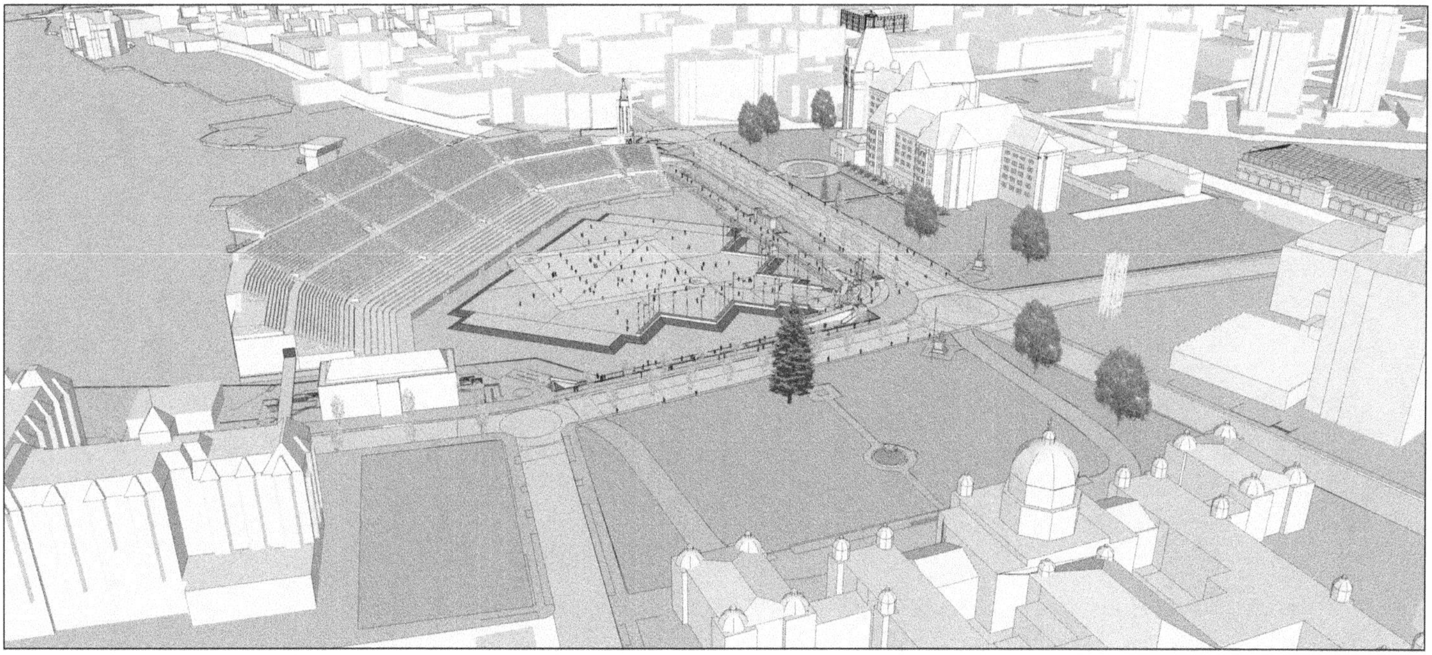

Fig. 12-10. A 3D visualization of the proposed floating bleachers and sports "field" in the Inner Harbour basin, drawn for the 1994 Commonwealth Games. [The wade williams corporation, image created by Chris Gower.]

the scaffolding framework supporting the extensive bleacher system.

Although various alternative and smaller layouts were also considered, in the end practicality persuaded the Games Society that the budget would be better spent on permanent improvements to facilities at the university than on two weeks of temporary spectacle. But the idea of entertainment on barges in the harbour took hold, and Victoria Symphony's annual Symphony Splash puts the orchestra on a barge and the audience arrayed around the Inner Harbour for what has become Canada's largest annual outdoor symphony event.

Chapter 13

Wharf Street Waterfront

Wharf Street was once the city's most important thoroughfare. It ran in front of the HBC fort and initially ended at Fort Street, the southern edge of the fort. In its heyday the waterfront was littered with wharves and warehouses (Fig. 13-1). As well as trading activity it saw throngs of gold seekers arrive during the Fraser River gold rush in the late 1850s, and it served as a passenger terminal from which, when there was a rate war on, a ticket to Seattle could be had for 25¢. As the city industrialized, factories, such as a fish-packing plant and a cement works, found a home on the land, and as resource exploitation boomed, the trading ships were joined by the sealing fleet, and in places the water was invisible under a carapace of log booms. By the end of the century, when Victoria was no longer the trading hub of the province, the harbour was inadequate for modern steam ships and the port moved to the outer harbour at Ogden Point. With the arrival of the electric railway and then the car, city development shifted eastwards away from Wharf Street, leaving it scattered with warehouses, most of them vacant, and utilitarian industrial buildings with all the pollution and general untidiness that that entails. Gradually this harbour activity waned too. Victoria's industries needed to modernize to compete, but they found it more advantageous to move to better locations in Vancouver and Nanaimo, and, in 1960, the terminal for ferries to the mainland moved to Swartz Bay — the abandonment of Wharf Street was almost complete.

In 1946 a start at cleaning up the Wharf Street waterfront was made by J.H. Todd & Sons, which owned the HBC warehouse and the land around it. Built inside the fort in 1859, at what is now the junction of Wharf and Fort Streets, the warehouse was the gateway for all the of the HBC's goods. The firm demolished the warehouse as part of its plans to build offices and docks for the Victoria

Barge Transportation Company. But only two warehouses and a lunch room were erected; the remainder of the site — from the Finlayson Building (Hartwig Court) to the Malahat Building, the former Customs House — remained vacant. Then, in 1964, there was speculation that the Department of Transport might use it as a ferry terminal, but speculation was all it was.

Enter J.A. (Sandy) Reid, a Vancouver property developer who by 1968 had amassed 1.2 hectares of land below Bastion Square and was proposing three twenty-five-storey towers of offices and apartments to be built on the waterfront (Fig. 13-2). Two towers were to be apartments, and the third would contain ten storeys of hotel rooms and ten of offices. A Mrs. J.C. Cox, in a letter to the *Victoria Daily Times* under the headline "Sudsy Tower Scorned," protested, "I'm sure the architects involved could have come up with something better than three detergent bottles between the Empress Hotel and Bastion Square." At the time there were few other howls of protest.

The land to the south of his development contained the Ocean Cement site and various warehouses — remnants of the industrial harbour, but still in operation — and not, Reid thought, a suitable neighbour for his upscale apartment-dwellers and hotel guests. He expected the city to clean up the area, get rid of Ocean Cement, which the city was not in a position to do, and provide his clients with an urban park on their doorstep. Although the mayor, Courtney J. Haddock, objected to city's having to spend $100,000 on land beautification as a condition of attracting Reid's project, he gave the scheme his enthusiastic backing. This may have had something to do with the projected income for the city of $300,000 a year in tax revenue.

Despite the announcement that the project would be under way by summer, not all council members were as convinced as Haddock that it should go ahead. Peter Pollen, newly elected to council in 1970, was particularly antagonistic to the scheme. Pollen and Alderman Tom

Fig. 13-1. The Enterprise Dock on the Wharf Street Waterfront after 1892. The Hudson's Bay warehouse stood at the junction of Wharf and Fort Streets. The heritage buildings on the east side of Wharf Street, south of Bastion Square are just visible, as is the top storey of the Board of Trade building, now hidden by the later addition of a third storey to the Rithet building at 107–1125 Wharf Street. [Collection of Greg Windwick.]

Christie suggested that the council need not rush and should take a second look at the entire project. Roderick Clack, a former Victoria planner who was then with the National Capital Commission in Ottawa, thought the project was wrong for Victoria; it would dwarf the surrounding buildings, it was not an inspiring design and may set a trend that the city would regret in the future, and it did not demonstrate any design excellence. Others, such as newspaper columnist Elizabeth Forbes, agreed — the harbour did not need a "Highrise Jungle."

By the middle of October, a petulant Reid announced that he had scrapped the three-tower project, but not necessarily his plans to build something on the site. He wondered if he might just build something that complied

Fig. 13-2. An aerial view of Reid's first proposal. The Empress Hotel and the Executive House Hotel are on the right-hand side, the Ocean Cement site is to the south, and round to the causeway is a manicured park. Published in the *Times*, January 28, 1970.

with zoning regulations, even if it did completely obscure the view of the Inner Harbour. Mayor Haddock envisaged a lawsuit if council tried, as some members suggested, to change the rules to prevent something so grotesque from being built on the waterfront. Reid singled out Peter Pollen as instrumental in his decision to abandon the three-tower scheme, and Pollen was proud to take the blame.

But the city had a problem and, for the moment, at least, Reid was not going away. City solicitor Terry O'Grady thought that buying the land was the only way that the city could control what was built on it. Haddock was alarmed at the potential expense of such an action; not only would the taxpayers have to pay for the land, but some use would then have to be found for it, and that would cost yet more. And then he considered the loss of property tax revenue, which city planner Geoff Greenhalgh estimated would be $700,000 annually. Unwilling to commit the city to such an expenditure, Haddock continued to negotiate with Reid; he was convinced that high-rises would be a "fact of life" for Victoria.

In an effort to exercise some control over this contentious issue, the city approved a set of development standards devised by the Victoria Advisory Planning Commission. The standards covered the entire Wharf Street waterfront, not just the Reid development. The main points were: an early start on renewal of the shore from the Johnson Street Bridge to the causeway; the use of private developers; the creation of a walkway all along the shore line; the city should buy the Ocean Cement property and hold it for future public use; and all development along the Wharf Street waterfront should fall under the Municipal Act and be subject to special development permits. With this new sense of purpose, the city also resolved to apply to the federal government for funding for the renewal.

The stalemate continued throughout the first half of 1971. The Chamber of Commerce wanted the Reid Centre, as did the mayor and some of the councillors. The citizens did not specifically indicate that they wanted it, but they refused to vote for the $2 million that would be needed to buy the land and stop it. Then the councillors grasped the nettle and refused the necessary permits for Reid's three-tower plan, but they did suggest that he come up with a more imaginative, and smaller, plan. This he did, with a proposal for two curving towers facing each other, much like the twin towers of Toronto's new city hall, which were positioned in such a way as to optimize views of the ocean from Bastion Square (see Fig.12-4). The proposal was greeted with approval by the city councillors and hoots of derision from the public gallery.

A year passed with no action on the site; the only action was the war of words. The full realization of what was planned for the waterfront galvanized protesters and pundits. The council's competence, and possibly even probity, was called into question, as was the glacial progress of the planners. And then rumours began to fly that Reid was trying to sell his property. In a blustering denial he said "the centre is undoubtedly the most spectacular development in North America in terms of land utilization and consumer service [it] will crystallize and engender in the city of Victoria a brilliant impetus to downtown revitalization … the Reid Centre will be Victoria's skyline … will be one of North America's very talked-about facilities."

Another year passed, and then the recently elected premier, David Barrett, weighed in, signalling the province's disapproval of the Reid plan. The entire Inner Harbour, including the Wharf Street waterfront is, essentially, the parliament buildings' front garden; imagine the Queen or the Governor General turning at the ceremonial entrance to acknowledge the cheering crowd and having their eyes assailed by three high-rise detergent bottles, or a pastiche of the Toronto City Hall. Barrett, and his government, were having none of it. Meanwhile, Reid had been trying to sell the property to Commonwealth Holiday Inns, and the city had approved the sale, only to find one week later that Barrett's words had turned into action and the provincial government had imposed development restrictions on the entire waterfront including the Reid Centre, and bought Reid's land.

What to do with the site? The Chamber of Commerce was pleased by the government's decision to purchase the property, even though it had been in favour of the Reid development. The chamber's main concern was that something was done that would boost Victoria's economy and be of aesthetic value as well. After all the vacillation and delay, it wanted a speedy decision, and suggested that the site would be ideal for a convention centre.

In the meantime, Sam Bawlf, a provincial politician at the time, and in charge of Inner Harbour development, proposed a market, something between a supermarket and a farmers' market, with over nine thousand square metres of small retail shops and underground parking for two hundred cars. Perhaps Bawlf had in mind the Granville Island redevelopment scheme then under way on former industrial-harbour land in Vancouver, and funded by the federal government; but Bawlf called for proposals from private developers. The plan was to provide pedestrian access to the market via a skywalk across Wharf Street from Bastion Square, and this did not meet with the city's approval. This, coupled with a lack of interest from developers, killed the project.

The chamber of commerce weighed in again with its convention centre proposal. Architect Paul Merrick drew plans and the project even went so far as to see Premier Bill Bennett, resplendent in business suit and a hard hat, jack-hammer the tarmac of the site (see Figs. 5-6, 5-7). But as residents and visitors know, the convention centre was not built on land at the foot of Bastion Square, nor has anything else disturbed that ground in the nearly forty years that have elapsed since Sandy Reid left town. In 1970, when the city was deliberating on what seemed the only solution to gaining control of the site's use and development, Haddock said that turning the land into a park was "impracticable and undesirable" — he surely could not have imagined that that was precisely what it would become, and remain, albeit a park for cars.

Although nothing has been built on the land, there have been various studies. In the late 1980s the city and the Provincial Capital Commission (PCC) commissioned an "issues and design brief" for the Wharf Street Waterfront — all the land on the harbour side of Wharf Street stretching south from the Finlayson Building to the visitor centre in front of the Empress Hotel. The report proposed that the waterfront be looked at as two sites: the north site, still referred to as the Reid site, testament to the lasting memory of Sandy Reid; and the south site, comprising the Ocean Cement property and Ship Point. A panel of waterfront-development consultants and designers reviewed this document and suggested a general plan for land use by organizing the site into a series of "activity nodes" (Fig. 13-3).

Following on from this study and its review, the city commissioned a site design brief. Although this accepted, in general, the conclusions of the review panel, it proposed that the waterfront be treated as having three components — the Reid Site, the Ocean Cement Site, and Ship Point — and that it be divided into areas for discrete activities. The Reid site would be business-oriented with commercial and office space; the Malahat Building and the park surrounding it, a federally owned site, National Historic Site of Canada, would serve as a link between the Reid and Ocean Cement site. The brief also considered transportation requirements and decided to concentrate ferries, catamarans, and float planes at the Reid site with a one-way loop of pick-up and drop-off traffic entering the terminal just south of Finlayson Building and exiting in line with Fort Street. This plan had the advantages of keeping traffic away from the public entertainment area to the south, and would reduce the risk of conflict with pleasure craft by keeping all ships and aircraft to one side of the harbour

The Ocean Cement land would be a cultural and civic site, housing a museum and a civic plaza at the Wharf Street level. It was considered the ideal location for the Maritime Museum. Not only was a harbour site more in keeping with the mission of the museum — then, as now, in Bastion Square — but this location would allow

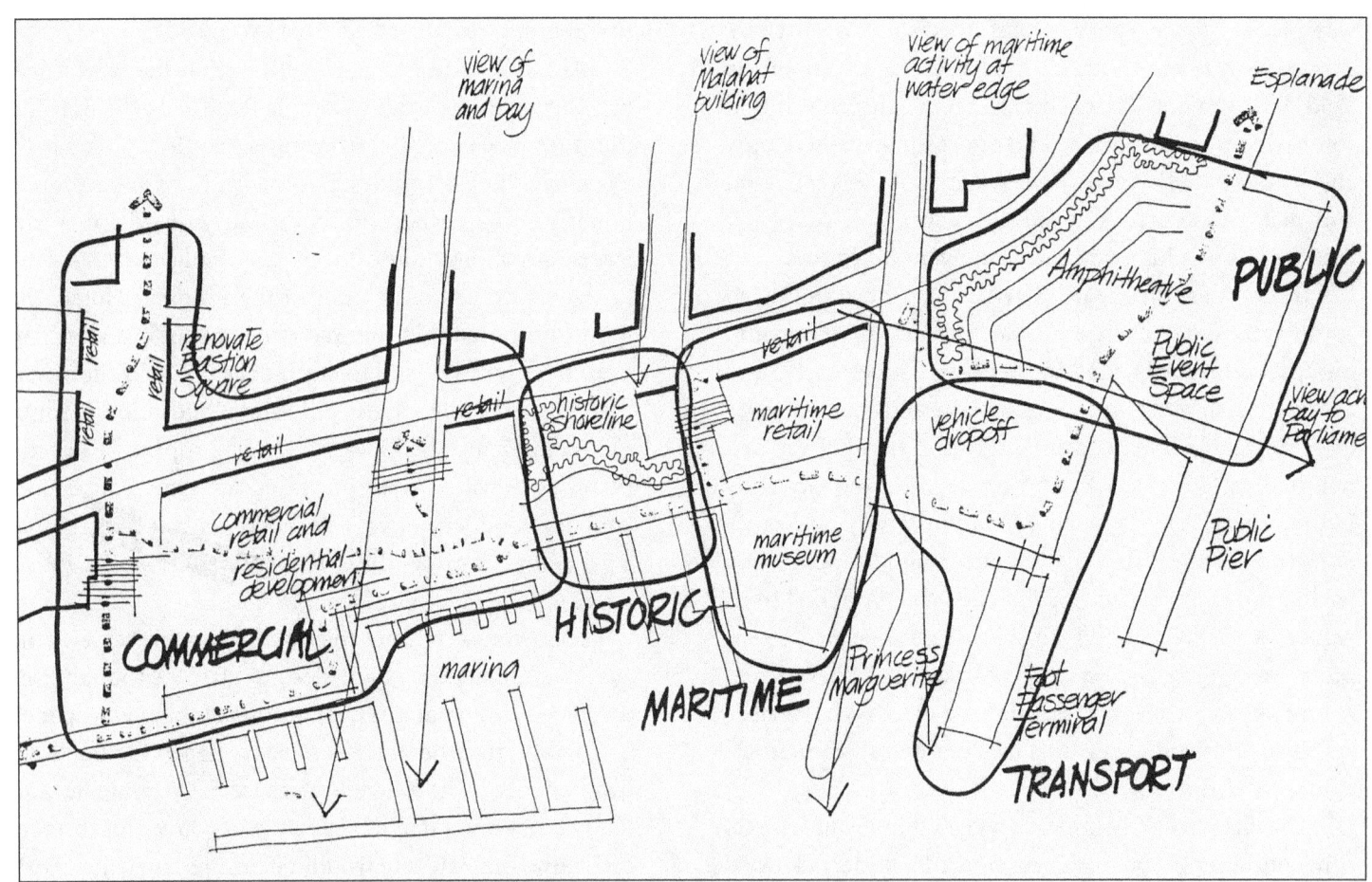

Fig. 13-3. A plan of the suggested uses for the various areas of the waterfront prepared by the review panel. [CVA, CD 137.]

its artifacts to "spill out" into the public domain, giving visitors the opportunity to participate in the history of the harbour. Ship Point would be a public space with facilities for festivals and concerts that would offer "picture post-card" views of the Inner Harbour's architectural splendour. An amphitheatre, able to accommodate four thousand people, facing the parliament buildings and the Inner Harbour, would be a terrace of seven-foot-wide grassy levels rising from the water's edge — where the stage would be — to Wharf Street. The terraces would be faced with the same granite as the causeway so as to integrate them with the entire sweep of the Inner Harbour walls. And all would be connected by a waterfront walkway from the Regent Hotel to Ship Point.

The brief was prepared with extensive public input, and it emerged that, for Victorians, the most important consideration for any development was the preservation of the views, from Laurel Point and the Old Songhees Reserve, of the heritage buildings along Wharf Street. But even so, a surprising 85 percent of the participants at the public workshop were in favour of a modern architectural aesthetic rather than simulated historic styles. As a result of this collaborative process, the brief concluded with an illustrative site plan (Fig. 13-4).

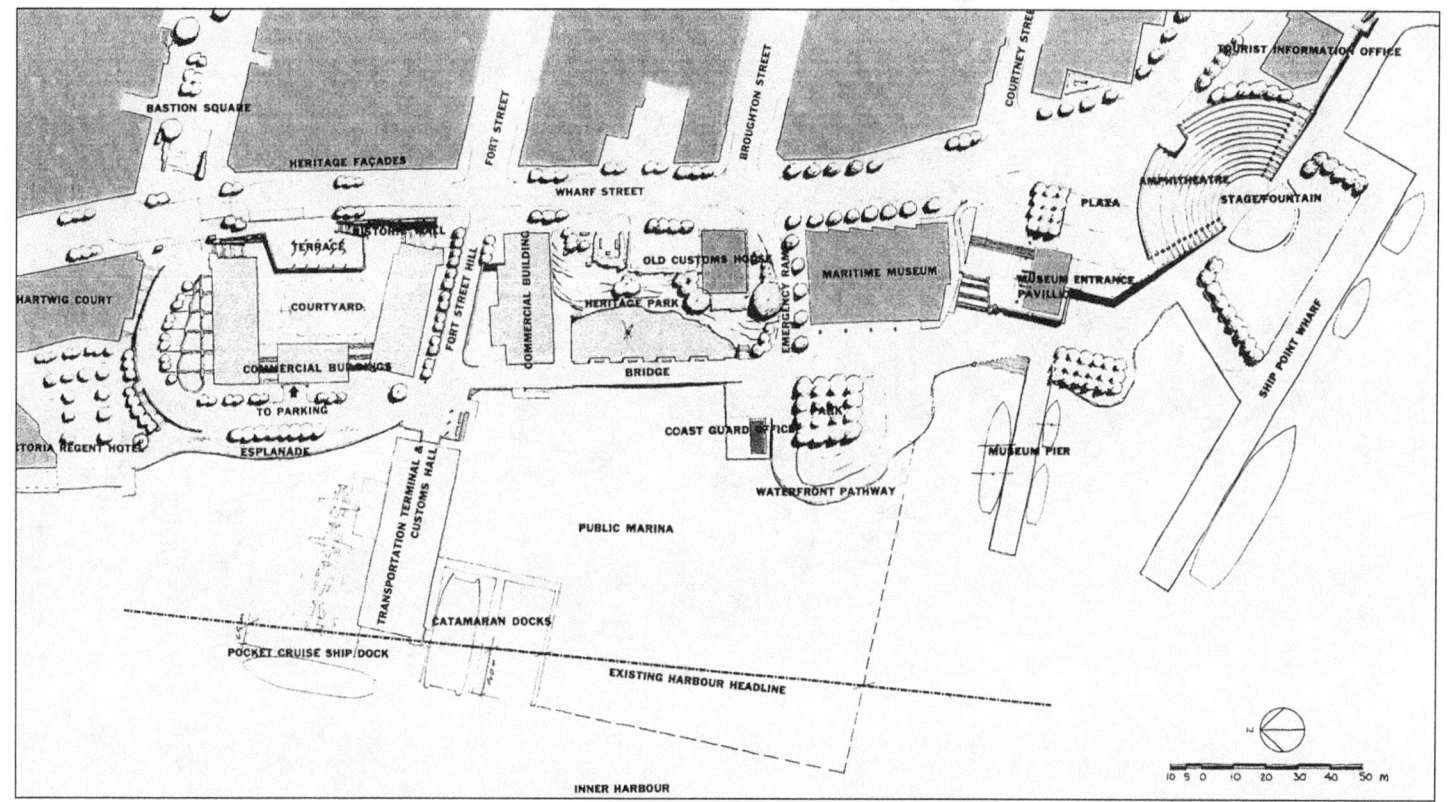

Fig. 13-4. The illustrative site plan, from "Wharf Street Waterfront Project: Site Design Brief," p. 57. [CVA, CD 139.]

Enthusiasm for doing something about the Wharf Street waterfront was spurred by the prospect of exposing it to the world, or at least the Commonwealth. The city was to host the Commonwealth Games in 1994, and the cornerstone of its winning bid was holding the opening and closing ceremonies in the Inner Harbour basin. The review panel thought this event could be an incentive to find the funding to improve the waterfront and sell Victoria as Expo '86 had showcased Vancouver. But the site of the ceremonies was moved to the University, and momentum, in general, flagged.

Ship Point, however, continued to be a "controversial piece of property." Its proximity to the parliament buildings had resulted in its inclusion in the improvements

Fig. 13-5. The scheme for a performing arts centre on Ship Point, 2001. [Paul Merrick Architects.]

covered by the Victoria Accord. In 1993, architects de Hoog D'Ambrosio Rowe prepared a feasibility study for an amphitheatre; public comment on earlier schemes had indicated a preference for a green landscaped area over a hard formal amphitheatre. The firm's study suggested a hybrid design with generous areas of lawn and retaining much of the existing landscape and trees, and recognized the importance of both conceptual and material compatibility with Rattenbury's formal harbour ensemble. Mayor David Turner was all in favour, and hoped for funding assistance from the Commonwealth Games Society, but since the society had changed its mind about the ceremonies in the harbour, it declined.

After the failure of Robert Wright's plan for a performing arts centre on the Y-lot, a consortium of performing arts entities, spearheaded by the Pacific

Fig. 13-6. A commercial scheme for Ship Point, 2005. [Bing Thom Architects.]

Opera Victoria, began fundraising for an arts centre on Ship Point. Paul Merrick Architects prepared a conceptual drawing for the $45 million project, which would include an 1,800-seat main theatre, a stage-sized rehearsal hall, an outdoor amphitheatre, tiered walkways, shops and restaurants, underground parking, government offices, and some residential units, all in extensively landscaped public space that extended north to the Malahat Building (Fig. 13-5). Funding was to come from a $30-million Canada–B.C. infrastructure grant, local governments, and donations. But, as ever, the money was not forthcoming. The provincial government began to lay off thousands of staff at the end of the year, and federal funding was increasingly directed to "green" projects.

The next idea was for a speculative commercial development. Bing Thom Architects of Vancouver prepared renderings for a mixed-use scheme including a hotel, offices, retail, restaurants, a seaplane terminal, a marine adventure centre, a maritime heritage harbour and centre, a sea-walk, and a Festival Plaza, sheltered with a transparent sail, for civic celebrations. Although this scheme had a greater emphasis than others on commercial activity, it had plenty of public space as well, and the buildings were carefully massed so as to preserve the sight lines to the water and the parliament buildings (Fig. 13-6). In the end the various parties involved could not agree and the project did not get off the ground.

Now it seems that the Wharf Street waterfront is a suitable topic for theoretical study. The Downtown Victoria

Fig. 13-7. A scheme for a harbour market on the Reid site, at the foot of Bastion Square. [D'Ambrosio urbanism + architecture.]

Community Alliance, a non-profit society formed in April 2003, initiated a conference series — Downtown Victoria 2020 — that brought together representatives of the city, the general public, and professionals. The conference's main themes were the challenges and opportunities in our downtown, and means and methods to create and implement a plan to restore downtown's lustre, economic vibrancy, and social health. In response to a call for proposals for unused sites, D'Ambrosio urbanism + architecture prepared a conceptual design for the Reid site (Fig. 13-7). The scheme was for two classic glass-enclosed market halls flanking a 2.8-square-metre plaza level with Wharf Street. Here fountains, art installations, and seating would create a very public space that could be used informally or for special events and provide a frame for views both of the harbour and of the heritage buildings from the harbour. Parking would be underground, and along the water's edge, shops and cultural spaces would line an expanded dockside walkway. D'Ambrosio envisioned that the Victoria Harbour Market could become a tourist attraction, a showcase for local food, products, and talent, as well as an amenity for the residents. But it was all theoretical.

Chapter 14

Old Songhees Reserve

WHEN THE HUDSON'S BAY COMPANY began to build its trading fort, the man in charge, Chief Trader Charles Ross, noted that a group of Aboriginal peoples had moved from their village on Cadboro Bay and were camping around the fort. The newcomers were useful to the company, labouring at fort-building and farming, but it was an uneasy arrangement. When a fire destroyed the woods near the encampment, between Johnson and Fort Street, the company decided that the Aboriginals had to go and moved them across the harbour onto land that in 1850 would become the Songhees Reserve.

For over sixty years the Songhees Nation lived on this piece of land. Over that time there were encroachments by the railways; the Canadian North Pacific Railway had a right-of-way at the northern end, and the Canadian Pacific Railway, now running the Esquimalt and Nanaimo Railway (E&N), operated at the south end. The provincial government wanted the remainder, particularly the waterfront, for shipyards, docks, and industry. In April 1911 the Songhees Nation formally handed over their reserve land in exchange for a new reserve on Esquimalt Harbour, and the following year all the Songhees buildings were demolished, leaving a wasteland.

After another sixty years the Old Songhees Reserve had become a blot on the landscape — a scene of industrial decay and dereliction. Imagine the tourists' impression on stepping out of the Visitor Centre: to the south and east are the iconic images of the city, the magnificent view of the parliament buildings and the Empress Hotel, but just a few steps up Wharf Street and their gaze would be assailed by this scene of industrial blight just across the water, but so close to the city. Something had to be done.

Arthur Erickson Architects prepared a development theme study, in 1982, which suggested, as his Inner Harbour study had in 1973, that apartments and multi-family housing for a variety of income groups would be a suitable use. Defining an area bounded by Bay Street, Kimta Road, and Tyee Road, Erickson proposed the creation of a complete community with commercial activities and a recreation area centred on the existing Victoria West Park, with playing fields, lawn bowling, tennis courts, and a children's playground. The park was to be linked with other landscaped areas — public, commercial, and recreational — to create a linear focus with spaces of varying shapes and sizes stretching across the entire width of the peninsula. The hub of this system was to be the historic brick roundhouse that would be renovated and converted to new public-oriented retail or cultural uses. Through traffic would be minimized by channelling traffic going westwards onto an improved Kimta Road and downgrading Esquimalt Road (Fig. 14-1).

The residential component of community was defined in layers rising up from the waterfront where there would be mid-rise apartments and hotels, with good views from each suite. At the next level, stacked town houses and low-rise apartment buildings would provide family accommodation. Mid- to high-rise apartments for singles, couples, and the elderly — but no children — would be placed at the top of the hill. No architectural theme was suggested. An overriding theme was the maintenance of view corridors, and this was achieved by the radial arrangement. The community was to have a strong pedestrian focus and to support this Erickson recommended that the harbour walkway be extended round to Lime Bay — the only recommendation that has been followed.

A study for the provincial Ministry of Lands, Parks and Housing suggested that the area would be a suitable place for the development of festival retailing, such as farmers' and public markets, and a complex of specialty shops, something like Granville Island in Vancouver or Pike Place Market in Seattle. There would be some five thousand residents in this "diversified urban development," and it would be "the place to be" in Victoria.

The prospect that the old reserve would be covered with a residential development did not sit well with the Victoria Waterfront Enhancement Society (VWES). The organization, formed in August 1980, was opposed to private use of the waterfront and wanted to ensure that access was available to all; it feared that residential developments would allow the general public only "token" access. As well, this dormitory for the city would do nothing to revitalize the economy and create jobs, except in the short term while building was underway. So the VWES prepared a report offering an alternative use — the Songhees Living Historic Village (Fig. 14-2).

Its concept included a park with plenty of green space and open water access, a Songhees Native display (Fig. 14-3), a reconstruction of Fort Victoria, a heritage village of replicas of early farms and houses, and a downtown street scene from the gold-rush era with outfitter's shops exhibiting all the necessities for the miners' expedition to the diggings. There would be a maritime village with tall ships moored at Lime Bay, and a railway museum centred on the old E&N roundhouse and its out buildings — declared a national historic site in 1992. Automobile access was to be discouraged: instead visitors would use water taxis, or, perhaps, heritage trolley buses crossing the Johnson Street Bridge.

Hotels in the historic village would make the facility open all hours and give it a lived-in ambiance, and three were proposed, each replicating an actual hotel that once stood in Victoria: the Driard, the Dallas, and the Mount Baker (Fig. 14-4). The Driard, once the most fashionable hotel north of San Francisco, stood at Broad and Yates

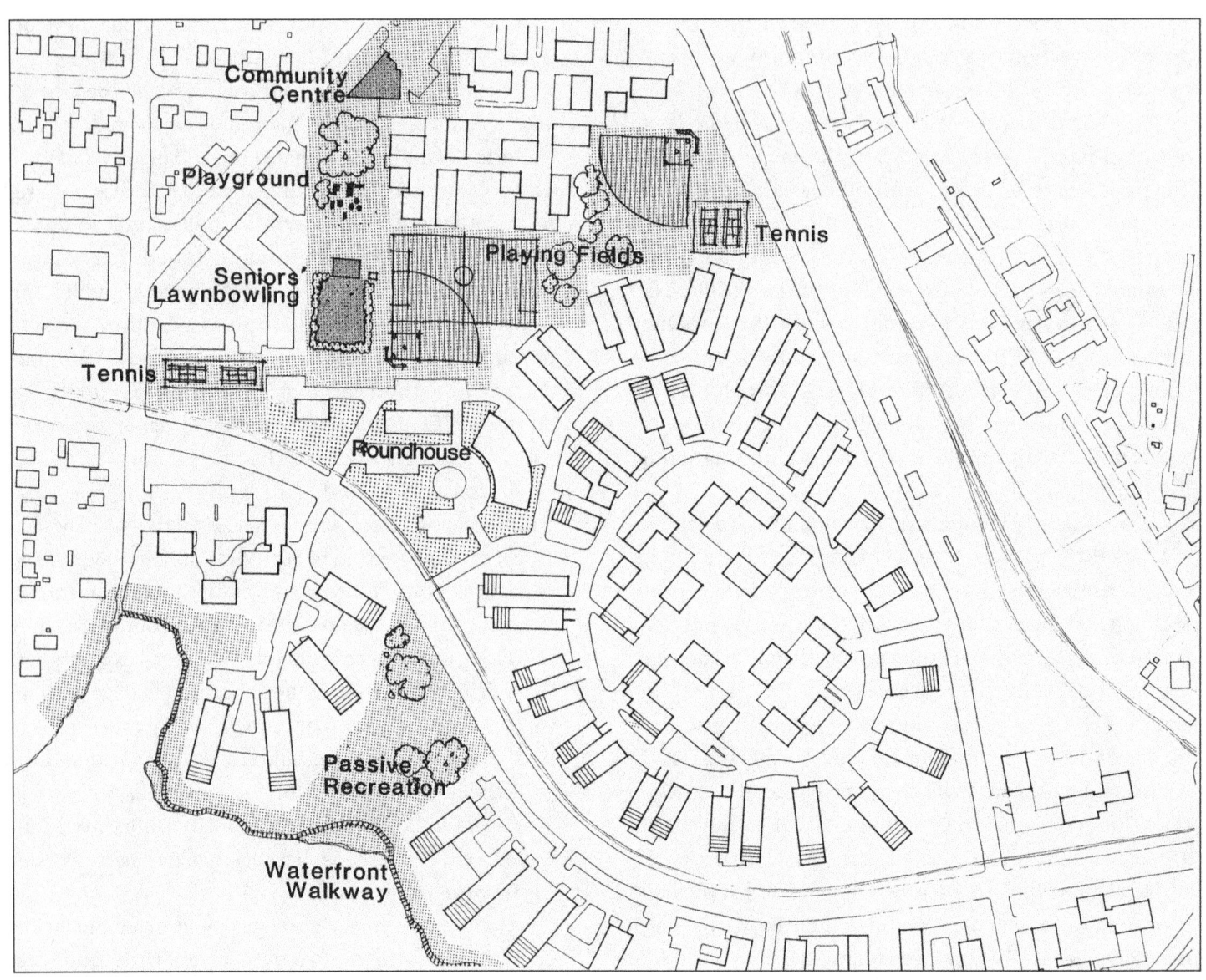

Fig. 14-1. A suggested plan for the Old Songhees Reserve, from Songhees Development Theme Study, Arthur Erickson Architects. [CVA, CD 103.]

Streets, and its reconstructed facade has now been incorporated in the Bay Centre. The Dallas, on Dallas Road, and the Mount Baker, in Oak Bay, are now gone. The proposal had support from such quarters as the Songhees Nation, railway enthusiasts, and university professors. Peter E. Murphy, Associate Professor in the Department of Geography at the University of Victoria, suggested that the village could be a revenue-generating outdoor museum along the lines of the Polynesian Cultural Centre in Laie Hawaii and Colonial Williamsburg, in Virginia, but it would have to be enclosed and an entrance fee charged. It was a suggestion that would have negated the aims of the society for free access, but one that the society chose to include in its report. The entire scheme was to be built with public funds, with the exception of the hotels, and the cost was projected at $21 million.

The following year, 1985, a group of individuals from all levels of government, industry, and the arts at the

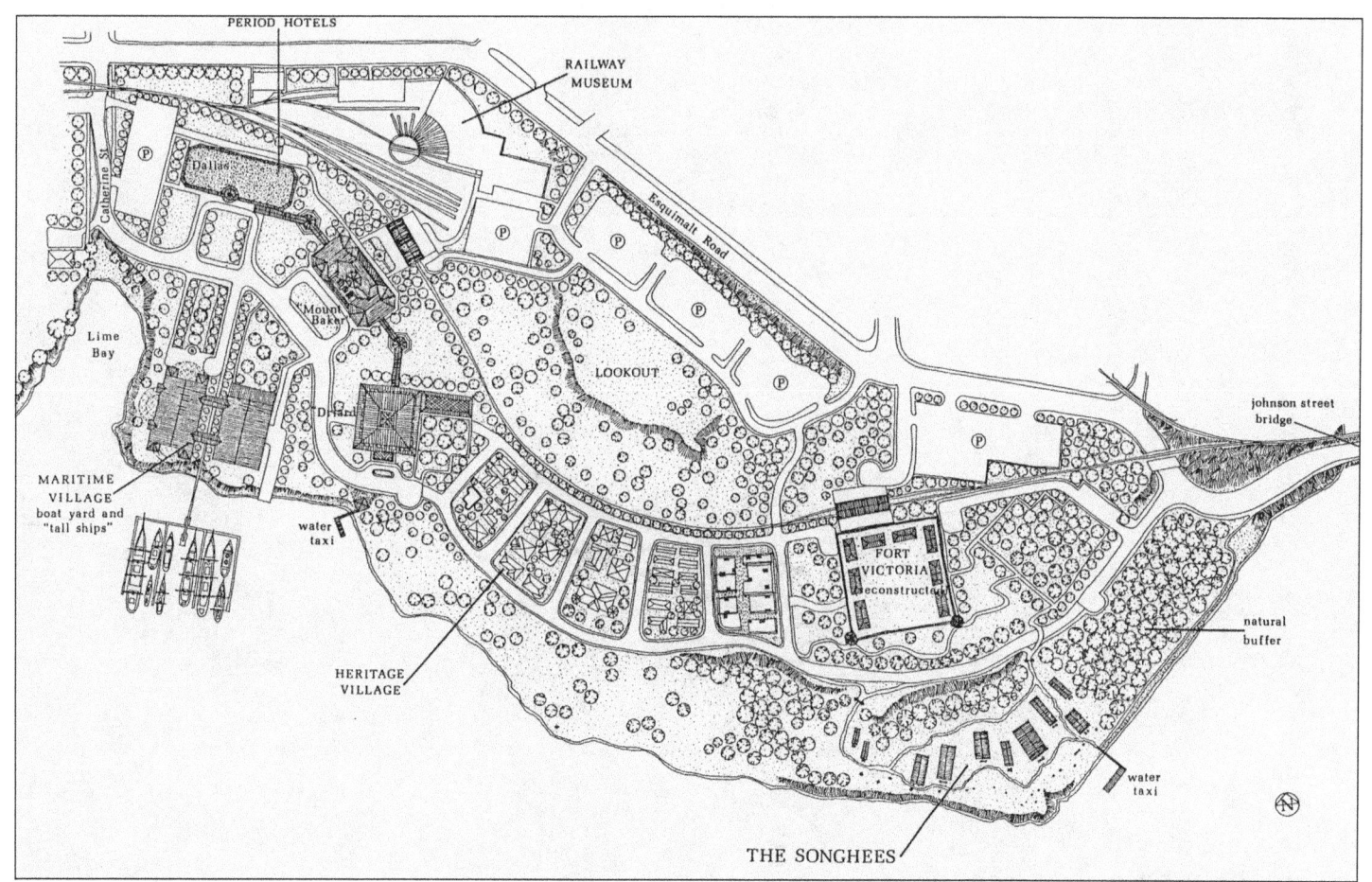

Fig. 14-2. A plan for the Songhees Living Historic Village by the Victoria Waterfront Enhancement Society, 1984. [CVA, CD 193.]

Fig. 14-3. A sketch of the proposed Native display. [Donald Luxton.]

Fig. 14-4. A sketch of proposed period hotels. [Donald Luxton.]

local, provincial, national, and international levels came together to propose the creation of an institute devoted to education and the arts. Pacific National Investments Ltd. hoped to build a comprehensive, mixed-use community on the southern end of the Songhees peninsula, from Songhees Point north to Bay Street. The scheme would combine commercial, marine, recreational, residential, resort, and visitor facilities, all as a complement to the arts and education institute.

The group was of the opinion that both B.C. and Canada were lagging behind in cutting-edge technologies such as robotics and microelectronics, and that the country was "light-years behind countries which until recently were third-world have-nots." For Canada and B.C. to catch up we needed to strengthen our connection with the emerging powerhouses of these technologies, the countries of the Pacific Rim, and the proposed institute would achieve this. During the academic year,

Fig. 14-5. A rendering of the hotel at Songhees Point, as part of Pacific Nations Place. [Wagg & Hambleton.]

top executives from government and major corporations from all Pacific nations would attend intensive eight-week courses in international trade; the latest computer-aided techniques in learning and instruction would be used. Following this the students would be led on an international mission to Pacific Rim countries with trade potential; a mission, it was anticipated, that would highlight Victoria as a "major force in world trading affairs." In the summer the facility would be given over to an international school for the arts, which would emphasize the art of the Pacific nations and would attract performers and artists from all disciplines (Fig 14-5).

The promoters suggested that education was the ideal "industry" for the city, and pointed to the University of Victoria, Camosun College, and the Lester B. Pearson United World College of the Pacific; the Pacific Executive Program of Pacific Nations Place would "round out" this stellar group of educational establishments. And to round out the entire scheme, there would be a hotel and a conference and performing arts centre. The projected performing arts centre would offer year-round entertainment on a par with the Sydney Opera House, the Royal Festival Hall in London, and the National Arts Centre in Ottawa — all spectacular venues in a waterfront location, just as this would be, for both residents and visitors. These were all lofty goals that would benefit the citizens of Victoria, the province, and the country economically, culturally, and educationally, but local opposition to the marina complex killed the project.

The city took another look at what to do about the unsightly mess on the Old Songhees Reserve in the late 1980s and issued a policy plan and design guidelines. This document echoed many of the principles defined in the earlier report, such as the maintenance of view corridors, a variety of building scales, a pedestrian focus, and the provision of recreational and commercial spaces, but it was prescriptive. Its aim was not only to create a new community across the harbour from the old city, but to integrate this community into the city. To do this it proposed that the architectural style of the new buildings should be the same as that across the harbour: Victorian and Edwardian detailing, and pitched roofs with spires, turrets, and domes providing an interesting skyline (Fig. 14-6).

It was this policy that guided what has been built on the Old Songhees Reserve, developments that have been described as "hokey, pathetic, jimcrack, pastiche architecture, Disneyland-north, and ghastly." One planner suggested that the only answer to this architectural and planning disaster was a shipload of explosives. Another suggested that mirrors might hide the site and create spectacular reflections of the Empress Hotel and the old town — perhaps he was remembering John Wade's suggestion

Fig. 14-6. The suggested architectural style for development, proposed by the city. [CVA, CD 106.]

for the completion of Christ Church Cathedral. Would any of the rejected schemes that came before have been better? The stated aim of integrating the Old Songhees Reserve with the old city is laudable. The reserve lands had long been separate — both physically and functionally — but would having the same architectural idiom really make it part of the old town?

Chapter 15

Belleville Street Waterfront

Unlike waterfronts of Wharf Street and the Old Songhees Reserve, the shore on the Belleville Street side of the harbour, from the parliament buildings to Laurel Point, did not witness industrial development on any great scale. The James Bay neighbourhood was the city's first residential area, a trend that started when James Douglas built his home — James Bay House — on the site of what is now the Royal British Columbia Museum. Later wealthy industrialists such as soap and paint manufacturer William J. Pendray, and furniture maker Jacob Sehl built large houses along the waterfront. Pendray's house, an elegant Queen Anne Free Classic, still stands at the corner of Belleville and Pendray Streets. There was some industrialization. In 1885, Sehl built his Gothic Revival mansion with a tower and lookout, costing $34,000, next to his factory at Laurel Point, and later Pendray moved his factories to the site. But, in general the waterfront did not see the jumble of wharves and warehouses, and the hustle and bustle of Wharf Street, nor the noisy industry of the Old Songhees Reserve.

In 1904 Francis Mawson Rattenbury built a wooden marine terminal for steamships of the Canadian Pacific Railway, replaced in 1923 by the stone terminal building that still stands at the foot of Menzies Street. The CPR owned much of the land, and once it had built the Empress Hotel this was a convenient landing place for its guests, who would be driven the short distance to its hotel in horse-drawn cabs. From the beginning of the twentieth century, the Belleville Street waterfront served as a transportation hub, first for the CPR and later for other ferry companies.

After the debacle over Sandy Reid's proposals for the Wharf Street waterfront, the city reviewed land use in the harbour and decided that the working harbour should be confined to the area north of the Johnson Street Bridge. South of the bridge was deemed to be in transition, and it commissioned Arthur Erickson Architects to undertake a study of the entire harbour south of the bridge, considering it as a tourist, recreational, and ceremonial precinct, as well as an important transportation hub. But what many saw as the province's high-handed behaviour towards the city in its unilateral action over development in the harbour and the purchase of the Reid site, also extended to land on the Belleville Street waterfront. And this tug-of-war between the city and the province was just one of the factors that contributed to the virtual inertia on the south side of the harbour, and resulted in what has been termed "cramped, Spartan and unwelcoming" ferry facilities.

Under Mayor Peter Pollen the city does seem to have tried to reach some accommodation with the provincial government. After lengthy negotiations with Marathon Realty, the real estate arm of the CPR, the city had agreed to buy its land on the Belleville Street waterfront for $1.2 million, only to find that the provincial government "in their enthusiasm for controlling the situation" decided to take over because it wanted the site. Eventually the province paid $2.4 million for it. Pollen wrote to Premier David Barrett, congratulating him on the acquisition and asking for assurances that development in the Inner Harbour would be undertaken in a "spirit of co-operation between the provincial government and the city." He hoped that "in the name of intelligence and in the spirit of co-operation, and, above all, in the interests of our total community," that the two levels of government could coordinate their efforts. This was 1975.

But such cooperation was not so simple. Other organizations and agencies had an interest in what happened at this transportation hub: the safety and security rules and regulations of Transport Canada had to be taken into consideration; customs and immigration agencies from both Canada and the United States each had requirements, which became even more stringent after 9/11; and Tourism Victoria had concerns about ensuring that this gateway to the city be as welcoming and spectacular as possible. Despite all the competing interests, there have been at least four proposals for the development and beautification of the Belleville Street waterfront spanning the nearly forty years since Arthur Erickson's overall study of the Inner Harbour.

Erickson recommended that the Belleville Street waterfront area should be the site of ferry and seaplane terminals, and also a place for recreation for the residents of the James Bay neighbourhood. From the park at Laurel Point a continuous tree-lined promenade would lead to the CPR steamship office. Vehicle ferry traffic would be underneath this promenade. The seaplane docks were to be near the CPR steamship terminal, which would be used for offices, waiting rooms, and other facilities of the seaplane companies. Parking for seaplane travellers would also be underground. Erickson suggested that if, in the future, vehicle ferries moved to the outer harbour, the superfluous underground parking area could be developed into a waterside park.

The bicentennial of Captain Cook's visit to Vancouver Island in 1778 was cause for celebration — and the availability of federal and provincial funding. The PCC moved the Black Ball ferry dock from Ship Point to the western end of the Belleville Street waterfront, where it is today. And the Air BC terminal was moved from Belleville Street to the old Ocean Cement site, a move that did not conform with Erickson's suggestion of a transportation hub on the south side of the harbour. The Black Ball company, in concert with Marathon Realty, commissioned John Di Castri to prepare a scheme for the waterfront westwards from the foot of Menzies Street. This follows Erickson's concept to some extent. It is a ferry and seaplane terminal, but there is no waterside walkway or the extensive landscaping for the residents of James Bay neighbourhood (Fig. 15-1). Di Castri has modified Erickson's bridge across the mouth of the bay with a jetty structure housing parking and a restaurant (Fig. 15-2). The prospect of dining, or even just having a cup of coffee, in such close proximity to seaplanes, ferries, and cars manoeuvring to park, would seem to have limited appeal. No matter, the project was dropped.

In 1981 the city commissioned The wade williams partnership to prepare a study examining how the Black Ball and the Princess Marguerite ferry terminals could be accommodated on the south shore. A seaplane terminal was to be to the west of the ferries. The goal was to consolidate water traffic and a tour-bus terminal, provide secure customs and immigration facilities, and create a community park as an extension of the Inner Harbour walkway, much in the manner that Erickson had proposed (Fig. 15-3). Vehicles lining up to board, or waiting for customs, would be housed in a lower level. Again, as Erickson had suggested, this would allow for an upper promenade, stepped up from street level, with landscaping and fountains as a buffer against street noise. At night concealed lighting

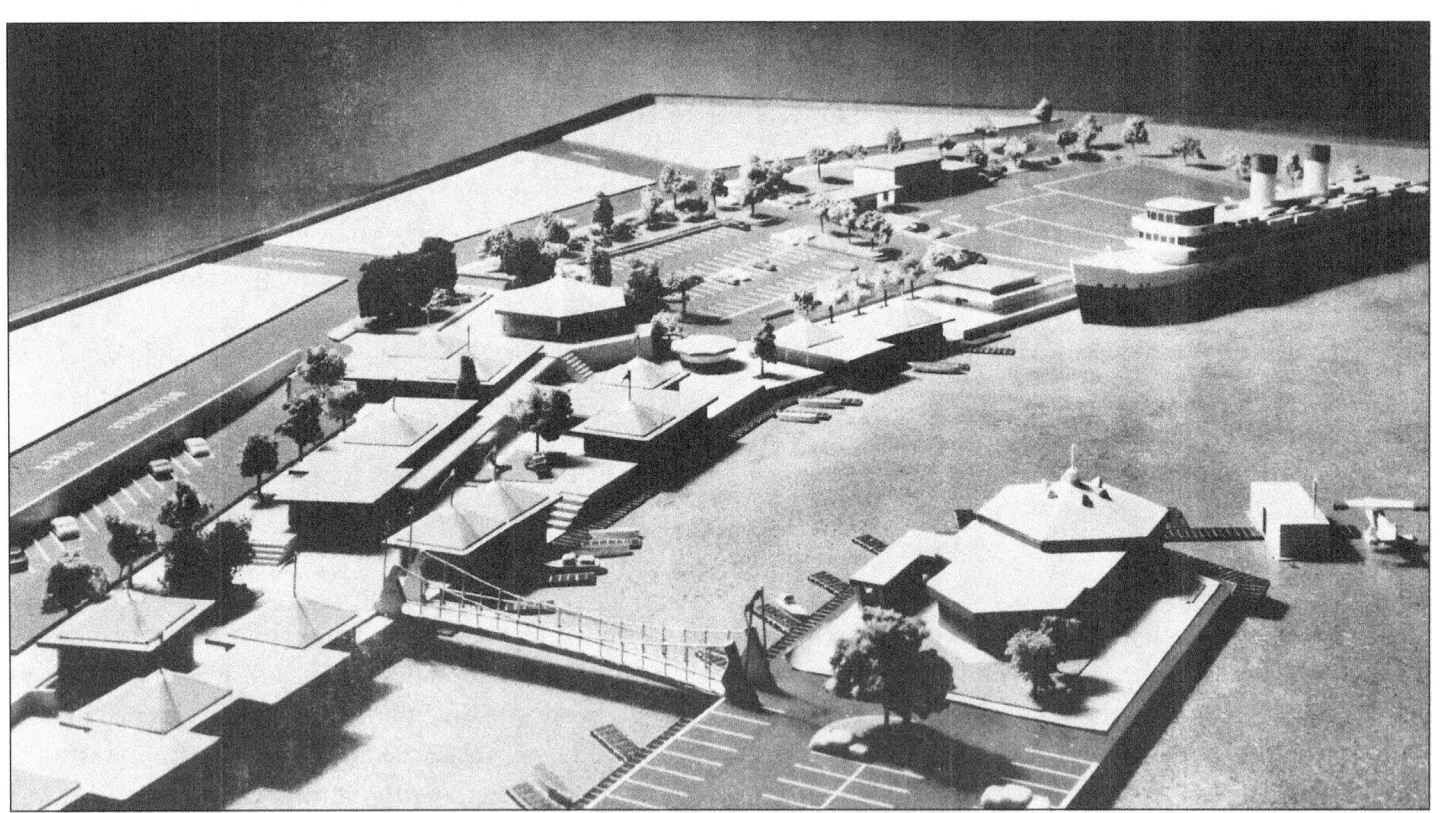

Fig. 15-1. A model of the proposal for Marathon Realty by John Di Castri. [University of Victoria, John Di Castri Fonds, 4.38.]

would illuminate these, creating focal points. Also on the upper promenade, an observation deck, terrace, and restaurant would make for a vibrant and attractive transportation terminal and community facility (Figs. 15-4, 15-5). The proposal also included planting on the lower deck to reduce the vast expanse of asphalt in the marshalling lines. The lower causeway would continue round to the north of the old CPR steamship terminal — at the time home to the wax museum and destined to stay that way as it had a long-term lease — and then access the upper promenade, which would allow pedestrians to continue walking to the end of the terminal and into Centennial Park, which was to be constructed beyond Pendray Street.

Although from a planning perspective this proposal could have been implemented, it was not clear which organization would own and operate the facility, and the ferry operators showed little interest in the change — it would not, after all, benefit their business. People wishing to travel, would, as they do today, put up with whatever surroundings the travel terminal provides in order to make their journey, and arriving at a vibrant and exciting terminal would probably improve the travellers' well-being, but would hardly be a reason to choose that destination. The study was not well circulated, and was retired to the archives.

And there the matter rested; in 1994 the three levels of government spent $1.3 million upgrading the

Fig. 15-2. The proposed restaurant alongside the ferry terminal, by John Di Castri. [University of Victoria, John Di Castri Fonds, 4.38.]

terminal, but this was not in the cause of creating a lively civic space, but rather to improve the docks and replace some temporary trailers. But the opening did provide a photo-op for the politicians who took a ten-minute ferry trip across the harbour, prompting Victoria MP David Anderson to comment that it was "one of the shortest trips we politicians have taken and appropriately most of it was backward."

New impetus to do something about the harbour came when the federal government handed over control of some of its land holdings to a new harbour authority. The PCC and the harbour authority committed almost a million dollars to a planning and consultative process for the Belleville Street waterfront and commissioned Paul Merrick Architects, with others, to undertake the study. The authority's general manager, Michael Cormier, stressed that the development "must make financial sense," and would be designed to be economically viable without the need for subsidies. At the same time, the fate of the wax museum was under discussion, and architect Arthur Erickson — whose study for the Inner Harbour, by this time thirty-years old but still the most comprehensive — argued strongly for the building's return to its original use.

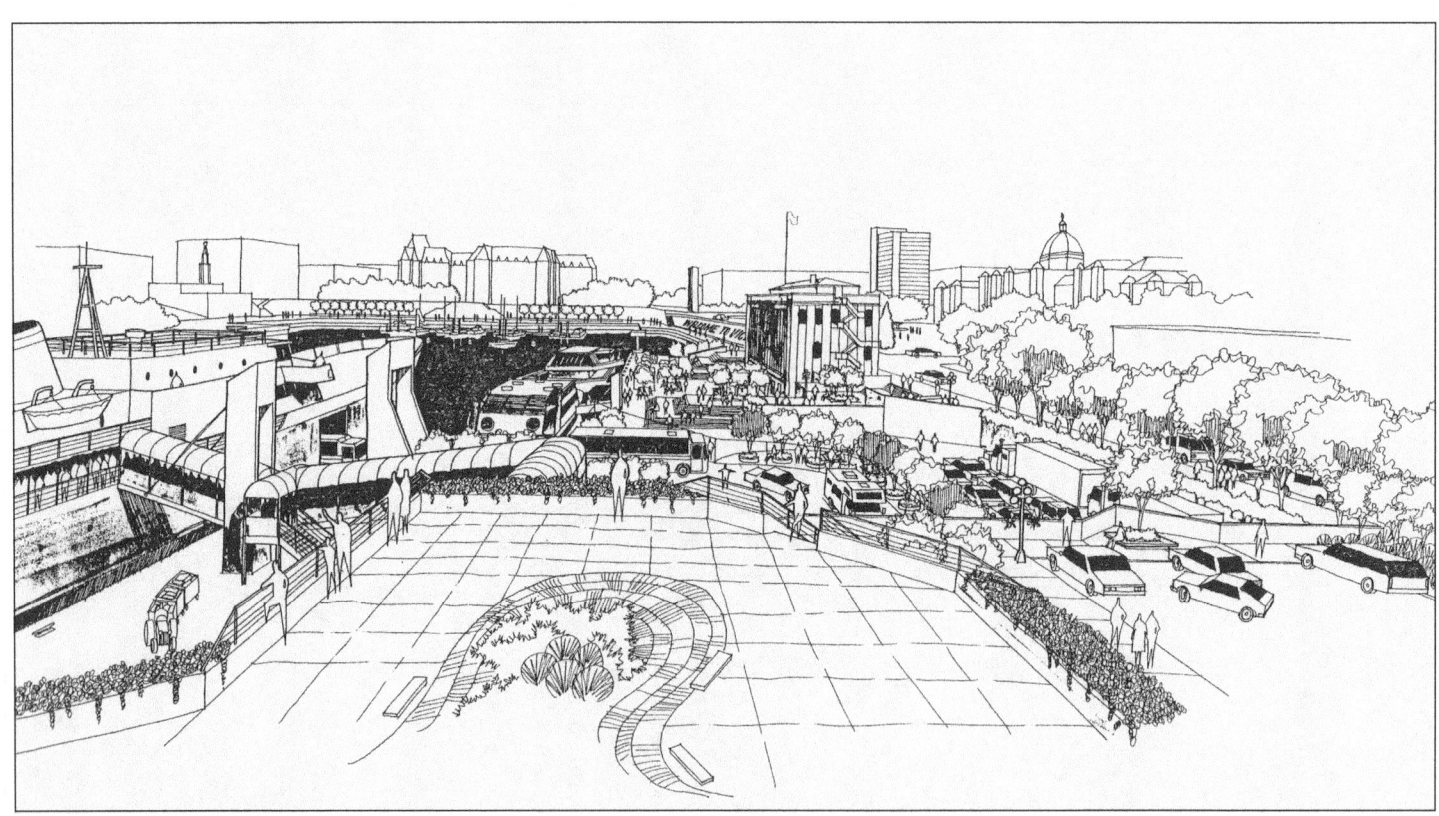

Fig. 15-3. A perspective view of the upper deck, 1981. [CVA, CD 285, the wade williams partnership.]

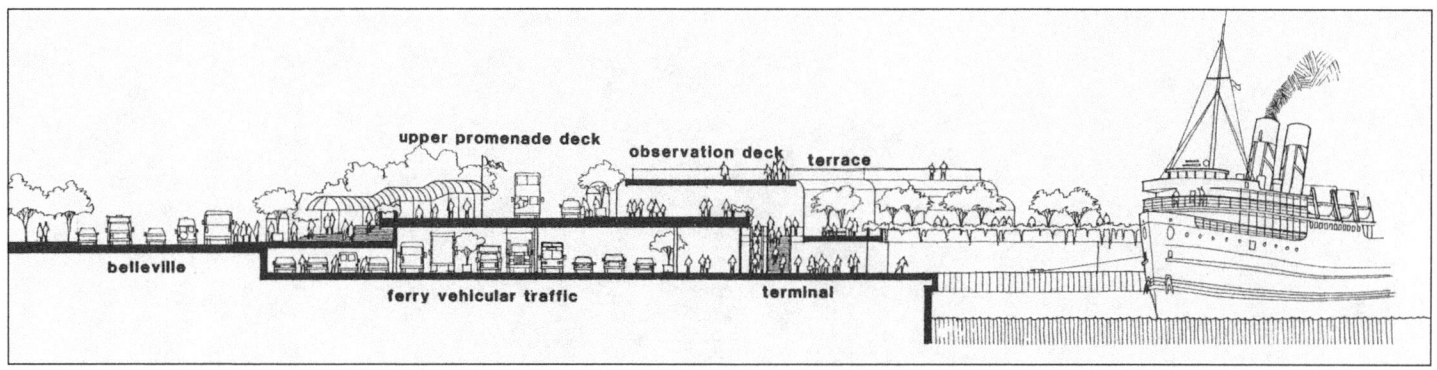

Fig. 15-4. A schematic cross-section showing the two levels. [CVA, CD 285, the wade williams partnership.]

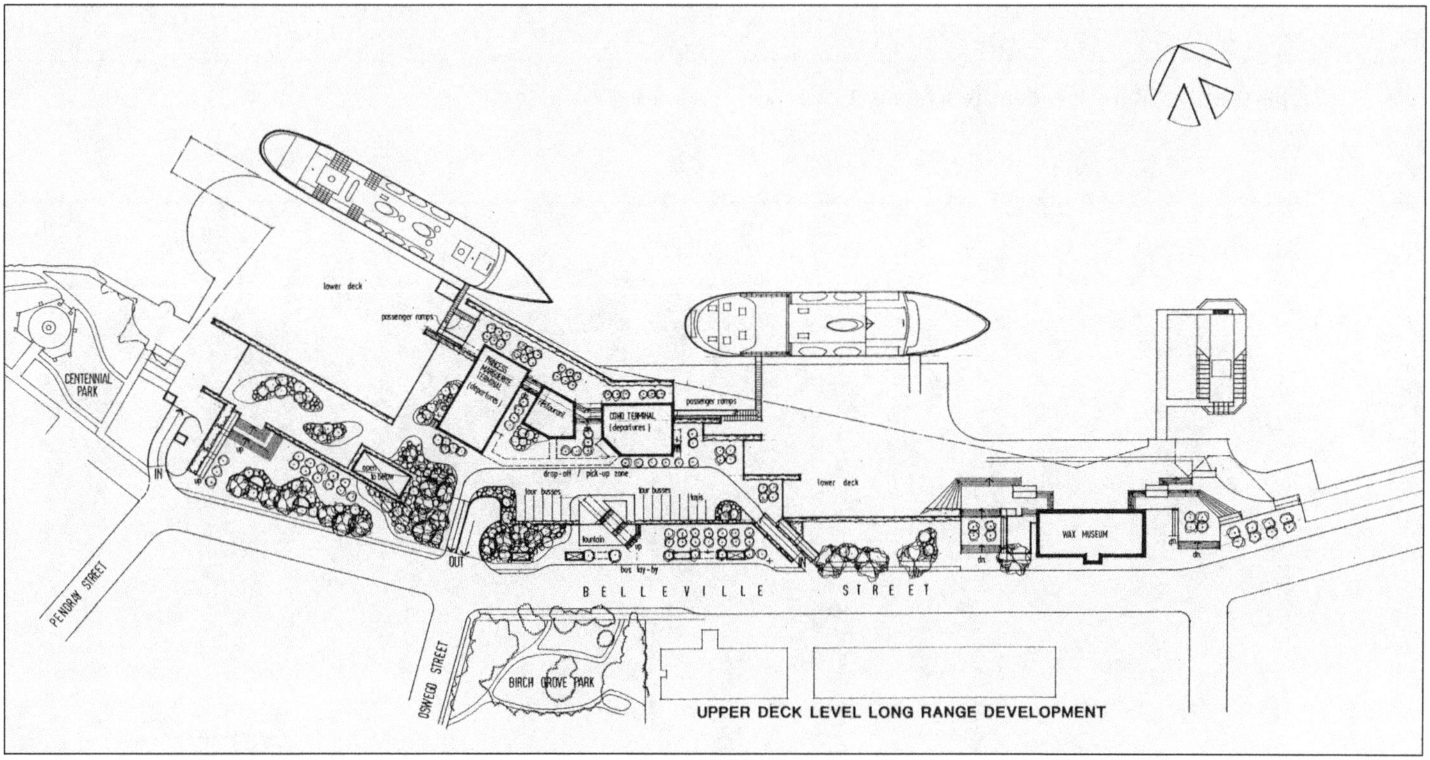

Fig. 15-5. The upper-deck level, long range plan. [CVA, CD 285, the wade williams partnership.]

[138] Unbuilt Victoria

Fig. 15-6. A perspective of the low-density scheme, 1994. [Paul Merrick Architects.]

Fig. 15-7. A perspective of the high-density scheme, 1994. [Paul Merrick Architects.]

Merrick designed three schemes which were presented for public consultation in March 2005 (Figs. 15-6, 15-7). All the schemes utilized the old steamship terminal, connecting it to a hub for smaller craft. Vehicle ferries, to the west of this hub, would load and unload at a lower level, leaving the upper level available for facilities such as shops, restaurants, and an observation deck, as well as landscaping. The low-density option left open much of the waterfront to the west of the CPR terminal, the medium-density option extended Oswego and Pendray Streets down to the waterfront forming a triangle of land with a seaplane terminal at its apex, and the high-density option added another terminal hub at the apex. When the three schemes were ranked according to long-term economic benefit and return on investment, the high-density option was considered to be the most beneficial, and the low-density was next. As with earlier schemes, these too were quietly forgotten.

In 2006 D'Ambrosio architecture + urbanism prepared yet another concept (Figs. 15-8, 15-9). Once again a two-level terminal was integral to the design, but this scheme called for a transit station, parking, and vehicles for the ferries all to be on the lower level, leaving the upper level at Belleville Street for civic amenities and facilities. Here the there would be a public plaza, gardens, a public waterfront esplanade, a First Nations cultural centre and trail of totems exhibit, an amphitheatre, and, providing the economic engine for this proposed redevelopment, a multi-storey hotel with a stepped tower over a podium containing retail shops, restaurants, and other amenities, along with secure facilities for the Canadian Border Services and US Homeland Security. The historic CPR terminal building would be renovated and repurposed as the visitor centre, and the wax museum could be housed at the level of the causeway. This was a concept, not a proposal, and nothing was done.

More recently, a modern and innovative scheme for condominiums to replace the Admiral Inn at the junction of Belleville and Pendray Streets was proposed by a Calgary-based developer. Hughes Condon Marler Architects (HCMA), Warner James Architects and CitySpaces Consulting Ltd., devised a scheme employing a new building typology. It was to be a shell with no interior fittings, and the units were to be completely customizable by the purchaser. The theory behind the concept was that purchasers of high-end condominiums frequently found the décor, provided by the developer at considerable cost, was not to their taste. In this building buyers would design the layout of the condominium, buy as much space as they wanted, and not have to spend money on interior fittings which they then proceeded to throw away. Between each storey, forty-centimetre voids would allow for the flexible placement of services.

To be called the Landmark (Fig. 15-10), this building would indeed have been a landmark. The plan took into consideration its location on a corner site and was angled so as to preserve sight lines and sun exposure to adjacent properties and public spaces, but was still too large and close to the lot lines to please the city's councillors and planners, and some local residents. At over forty metres tall, it would have been marginally taller than the Empress Hotel, but not so tall as one of the hotels on Belleville Street, to which it would have been closer. And the modern architectural style was considered inappropriate by some, with one letter to the editor going so far as to call it an "offence to the historical character of James Bay."

In the end, the criticisms that the building, which had been dubbed the "pyramid" by the local press, was too tall, too large, and not the approved architectural style, became an irrelevance — the economic woes of 2008 caused the developer to withdraw his application for rezoning.

[140] Unbuilt Victoria

Fig. 15-8. Aerial view, 2006. [D'Ambrosio architecture + urbanism.]

Fig. 15-9. The perspective from the Old Songhees Reserve. [D'Ambrosio architecture + urbanism.]

Fig. 15-10. A computer rendering of the Landmark "Pyramid" on Belleville Street, just east of the Pendray house, 2008. [Hughes, Condon, Marler.]

Take a walk along what of the lower causeway has been built, and behind the steamship terminal one is confronted with menacing black iron railings, topped with prison-like curved spikes, guarding the barren, fortress-like facilities of the Canadian and American customs and immigration services and the unrelieved blacktop of the ferry terminal. Tourism Victoria is adamant that the Inner Harbour must have a ferry service, but why? Cruise ships too large to enter the Inner Harbour dock at the outer wharf at Ogden Point, and the city's pedicabs, taxis, and horse-drawn carriages do a roaring trade bringing passengers to all the tourist delights. Could not the ferries plying international waters dock there too? The asphalt of the ferry terminal on Belleville Street would then be superfluous, as would an expensive multi-level terminal, and the Belleville Street waterfront could become the attractive and bustling place that so many architects have tried to make it.

Chapter 16

Oak Bay and Sidney Harbours

The distance overland from Victoria harbour to the waterfront at Oak Bay is some five kilometres, and with the arrival of the British Columbia Electric Railway Company's street cars in the early 1890s, it became an easy journey. Oak Bay was a popular holiday spot, away from the noise, heat, and, from time to time, smallpox of the city. A wealthy few built large houses close to the beach, but, until the arrival of the railway, most stayed under canvas in "tent villages." Now, with such ease of access, a group of investors formed the Oak Bay Land and Improvement Company (Limited), which had a grand plan to open the area of Oak Bay beach for development as a resort. The company proposed to build roads and sidewalks, to construct wharves, and to build a large and expensive summer hotel. It also planned to make the harbour a deep-water port and marina attracting steamers from Vancouver and Puget Sound, as well as visiting boaters who would save an hour's sailing time by not having to navigate the southern tip of the island and negotiate the entrance to Victoria harbour.

A plan was published (Fig. 16-1) and real estate agents Bowker & Smith were fulsome in their praise for the benefits of the bracing sea air, which would make the "sick well, and the strong even more vigorous and robust." They were convinced that the area was destined to become the most beautiful and attractive in the city, and urged interested parties to view the property before investing. Few must have done so, and the economic depression of 1893 cannot have encouraged sales; by the time there was some interest in the lots, towards the end of the century, the plan seems to have been forgotten, although parts of the subdivision still exist near Windsor Park, which includes some of the proposed lots. Although the harbour is a favoured port of call for boaters, it has no facilities for steamships.

A few kilometres north and a many years later in 1984, the town of Sidney was deliberating a proposal for a small commercial marina on its waterfront. At the same time, architecture student Chris Gower was preparing his graduation thesis for the University of British Columbia School of Architecture. Gower expanded on the contemporary plans to construct a breakwater to shelter a new marina on the town waterfront, to create a scheme for a civic harbour with a variety of marina docks surrounding an open civic harbour basin. His proposal made the case for the town's developing its role as an international centre for recreational boating.

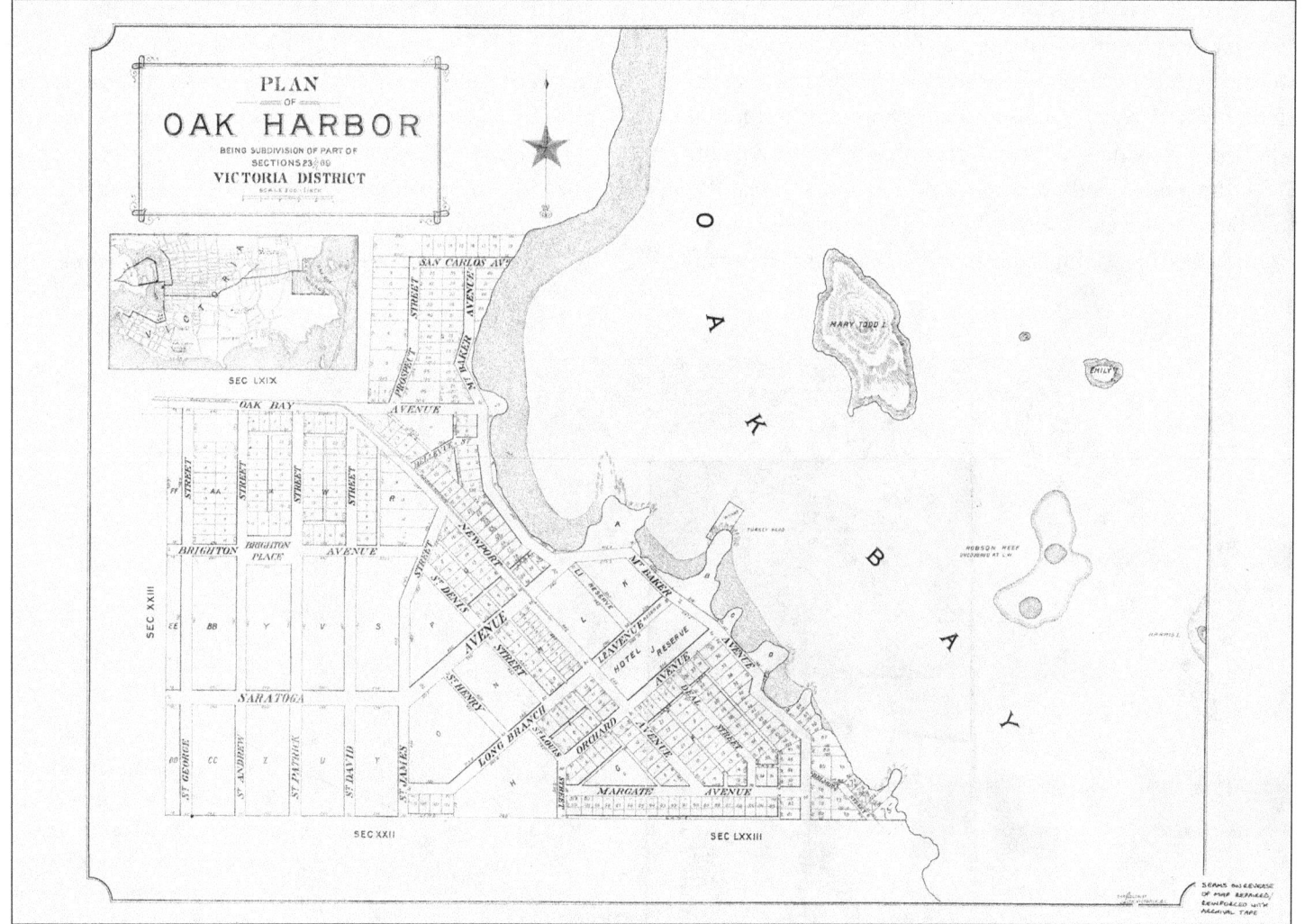

Fig. 16-1. A plan of "Oak Harbor," showing the proposed subdivision. [Glenlyon-Norfolk School Archives.]

The marina would be sheltered by the twin arms of a breakwater constructed of concrete caissons, each cast separately and built on-site using a series of construction rails on top of the breakwater using a system that had just been pioneered for the Brighton Marina in England. The top deck of the breakwaters would be open to vehicles and would terminate at lighthouses marking the harbour entrance (Fig. 16-2).

As well as facilities for boaters, the marina was to contain all the amenities to make it a community benefit and tourist attraction. For the boater there would be customs, fuelling, and repair facilities; for visitors and the locals the plan provided a formal central public waterfront, with esplanades and an outdoor entertainment area, the old Sidney Pier and fish market would be retained at the foot of Beacon Avenue, and support an expanded public market. A two-level floating public wharf reaching out into the marina would provide an opportunity to stroll out into the marina, appreciate the views of the Gulf and San Juan Islands, watch the wildlife in and above the water, perhaps have a closer inspection of the visiting vessels, and then visit the restaurant at the end of the wharf. Within the basin would be docks for shuttle boats and foot ferries connecting to the Gulf Islands.

The backdrop was to be a new hotel on the site of the old Hotel Sidney at the foot of Beacon Avenue, with signature chateau-style roof-profile creating a landmark for Sidney Harbour — the town's answer to the Empress Hotel (Fig. 16-3). This was an academic project, and had little chance of being executed in its presented form. It might, however, be an inspiration for a vibrant tourist attraction and give an economic boost. The pioneering

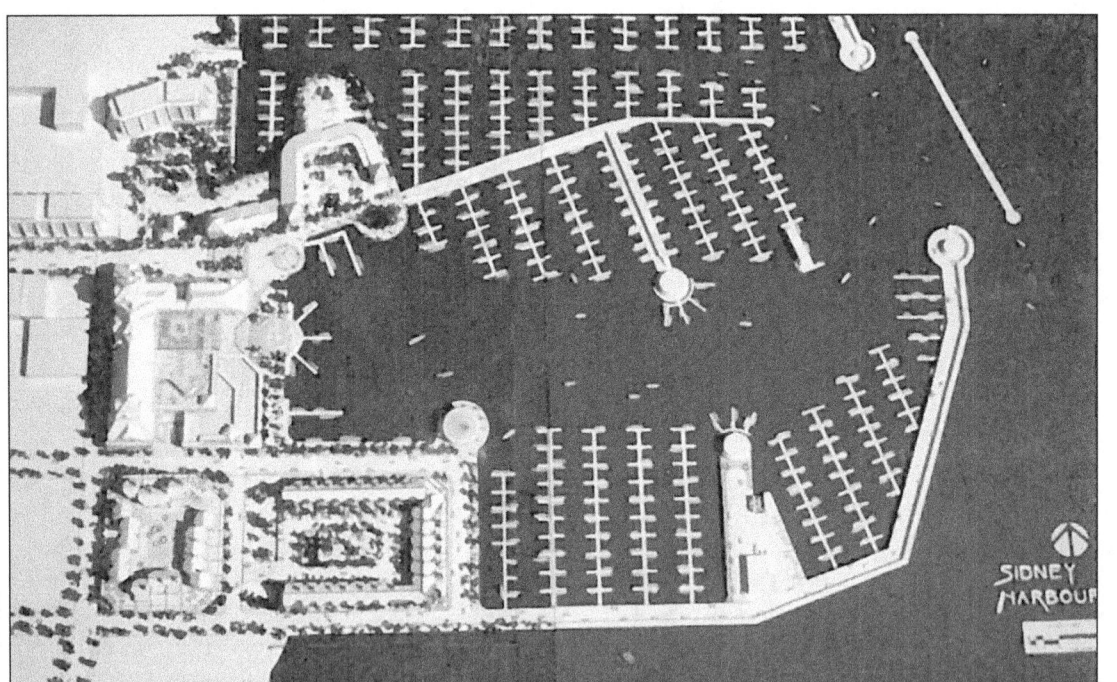

Fig. 16-2. An aerial view of the model of the proposal for a marina in Sidney, showing the harbour wall embracing the marina and the entrance protected by a linear breakwater. [Chris Gower.]

Brighton marina is now one of the most successful in the United Kingdom, but initial construction costs nearly killed the project. It was not until the public facilities such as shops, markets, entertainments, and hotels were an integral part of the scheme that it saw success and profit. With these sorts of amenities, even the most committed land-lubber might be attracted to such a destination.

Fig. 16-3. The proposed Hotel Sidney at the foot of Beacon Avenue, showing the circular entertainment pavilion to the south of the hotel and the market building to the north. [Chris Gower.]

TRANSPORTATION SCHEMES

Chapter 17
CPR Terminal

EVER SINCE THE FIRST WORLD WAR, THE progress, economic condition, and the built environment of the City of Victoria has been a response to just one project that was not built in the city — the transcontinental railway terminus on the Pacific. When British Columbia became a province of the Dominion of Canada on July 20, 1871, one of the terms of the agreement made with Ottawa was that the Dominion government would build a railway to the Pacific seaboard within the first ten years. Although the location of the Pacific terminus was not spelled out, it was obvious to Victorians that the only possible site was on Vancouver Island.

Surveying for the route to the Pacific began in the summer of 1872, with Sandford Fleming (later Sir Sandford Fleming), engineer-in-chief of the Pacific and Intercolonial Railway, leading the expedition. Fleming had identified the Yellowhead Pass as the best path through the Rockies, and this led to Bute Inlet, some 150 kilometres north of Vancouver, which earlier surveys by Alfred Waddington had suggested gave the best access to the interior. From Bute Inlet the route would cross the islands of the Discovery Group and Seymour Narrows to make landfall somewhere near Campbell River, and then on to the chosen terminus. Victoria, Esquimalt, and Alberni were all contenders, although Fleming favoured Alberni for its harbour, the deepest of the three, and more easily accessible for ocean-going vessels.

Preposterous as such a plan might seem to those who know Vancouver Island, and know that the only ways to get to the mainland are by air and sea, it might have been possible. The technology and engineering know-how required to build bridges from island to island linking the mouth of Bute Inlet to Vancouver Island was already available — the Brooklyn Bridge, which opened in 1883 after thirteen years of construction, has a span over the East River of 486.3 metres. According to William Fraser Tolmie, Hudson's Bay Company officer and staunch supporter of the Bute Inlet route, the distances to be bridged were 183 metres to Stewart's Island (Stuart Island), 275 metres to what he called Valdez Island, and 548 metres across Seymour Narrows to Vancouver Island. But there was a rock, Ripple Rock, in the middle of the narrows, and Tolmie thought that this would make an ideal foundation for a supporting pier for the bridge (Fig. 17-1). But whether the technology and engineering skill to work in such treacherous waters was available is another matter.

The short distances, which made bridging such an attractive option, were themselves a hazard; tidal rushes through the narrows were treacherous. The final bridge to the island was planned to cross Seymour Narrows, which was, according to George Vancouver, "one of the vilest stretches of water in the world." Over the years, 119 ships sank in these waters. Even in the 1930s there was still the hope that the narrows would be bridged and that the railway would come to the island, so the proposed destruction of Ripple Rock met with some opposition from those who still saw it as a potential bridge support for the railway link. The lingering dreams died on April 5, 1958, when "the world's largest non-nuclear peacetime explosion" demolished the rock.

The cost to bring the railway across to the island would have been exorbitant, but Amor De Cosmos, MP for Victoria, supported an Order in Council, passed in Ottawa on June 7, 1873, that approved the Bute Inlet route. Prime Minister Sir John A. Macdonald named Esquimalt as the Pacific terminus. Rails were ordered from the United Kingdom and delivered to Esquimalt, where they languished and rusted before eventually being shipped to the mainland.

The final decision on the site of the terminus was not made until December 1877, when it was decided that Port Moody would be the western terminus. For the country it made good economic sense to adopt a more southerly route — the Americans were building the Northern Pacific Railway running from Lake Superior to Puget Sound, a line that would take Canadian business if there were no competition along the border. For the Canadian Pacific Railway Company it was good business sense to prefer the route through the Fraser Valley. It had been promised $25 million and twenty-five million acres in return for taking the financial risk of building the railway. The route down the Fraser Canyon to the rich valley land was a real-estate bonanza not to be sneezed at, and one that earned the company money for the next fifty years.

Shortly after deciding that Port Moody, at the head of Burrard Inlet, would be the terminus, the CPR saw financial advantage in moving it slightly westwards to the townsite of Granville, which was a deep-sea port offering better access to trade with the Orient. But the president of the CPR, William C. Van Horne, wanted the name changed, arguing that people back east in Toronto and Montreal had never heard of Granville but would recognize the name Vancouver. In Victoria this was seen as yet another snub; the mainland had "stolen" the terminus that should have been on the island and now it had stolen its island's name. But the CPR and Van Horne were powerful and influential. The City of Vancouver was incorporated on April 6, 1886, and the first transcontinental train rolled into town on May 23, 1887. The fate of the city of Victoria as the entrepôt for western Canada and the country's major city on the west coast was sealed.

Imagine what the southern tip of Vancouver Island would look like today had the Bute Inlet route been chosen and CPR terminus built here. It would doubtless look like most North American cities, windy canyons lined with high-rise offices, not a Victorian or Edwardian building in sight, not a farm remaining on the good flat building land of the Saanich peninsula, suburbia all the way to Sooke — and no ferry line-ups. There would be no city of Vancouver on the mainland, but rather the city of Granville, and when Victorians, and islanders, wanted big-city amenities they would go to downtown Victoria, not Granville. Instead we have a city that has retained one of North America's finest collections of Victorian and Edwardian buildings, a relaxed and welcoming atmosphere, only a few kilometres of freeway, and none of that downtown — and a city with remarkably little modern architecture.

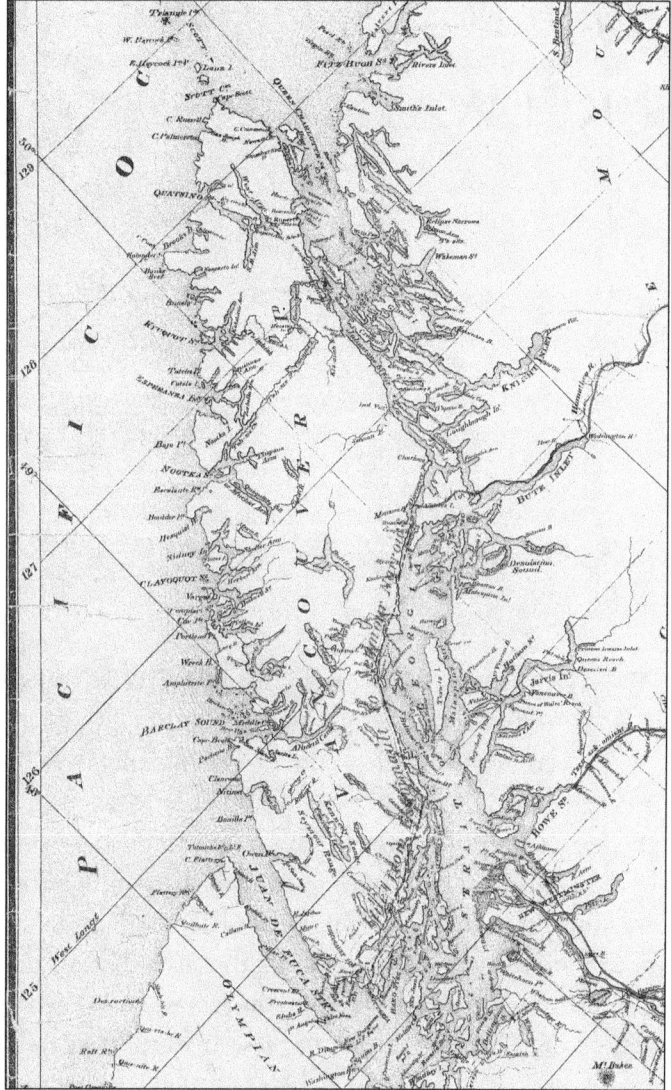

Fig. 17-1. Sir Sandford Fleming's proposed route of the railway, down Bute Inlet and bridging across the Discovery Islands onto Vancouver Island and then down to Esquimalt. [Part of "Map from the Pacific Ocean Across the Rocky Mountain Zone to Accompany Report on the Exploratory Survey; Canadian Pacific Railway January 1874," 52 Tray 1 Original Maps. Office of the Surveyor General, Surveyor General Division, Land Title and Survey Authority of British Columbia.]

Chapter 18

Freeways

VICTORIA HAS ONLY A FEW KILOMETRES of freeway — multi-lane divided highway with controlled access. But if the planners of the 1960s had had their way, there would be a freeway out to the ferry terminal at Swartz Bay, another along the route of the Trans-Canada Highway, and, most alarmingly, one snaking through Victoria West and James Bay neighbourhood to form a loop encasing the city's central core.

The 1960s was a time of urban renewal and revitalization, and Victoria began to recover from its years of stagnation. Centennial Square was created and became, for a while, a vibrant civic space, and other beautification programs improved the downtown business district. Anticipating population growth throughout the capital region, and with it a changing role for Victoria as the region's hub, the capital region's planners turned their attention to an overall plan for the city, and much of this addressed region's transportation needs.

The most important concept of the planners' report — a comprehensive eighty-four page document — was the need for Victoria to become the centre of the region. The city's workforce had expanded by 32 percent in the decade from 1951 and was expected to have increased by over 50 percent by 1981; this additional population would live in the surrounding municipalities and, in general, travel into the city for work, entertainment, shopping, etc. And, if Victoria was to become the beating heart of cultural and commercial activity of a region stretching from Sidney to Sooke to Shawnigan Lake, then it had to have good roads to connect all the parts.

At the time there were two main routes connecting the city to its region. Quadra Street, which connected at a Y junction with East and West Saanich Roads in the vicinity of Royal Oak Drive, was the main route to the communities on the Saanich Peninsula and was the only way to get to the airport at Patricia Bay and the Swartz

Bay ferry terminal, which opened in 1960 (Fig. 18-1). The Island Highway took the route of what is now the Old Island Highway and Goldstream Avenue, connecting to communities to the west of the city and then to the main body of the island. Both of these were obviously inadequate for the needs of a growing commuter population, and anticipated increases in tourist numbers.

Early in 1965 a transportation study recommended the construction of four urban freeways (Fig. 18-2). The Patricia Bay Freeway would extend south from Telegraph Road to Tolmie Avenue where it would connect with the Blanshard Street extension — at the time Blanshard Street only ran as far north as Hillside Avenue. This route from the Swartz Bay terminal to downtown has essentially been

Fig. 18-1. Quadra Street looking south towards Cloverdale Avenue at Cook Street, 1959. [Saanich Archives Number: 1980-015-191a.]

completed, although it is peppered with traffic lights and is only a freeway in a couple of places. The Trans-Canada Highway would extend from the Thetis Lake Interchange — which was a two-lane highway to the north — along its present alignment to Wilkinson Road where it would branch in a north-easterly direction and join the Patricia Bay Freeway somewhere near its junction with McKenzie Avenue. Later that year the city commissioned an overall plan for Victoria, expanding on the transportation plan, it proposed a "loop concept" encircling the downtown core. Part of this proposal has been completed, but the realignment along Wilkinson Road has not.

The West Victoria Freeway would run from the southern terminus of the Pat Bay Freeway at Tolmie and Blanshard, then over Douglas Street and then follow the CNR right of way, now the Galloping Goose Regional Trail, south over the Selkirk trestle, through Victoria West and then bridge the harbour from the Songhees to Laurel Points, terminating near the parliament buildings in James Bay (Figs. 18-3, 18-4). And the Island Freeway (Route 1A) would extend from the Thetis Lake interchange on the Trans-Canada Highway along what is now the E&N rail trail to Craigflower Road at Admirals Road providing a link between Langford and Colwood with Esquimalt and downtown Victoria.

The overriding philosophy of the freeway plan was to move people and goods swiftly and efficiently into and out of the downtown core, and at the same time minimize congestion there. Particular attention was paid to what was probably the most radical of the plan's proposals — the West Victoria Freeway. It would allow logging trucks to bring their cargo from the up-island logging areas via the Trans-Canada Highway and West Victoria Freeway, over the bridge, and then to the outer wharf at Ogden Point without going anywhere near the core. The planners were confident that this proposal would not invite public protest as it would use the railway right-of-way and there would be no destruction of neighbourhoods. It would also

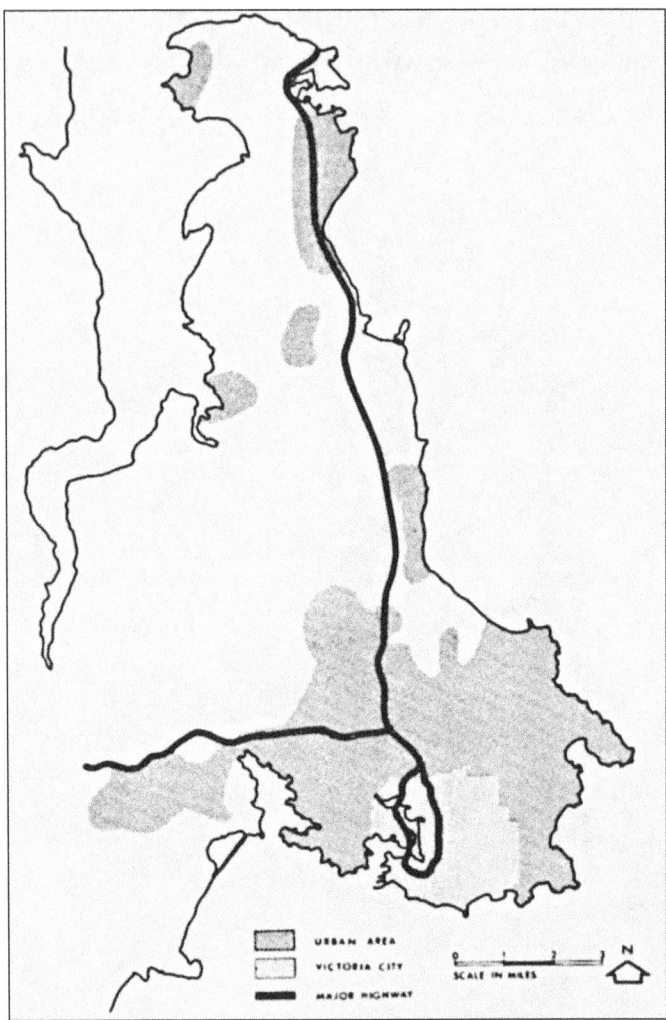

Fig. 18-2. The Regional Plan Concept for freeways, 1965, showing the loop around the city core, the Patricia Bay Freeway up to the ferry terminal at Swartz Bay, and the "Trans Canada Freeway" from the west, and linking at the level of McKenzie Avenue. [CVA, CD 120.]

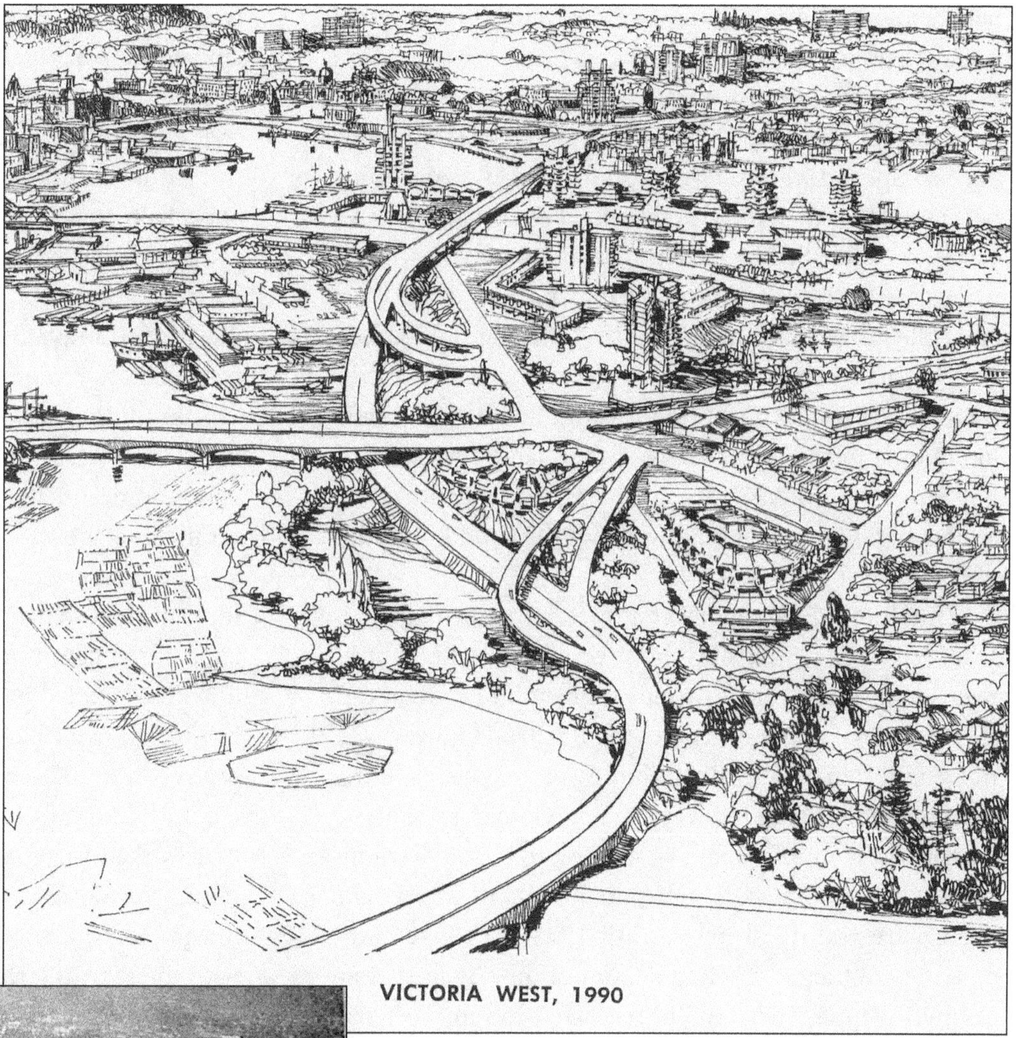

FREEWAYS [155]

Fig. 18-3. An artist's concept of Victoria West in 1990 after the completion of the West Victoria Freeway. [CVA, CD 120.]

VICTORIA WEST, 1990

Fig. 18-4. The projected bridge from Songhees Point to Laurel Point. Published in the *Times*, March 2, 1963.

benefit the increasing number of commuters to government offices in James Bay.

The artist's impression of what Victoria West would have looked like in 1990 had the West Victoria Freeway been completed is both alarming and intriguing. Alarming because of the extent of the envisioned ribbon of concrete as it leaps across Selkirk Water, at the bottom of the image, where the trestle is today, and winds its way, disgorging and collecting traffic, until it crosses the bridge into James Bay. What is intriguing is the perception, in 1965, that there would still be a working harbour in 1990; there are log booms in the upper harbour, and land between the Bay Street and Johnson Street Bridges is filled with what appear to be industrial buildings, not the condominiums of the Old Songhees Reserve.

The Island Freeway never attracted support, and the West Victoria would only have been viable had there been a continuous north-south connection between the ferry terminal and the city, but the Pat Bay Highway was not connected to the Blanshard Street extension until 1978, by which time freeways were no longer seen as an acceptable — or affordable — solution to the city's traffic woes. Connecting the Pat Bay to Blanshard Street had been a frustrating exercise; until 1978 Blanshard only extended to the northernmost limit of the city proper at Tolmie Avenue. The route of the extension to meet the Pat Bay was a surveying nightmare because the Town and Country shopping centre (opened in June 1961 and now redeveloped as Uptown) stood in the way. At least three routes were surveyed, including one that required an eight-hundred-foot-long tunnel under the shopping centre parking lot.

Eventually Blanshard Street was connected to the Pat Bay highway, but the completion of the loop around the city, connecting Blanshard Street to Laurel Point, was mired in controversy and interminable discussions. The Michigan Street extension, which would be in the loop's south eastern section, was stopped under the terms of the Beacon Hill Park Trust. With the waning enthusiasm for freeways, particularly their expense, experts turned their attention to alternatives. Public transit, improved arterial streets, and an integrated and coordinated system were what was needed, according to David E. Campbell of the city's traffic engineering and transportation planning department.

But little was done until mounting pressure for improved transportation into the city from the expanding communities to the west persuaded the provincial government to act. In 1993 MLA Moe Sihota stood up in the legislative assembly and said that the government believed that light rail was the solution to the transportation problems of the communities to the west of the city. He outlined the actions the government had already taken: land in Victoria West had been purchased to ensure that there was a continuous corridor for light rail from the western communities into Victoria, and the province and the city had worked together and formulated plans for a trolley system for downtown Victoria that would eventually be integrated with the light rail transit (LRT). Discussions with the federal government were underway with a view to getting an agreement to use the E&N and CNR rights-of-way to bring commuters all the way from Cobble Hill into the city. In the meantime, the Trans-Canada Highway would be upgraded and local bus services expanded — and that was all that happened; there is no LRT, there is no trolley system.

Some forty-five years after the planners created their grand freeway schemes, only a few kilometres have been completed, and little of it really merits the name "freeway" as there are numerous controlled, and even some uncontrolled, junctions at grade. The route up the Saanich peninsula to the ferry terminal has recently added a sixth intersection not at grade, and the Trans-Canada from Spencer Road to its terminus has only three. The failure to adopt the Wilkinson Road route from the Trans-Canada to the Pat Bay Highway is the cause of significant traffic delays — as well as a significant number of letters to the *Colonist* offering solutions to the Trans-Canada crawl. Should we regret the failure of these freeway plans? On the one hand the failure to build the West Victoria and the Island freeways, both of which would have used railway rights-of-way, has given us trails that are now heavily used, and much valued, by bicyclists and walkers. On the other hand we are facing increasing traffic congestion, particularly for those living in the communities to the west of the city and beyond, and the prospect of a solution that is ever more costly. As ever, the city's traffic woes are under discussion.

Chapter 19

Gordon Head Memorial Air Park

The trans-atlantic solo flight of Charles Lindbergh in *The Spirit of St. Louis* in May 1927 fired imaginations throughout the world, and for the first time the public began to realize that air travel was a real possibility. Victorians were not immune to this excitement, and in 1928 British Columbia Airways Limited was formed. It operated from Lansdowne Field, a rectangular parcel of flat land between Lansdowne Road, and Shelbourne and Richmond Streets, extending south to the level of Newton Street, where Lansdowne School is today. The site was no stranger to flight, as a plaque on the west side of Richmond Road, just south of Lansdowne Road, testifies; it honours William Wallace Gibson "who designed, built and flew the first all Canadian aircraft at this site on September 8th 1910."

After two years — and as many fatal crashes — Lansdowne Field, which was run as a private enterprise, attracted the attention of the city's Industrial Committee and the Chamber of Commerce, both of which wanted a municipal airport. After complaints about low and dangerous flying — the field was also used by private and student pilots of the Victoria Aero Club who were not above indulging in aerial acrobatics — the Dominion authorities ordered that Lansdowne was not to be used for commercial flights. The city then approved an airport by-law vote, asking the citizens to agree to the expenditure of nearly $250,000 for construction of an airport on Finnerty Farm in Gordon Head (Fig. 19-1). But in the midst of the Depression, the citizens were in no mood to fund what they perceived as "apparent luxuries for all of Greater Victoria," and the by-law vote was roundly defeated. Despite this defeat, there is evidence from aerial photographs that the land at Finnerty Farm was groomed with sand and gravel runways and used for air shows.

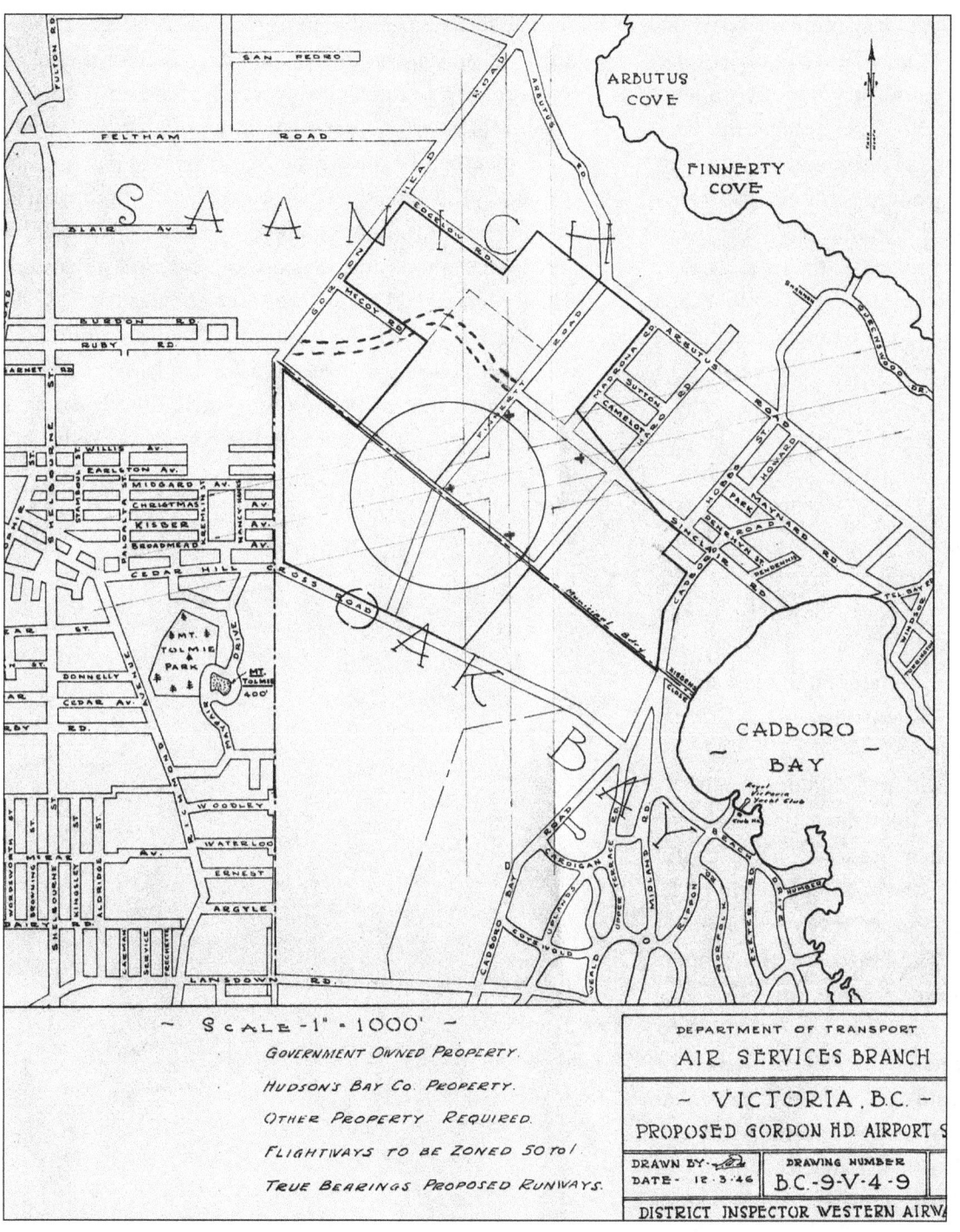

Fig. 19-1. The site plan of the proposed airfield, from Department of Transport, Air Services Branch, proposed airport site, 1946, amended to show the University Ring Road, and McKenzie Avenue. The 1931 airfield was located at the western end of Sinclair Road. [Saanich Archives.]

Victoria did eventually get a commercial airport for land-based craft courtesy of the Royal Canadian Air Force, which had carved an aerodrome out of farm land at Patricia Bay in the late 1930s. This became the base for Trans-Canada Air Lines operations in 1943, when it was declared the official western terminus for transcontinental service. The travelling public of Victoria were not overjoyed at the location; access up the winding East Saanich Road was considered too arduous. Two solutions were proposed: revive the plan for a municipal airport at Gordon Head, or spend the money on a decent road to the airport at Patricia Bay.

Support for the Gordon Head solution was particularly strong from the city's young aviators who had seen service in the war and wanted to continue flying for pleasure; they revived the Victoria Flying Club and started a campaign for the Gordon Head option. During the war the groomed sandy airstrips of the early 1930s had been built over by the Gordon Head Army Camp, but the city had an option to buy twenty-three hectares on the east side of Finnerty Road. The airport was to be named the Gordon Head Memorial Air Park in honour of the war veterans, and the city bought the land with the condition that it was eventually used as an airport. The flying club laboriously graded the runways, and in the process garnered a lawsuit for beginning the work before the re-zoning was in place. Only one plane ever landed there, in November 1948.

An airfield at Gordon Head also had the support of the Saanich bulb and flower growers who were prepared to buy their own planes and hire pilots to get their goods to market. "If we can get this airport it will be a big thing for Saanich" said A. E. Horner, president of Saanich Ward 1 Ratepayers Association. But Mr. Horner had not reckoned with the anger of the actual ratepayers themselves, who mounted a letter-writing and advertising campaign arguing that the airpark was for "a vociferous minority" and "designed for the selfish pleasure of a few amateur flyers who have absolutely no regard for the rights of the majority of property owners — but would like these property owners to pay for their project." The referendum to test the strength of feeling in the entire municipality of Saanich, in December 1948, went down to a resounding defeat. The Gordon Head Memorial Air Park was officially dead.

Perhaps it was for the best. When, a decade later, Victoria College went looking for land for its campus expansion, this conveniently-located tract was available, and eventually became the site of the University of Victoria.

Chapter 20

Gorge Inland Waterway

Although James Douglas thought that he had chosen an ideal harbour in Victoria, his judgement was flawed; and when the city became an international trading port, rather than a trading post of the Hudson's Bay Company, it soon became apparent that it was not capable of handling all merchant vessels. Ships needing deeper water docked at Esquimalt, and goods for Victoria had to be brought around Macauley Point. In August 1858 a proposal to build an inland waterway appeared in the *Victoria Gazette*. The idea was that a canal should be dug linking Thetis Cove, in Esquimalt Harbour, and Portage Inlet at the head of the Gorge Waterway. The route of this canal was a well-travelled one, having been used as a portage, probably for centuries, by the Songhees people. Goods unloaded in Esquimalt Harbour could be lightered through the canal, down the Gorge, and into the Victoria Harbour without having to go round Macauley Point; a journey of half the distance and without the risk of venturing into the open waters of Juan de Fuca Strait. The writer was convinced it would cost only a few thousand dollars, and hoped that the project "would be taken into consideration by some of our capitalists." It seems that none of them stepped up to the plate.

There were other proposals to build a canal linking the harbour and the inlet, but these were in order to use the tides of the harbour to flush the Gorge. However, the concept of linking the Gorge Waterway and Thetis Cove as a transportation corridor surfaced again when architect Chris Gower developed a plan as a contribution to the Victoria 2020 Conference in 2002. Organized by the Downtown Victoria Community Alliance, the conference was attended by professionals in numerous disciplines and the general public. Its objective was to examine and discuss ways to "create and implement a plan to restore downtown's lustre, economic vibrancy and social health."

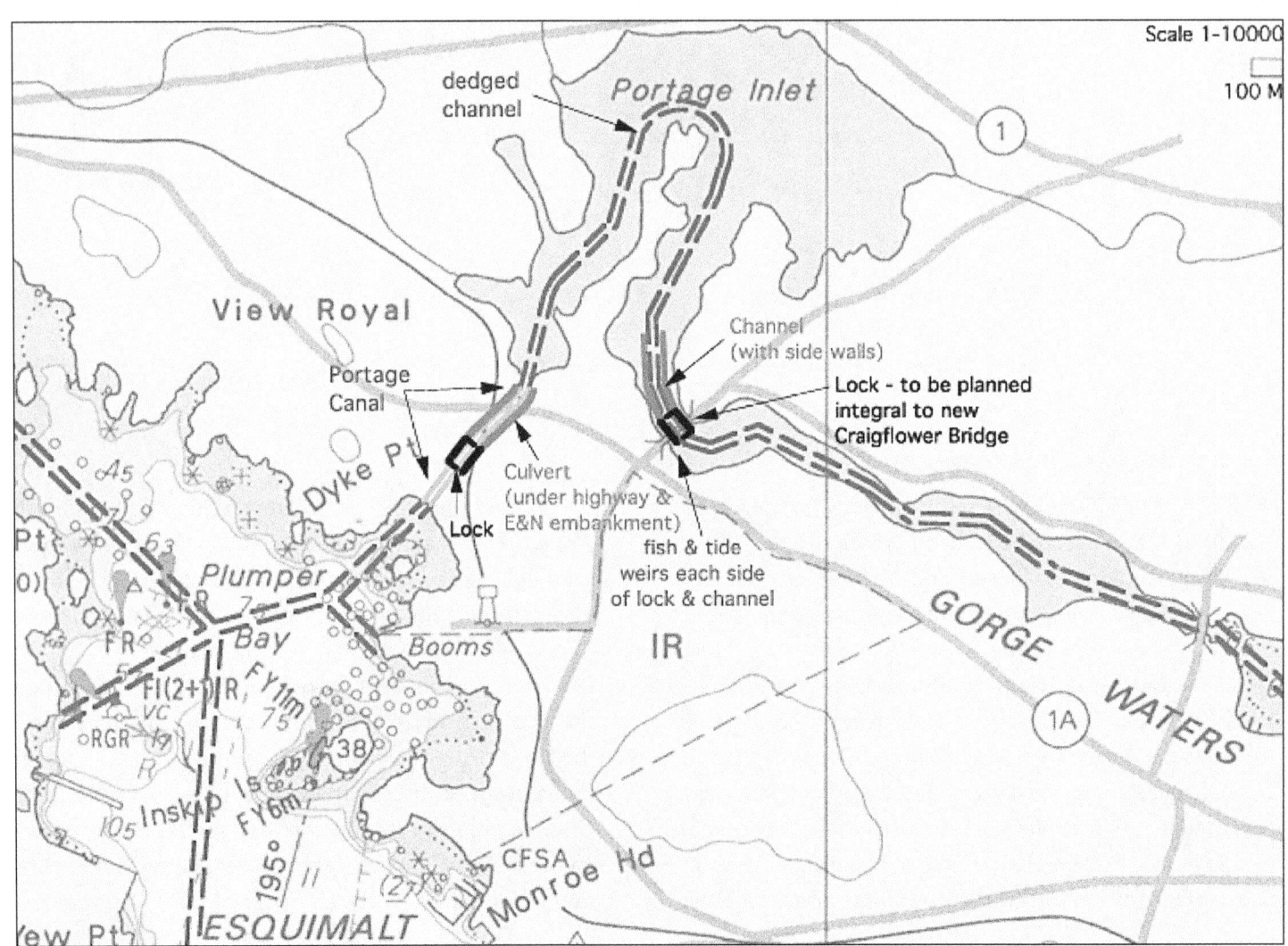

Fig. 20-1. A map showing the route of the inland waterway and the location of the locks and the dredged channel through Portage Inlet. [Chris Gower.]

Inspired by such canal schemes as the popular and well-used ocean locks leading from Elliott Bay to Lake Union in Seattle, by Venice's Grand Canal, and by the inland waterways of Europe, Gower suggested the concept of cutting a canal through from Thetis Cove to Portage Inlet to make such a waterway for Victoria (Fig. 20-1). A lock in the canal would be necessary, but its use would be limited to times of vigorous tides in Esquimalt Harbour, otherwise boats could pass freely. The canal would run in a culvert under the Old Island Highway and the E&N railway lines. A channel dredged through Portage Inlet would ensure enough depth for vessels such as tour boats and water taxis, and a second lock, underneath Craigflower Bridge, would control water levels in the inlet when necessary. Alongside this lock, open channels would allow fish, as well as small boats, to navigate at any tide.

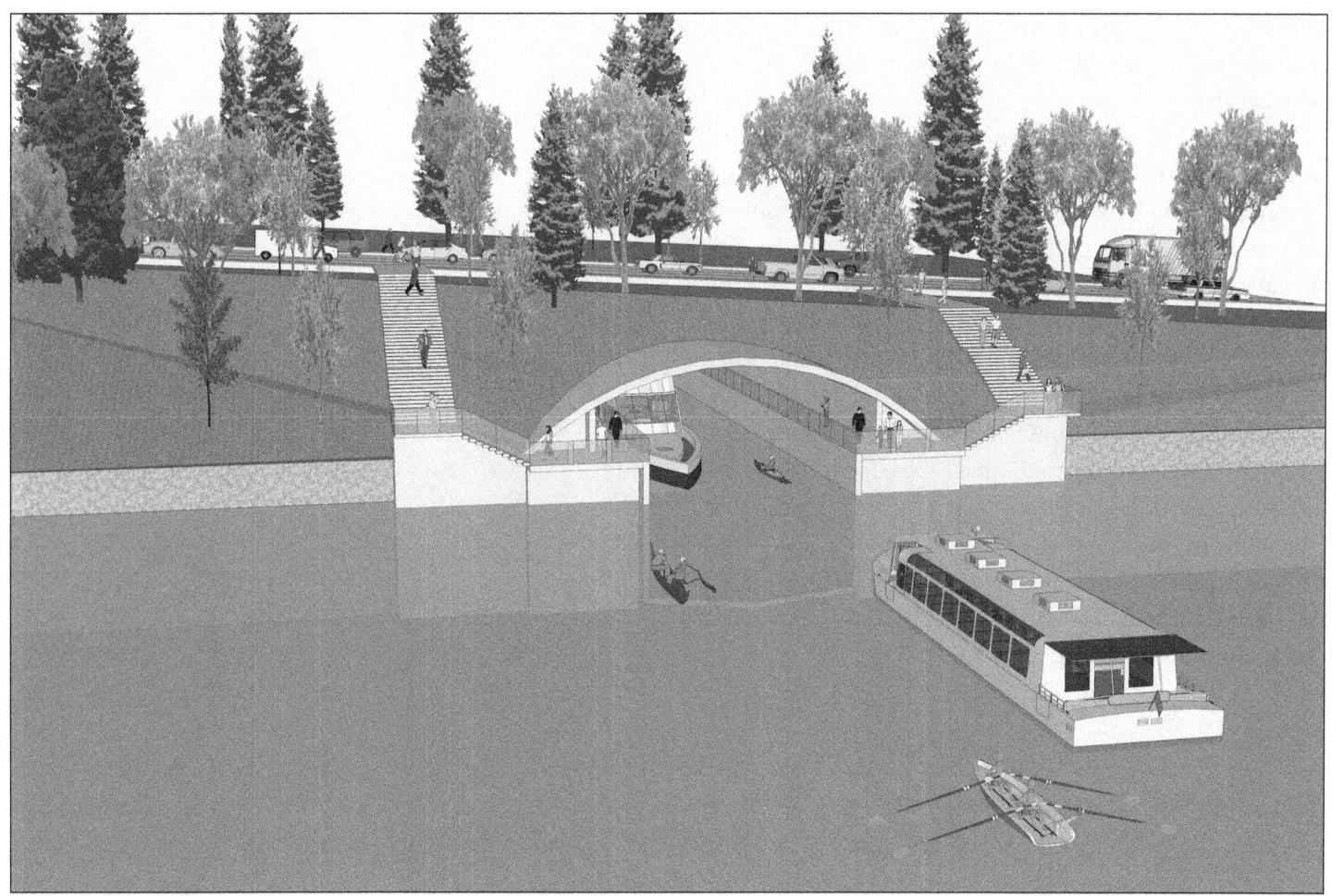

Fig. 20-2. A perspective of the tunnel under Old Island Highway. [Chris Gower.]

This proposal is technically feasible, although there would be significant cost in engineering a culvert under the railway and highway, but this endeavour might well be considered worth it by the thousands of commuters who make the journey into town from the western communities. One Metchosin resident recently claimed that his journey into town took one hour and forty minutes, most of that time spent idling on the Trans-Canada Highway; a water bus travelling through such a scenic route would surely be a much more pleasant and relaxing way to start and end the working day (Fig. 20-2). And even if it took half an hour, it would still be an improvement over the current journey time.

The cost of this waterway could not be justified if it only saw traffic at rush hour, but during the day and evening it could be used for scenic cruises. Tourists and residents alike could enjoy the wildlife and natural beauty of the Gorge, as well as see Fort Rodd Hill, the Fisgard Light, and Hatley Park from the vantage point of Esquimalt Harbour. If landing points at these, and other tourist attractions, were built, there would be a wider economic benefit in bringing more visitors, and the city's ship-building industry might reap the benefit from construction of the specialized shallow-draft vessels that would be needed.

All in all, it seems that the advantages of having such an all-season inland waterway are legion, but it has not been built, or even mooted, of late.

RELIGIOUS INSTITUTIONS

Chapter 21

St. Ann's Academy

"No factual work about Victoria would be complete without the inclusion of the Sisters of St. Ann and their contribution to education, healthcare, and the built environment of the city."

Founded in 1850 in Vaudreuil, Quebec, the Sisters of St. Anne are a religious congregation consecrated for the teaching of the young. In 1858 four sisters of the congregation travelled to Victoria at the request of the missionary Bishop Modeste Demers. After an arduous seven-week journey they arrived on Saturday June 5, 1858, and were installed in a "small, wretched house" the bishop had purchased for them, and there they opened their school the following Monday morning. From then until 1973 the Sisters of St. Ann, who had anglicized their name as a mark of respect for their new home, played a dedicated and vital role in education and healthcare, in the city, elsewhere on the west coast, and in Alaska. This first schoolhouse and home survives, and has been moved adjacent to the Helmcken House on the grounds of the Royal British Columbia Museum.

Over the years more and more sisters arrived and the congregation's work in teaching and health care increased. They bought land and erected convents and hospitals throughout British Columbia. In Victoria they built the first wing of St. Ann's Convent on Humboldt Street, and later, in 1886, a central entrance bay and the east wing was added. Architecturally, the building has its roots in Quebec; plans drawn by priest and amateur architect Father Joseph Michaud were sent from the Mother House in Lachine in 1871, and Charles Verheyden was the supervising architect for the construction. In 1886, architect John Teague continued in the same style. So, when the sisters wanted yet another addition in 1908, they understandably wanted a compatible work. The firm of Hooper & Watkins prepared a grand neoclassical design (Fig. 21-1). This scheme placed the addition right in front of the existing buildings, with the rear of its domed rotunda connecting to the original entrance bay. The sisters rejected this plan, as it was far too opulent and ornate for a congregation that had taken a vow of poverty. They decided to build only one wing, stripped of all ornamentation, and to place it at the west end rather than in front, where it survives and is known as the Hooper wing.

During the 1960s the sisters faced a number of problems. The academy was a private school with no government funding, which challenged their finances. Vatican II expanded the possibilities for those in religious life and many sisters and novices left the congregation, so teachers had to be hired, further stretching the sisters' resources. But perhaps the most insuperable problems were in the health care work. St. Joseph's hospital, opposite the academy on Humboldt Street, and owned and operated by the sisters, needed constant upgrades to meet advances in medical care. The Ministry of Health was obliged to fund this work, and in return took greater and greater equity in the property.

The provincial government considered a number of options to solve the problem of the city's shortage of hospital facilities, and one of them was to expand St. Joseph's, while another was to abandon it and build a brand new hospital farther out of town to accommodate the city's expanding population on the Saanich

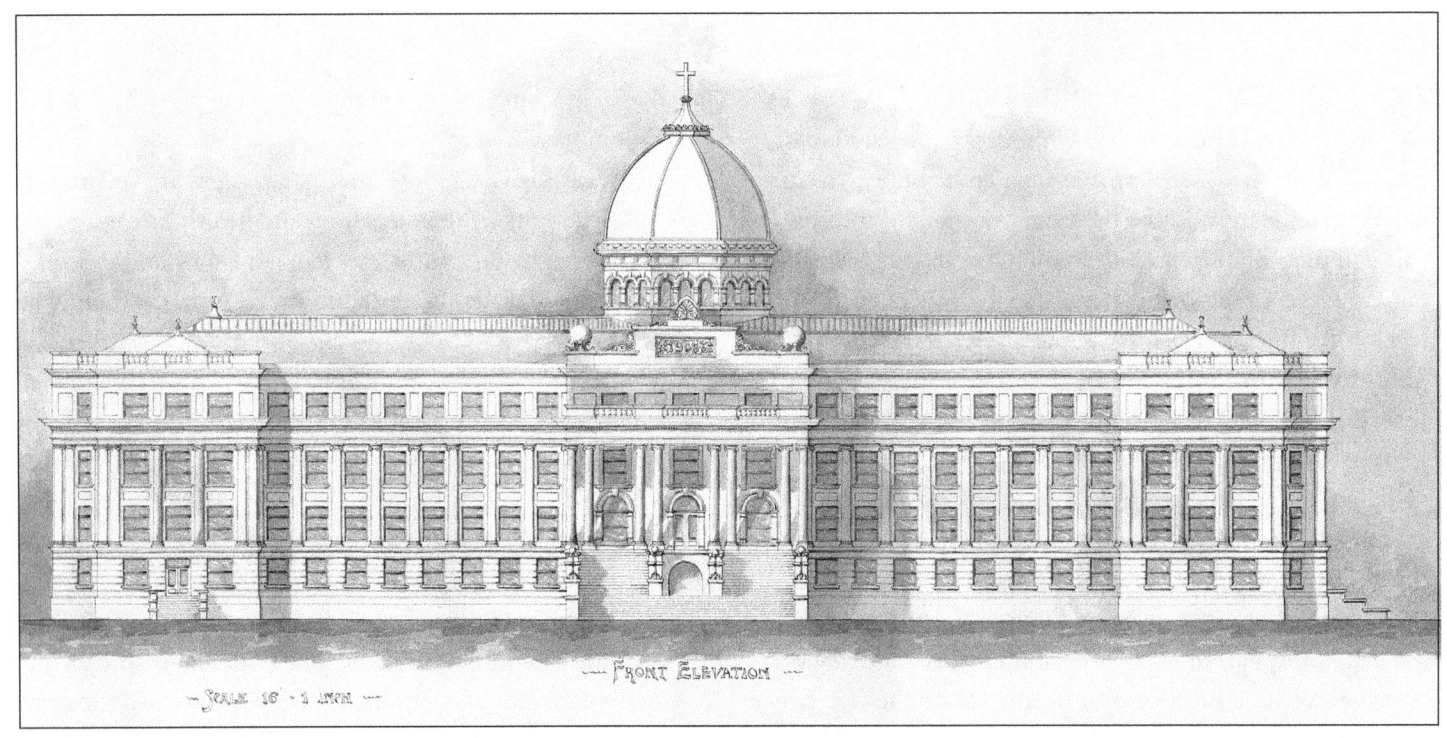

Fig. 21-1. A concept drawing by Hooper & Watkins for the addition to St. Ann's Academy, 1908. [Sisters of St. Ann Archives (SSAA), catalogue no. PL20-15-01.]

Peninsula. So sisters, and parents of students, were alarmed to read on May 15, 1968, that Fred Norris, chairman of St. Joseph's board of management, was proposing to build a new hospital on the grounds of St. Ann's Academy. Then, in late 1969, provincial politicians were considering a proposal to buy the academy for $1,587,000, demolish it, and build a new hospital. In this climate of uncertainty the sisters ultimately gave St. Joseph's to the city in 1972, with a covenant that the property only be used for healthcare purposes. The following day the city gave it to the province.

At the same time the city had a proposal to slice through the academy's front lawn with the eastward extension of Belleville Street (Fig. 21-2). If the hospital expansion were to proceed the city would have to close Humboldt Street, Heywood Avenue (now Academy Close), and parts of other streets in exchange for permission to extend Belleville Street. It would be far better, thought some politicians, to build a new hospital elsewhere, which is what happened with the construction of the General Hospital on Helmcken Road, and the eventual closure of St. Joseph's. Later the city abandoned its road-building scheme, leaving the property in limbo once again.

The writing was on the wall for the academy. After four years of vacillation about the fate of the property, the

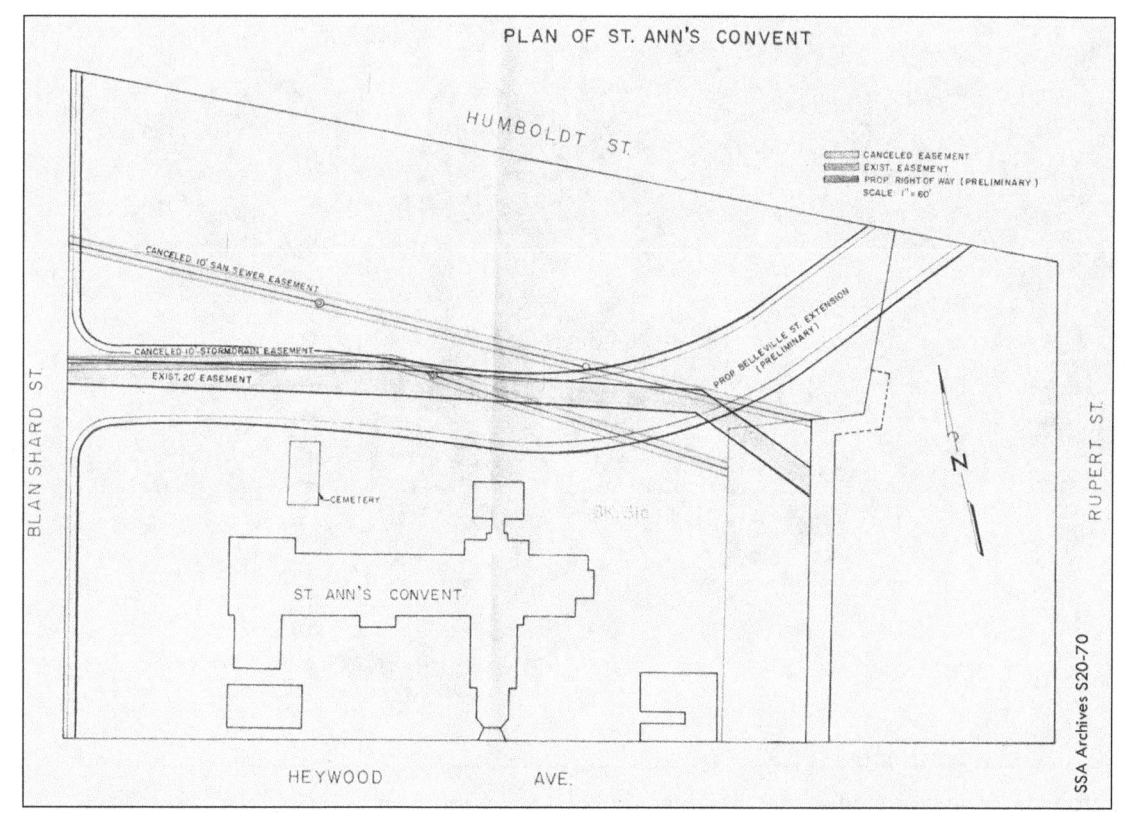

Fig. 21-2. A plan of the route of the Belleville Street extension through the academy grounds. [SSAA, PL-20-73-02.]

sisters closed the school and sold it to the province with no strings attached. The province gave responsibility for St Ann's Academy first to the British Columbia Building Corporation and, in 1982, to the Provincial Capital Commission (PCC). The building was used essentially as short-term rental space: for a time the Ministry of Education had offices there until it found something more suitable, the lawyers and the courts moved in for a year during the renovation of the law courts, and various charities and cultural organizations were allowed temporary office space. It seems to have been something of a white elephant, and without a clear future, the building was allowed to moulder and decay — even the cross on the chapel roof was leaning at an angle of eighty-degrees.

In 1984 the entire building was designated under the provincial Heritage Conservation Act, and the PCC commissioned a study for its restoration using historically accurate materials and techniques. It was assumed that the building would be returned to its former state and used as a school, but the $8.7 million price tag was

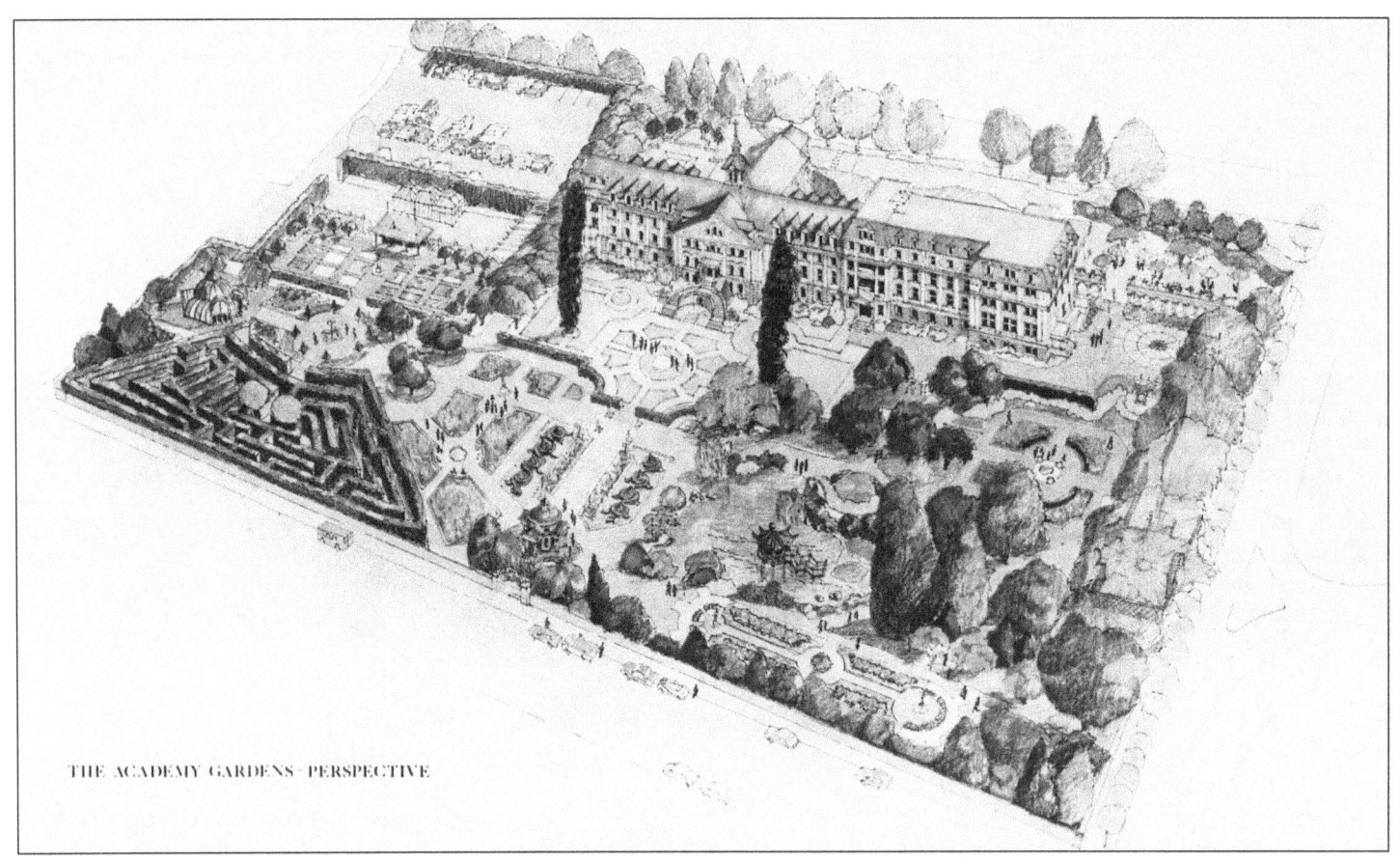

Fig. 21-3. A perspective of the grounds of the proposed Academy Gardens, 1988. [SSAA, Wagg & Hambleton.]

not an acceptable cost to create a building that was not revenue generating. So the PCC called for proposals to rehabilitate and use the entire site.

Five developers responded. The chosen proposal came from a consortium of Peter Daniel, a property developer, Jack Angus, a solicitor, both of Victoria, and Monte P. Nathanson of Winnipeg who proposed to form The Academy Gardens Corporation. With the local architectural firm of Wagg & Hambleton, and internationally recognized landscape architect John Lantzius, they presented an impressive scheme for "botanical gardens of world-class standards" occupying all the land in front of the building (Fig. 21-3). The chapel and the academy's exterior would be completely restored, but the interior would be gutted and filled with restaurants, art galleries, exhibits, and shops (Figs. 21-4, 21-5). The sisters were delighted with the plan, as the dilapidation and neglect of their former building was seen as a mark of disrespect for their century of service to the city; they cared more for people than bricks and mortar. This plan would both honour their contributions and the place would be "alive."

The garden, a sort of urban Buchart Gardens, "represents a nineteenth century Victorian garden based on fourteen individual gardens and plazas." Proposed garden features included a grande allée — an impressive avenue of trees — with topiary leading from the Humboldt Street entrance to a major plaza at the foot of the double stair entrance; a gazebo with a viewing platform on a high point at the northern edge of the property; a butterfly pavilion; a maze along the lines of the one at Hampton Court Palace; and a lake with a Chinese pagoda. Visitors to the gardens would be charged admission that would entitle them to any number of visits in a day, and it was suggested that visitors might enjoy the gardens in the daytime and return in the evening for the illuminations of the fountains and the floodlit building. Inside the building the ground and first floors would be converted into long hallways running the length of the building and the decoration would suggest a street scene — "much in the way historic scenes are recalled in the Royal British Columbia Museum" — the floor would have the appearance of cobblestones, and the shops "old-fashioned shop fronts."

Four of the five proposals were shown to the public at the Crystal Garden in April 1988; as well as the Academy Gardens scheme there was an integrated artists' studio area, seniors housing, and one with no specifics. Reaction ranged from guarded to outraged. The *Colonist* editorial called the proposal vague, and thought questions should be asked because British Columbians owned the property and "private interests want to lease it from us for commercial use." Although the promise of "195 permanent jobs and tax revenue of $250,000 to the city" was impressive, it speculated that it would be a "Fantasy Gardens" tourist-lure that attracted "hucksters and pedlars."

While the newspaper was skeptical, reserving judgement until more information was forthcoming, Bill Hockey, head of the restoration architecture section of Environment Canada, western region, made his opinion abundantly clear, calling the development a form of "vandalism" and a "national disgrace." In a strongly worded letter to Mr. Beres, the manager of the PCC, Hockey wrote, "If the resource has any chance of obtaining a federal grant of up to $1 million … it must be deemed to have national historic significance. This will never happen if the resource is developed as proposed, as all heritage value will be destroyed."

Throughout the summer of 1988 the PCC had discussions with the Academy Gardens Corporation. Meanwhile, politicians, editorials, and letter writers mused on alternative uses; MLA Robin Blencoe, was

Fig. 21-4. Interior scene of the ground floor of the Academy Gardens scheme. [SSAA, Wagg & Hambleton.]

Fig. 21-5. Interior scene of the second floor of the Academy Gardens scheme. [SSAA, Wagg & Hambleton.]

delighted to learn that the site was being considered for national designation, and hoped that the Academy Gardens proposal would be put on hold; he proposed to the National Sites and Monuments Board that the site could be a "national park and the buildings a cultural centre." Other suggestions included the central library, city archives, Kaleidoscope Theatre, and a downtown campus for the University of Victoria. The PCC's decision was expected by the end of September, by which time there was mounting opposition in the community. The *Colonist* opined that "if it fails it would be a reprieve for St. Ann's rather than a lost opportunity." Mark Madoff of the Hallmark Society said the project was "a short-term revenue-generating solution of doubtful benefit — but of certain destructiveness."

The city council eventually rezoned St. Ann's and gave the Academy Gardens scheme planning approval, the PCC agreed a long-term lease, and work began. But the company's financiers were becoming increasingly nervous, not about the plan or its developers, but about the possibility that the naysayers would stall, or even stop the project. By November 1990 the Academy Gardens Corporation was in financial difficulties, with builders' liens to the tune of $420,000, and, in consequence, a default of its lease agreement. Peter Daniel, company president, came up with a revised plan. But Ken Hill, chairman of the PCC, said that the new plan "would leave much of the originally agreed-to improvements undone, although it consumed the same amount of money," and the new plan was rejected in September 1991. Hill was saddened by the loss of the project as he, and other member of the commission "felt we had a method of restoring the building without tapping the public purse." Others, such as the St Ann's Rescue Coalition, the Concerned Citizens Association, and the Hallmark Society, were overjoyed.

The timing of this failure could not have been more opportune. The newly elected provincial government of the NDP had entered into a partnership with the city — the Victoria Accord — which was to develop schemes for revitalization of the city and beautification of the provincial capital; St. Ann's Academy was one of the accord's earliest concepts. It was proposed to restore the academy, both inside and out, and extend its grounds to be contiguous with Beacon Hill Park. The building would house an interpretive centre explaining the sisters' significance in the community and an auditorium. Outside, the original gardens would be restored with a rose arbour, fountain, and terraces, and a new courtyard would link the original building with a new structure housing the Victoria Conservatory of Music. All this would be paid for by property taxes from development on the Y-lot where high-rise high-density office blocks, a public park, and a new bus station would be built. Well, that was the plan.

In March 1992 Paul Merrick Architects was commissioned by the British Columbia Buildings Corporation (BCBC) on behalf of the PCC to undertake a detailed and comprehensive study of St. Ann's Academy's building and grounds, as well as publicly owned land in its vicinity. Unlike the Academy Gardens scheme, which was shrouded in secret sessions conducted by the PCC and in which citizen input was only solicited after the scheme had been chosen, this study actively encouraged public participation in exploring uses for the properties. The sisters, who had remained quiet during the rancorous Academy Gardens episode, offered their full support for any proposal that would restore the exterior, the chapel, and the grounds, and honour the history and outreach of their congregation. Merrick examined numerous options for use of St. Ann's Academy land, the Y-lot, and government-owned land south of Academy Close; these studies explored the possibilities for residential use (Fig. 21-6), a theatre, the school of music, and the art gallery.

After consultation with the public and various cultural organizations, Merrick reported that the Victoria arts community were the "only group that expressed a strong desire to focus their program aspirations on the grounds of St. Ann's." Accordingly, Merrick prepared plans and elevations for a new Provincial Art Gallery that took into account the "programmatic ambitions of the Greater Victoria Art Gallery" (see Fig. 10-1). The gallery would be at the east end of the grounds with its main facade facing west. In front of its concave entrance plaza would be an outdoor concert green, and a sculpture gallery along the north-western perimeter would lead to a public path to Cridge Park, just south of the Church of Our Lord. This concept was to give a new "public focus" to St. Ann's and

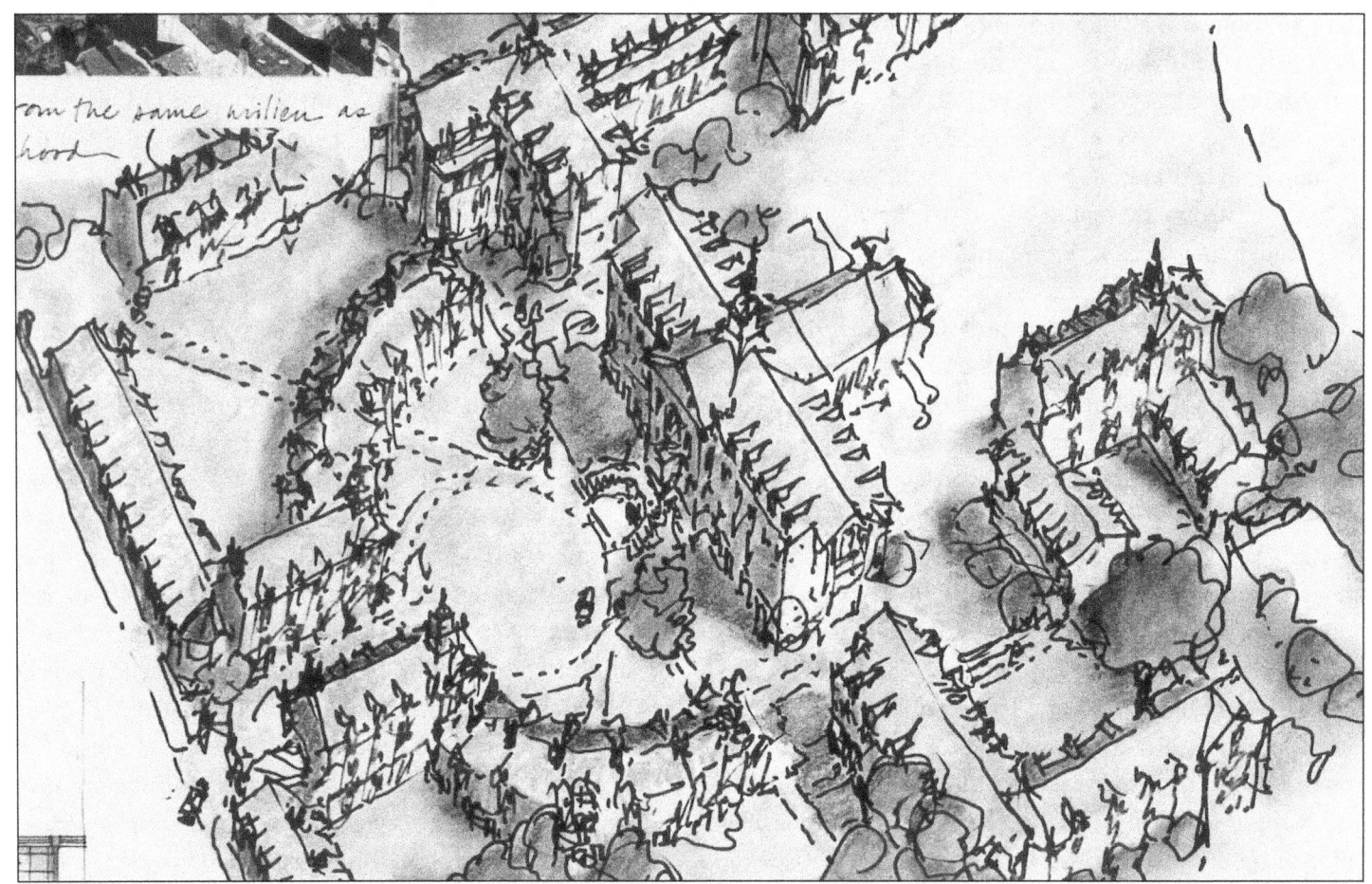

Fig. 21-6. A perspective of proposed housing in the academy grounds, showing a crescent of apartment buildings facing the academy, and blocks to the south. See also figure 10-1 for the proposed art gallery at right angles to the academy. [Paul Merrick Architects.]

make a "strong visual statement at the 'Headwaters' of the historic inlet" — an allusion to the fact that the stream feeding James Bay, before it was reclaimed, ran through the centre of the St. Ann property.

Funding for the work on the academy site was to come from revenue from the high-rise offices that the provincial government was proposing to build on the Y-lot; but after protracted discussions between the city and the province, the plans to build on the Y-lot were shelved — capital construction money could no longer stretch to the $100 million cost of the buildings. But the rehabilitation of St. Ann's, which had originally been contingent on the Y-lot development, had a gained such a level of public support that the provincial government found the necessary $17 million. The building is now home to provincial government offices, there are meeting and conference rooms, and the chapel is used for over one hundred weddings a year, catering to all faiths and denominations. However, apart from wedding guests and visitors to the interpretive centre, it has not achieved the "public focus" that had been the hope of the Victoria Accord, and which would have happened had the art gallery been sited there.

Chapter 22

CHRIST CHURCH CATHEDRAL

ARCHITECT JOHN CHARLES MALCOLM Keith (1858–1940) had to wait over thirty years to see a stone cathedral for the Anglicans rise in Victoria, and even then it was not his competition-winning design, nor was it complete. Anglicans in Victoria had wanted a stone cathedral since 1869 when the first Christ Church Cathedral went up in flames in under an hour in what the *Colonist* described as a scene of "indescribable grandeur." Within a week a committee had been formed with the objective of raising funds to rebuild, and this time it was to be in stone. George Hills, the Bishop of Columbia, while visiting London in the following year, commissioned plans from noted British ecclesiastical architect Benjamin Ferrey, architect to the diocese of Bath and Wells (Fig. 22-1). Ferrey's use of stone was sparing, just the walls, which would be of local limestone with freestone dressings. The roof would be wood shingles and the interior panelled in wood. Even with this economy in materials, and using a phased building program, it was unaffordable. So, local architect Hermann Otto Tiedemann was commissioned to design a wooden replacement; although roundly criticized by the *Colonist*, which said, amongst other criticisms, that it "had a sort of consumptive look about it." The congregation found it acceptable, as it was, after all, only temporary until a stone one could be built.

Two decades passed and the Anglicans were still worshipping in the wooden cathedral, but there were murmurings that it was time to replace the "unworthy wooden building" with a stone cathedral, so fundraising began. There was confidence that this time they would be able to afford a more suitable cathedral; the province was prosperous and the population had increased over the years, so surely the money could be raised. An international competition for the design was advertised, and the cost was not to exceed $150,000 — "a sum very inadequate for the purpose," thought *The Canadian Architect and Builder*. Nevertheless, a good number of architects wanted the opportunity to design such a prestigious building. Unopened, the entries were sent to London where Edmund Ferrey, son of Benjamin, selected ten that were exhibited in Church House, Westminster, and adjudicated by another noted British ecclesiastical architect, Sir Arthur Blomfield.

Before Blomfield's decision was made public, it was sent to Victoria for confirmation. *The Building News* (London) took the opportunity to make its own assessment of the ten submissions on display. These had been made under pseudonyms, supposedly to ensure impartiality on the part of the judge. The journal thought that the entry of "New and Old" (Fig. 22-2) was the most original and the best. Its second choice was "Duomo," (Fig. 22-3) where the "14th-century Gothic was handled with knowledge and dignity," and that looked like a "Colonial cathedral." Last on its list was "Fides," which it said was good "but hardly competes with those first described." However, Blomfield awarded first prize to "Fides," the motto of the Victoria firm of Evers & Keith (Fig. 22-4). Keith, a Scot, and Cecil Evers had moved to Victoria specifically to be well-placed to prepare their competition entry, but when it became obvious that a building start was not imminent, Evers left for New York. Keith stayed in the city for the remainder of his life and built a successful practice based on his reputation as the winner of the competition to design the cathedral.

Fig. 22-1. The stone cathedral designed by Benjamin Ferrey to replace the wooden one destroyed by fire in October 1869.
[Anglican Diocese of British Columbia Archives, Columbia Mission Report, 1870.]

[178] Unbuilt Victoria

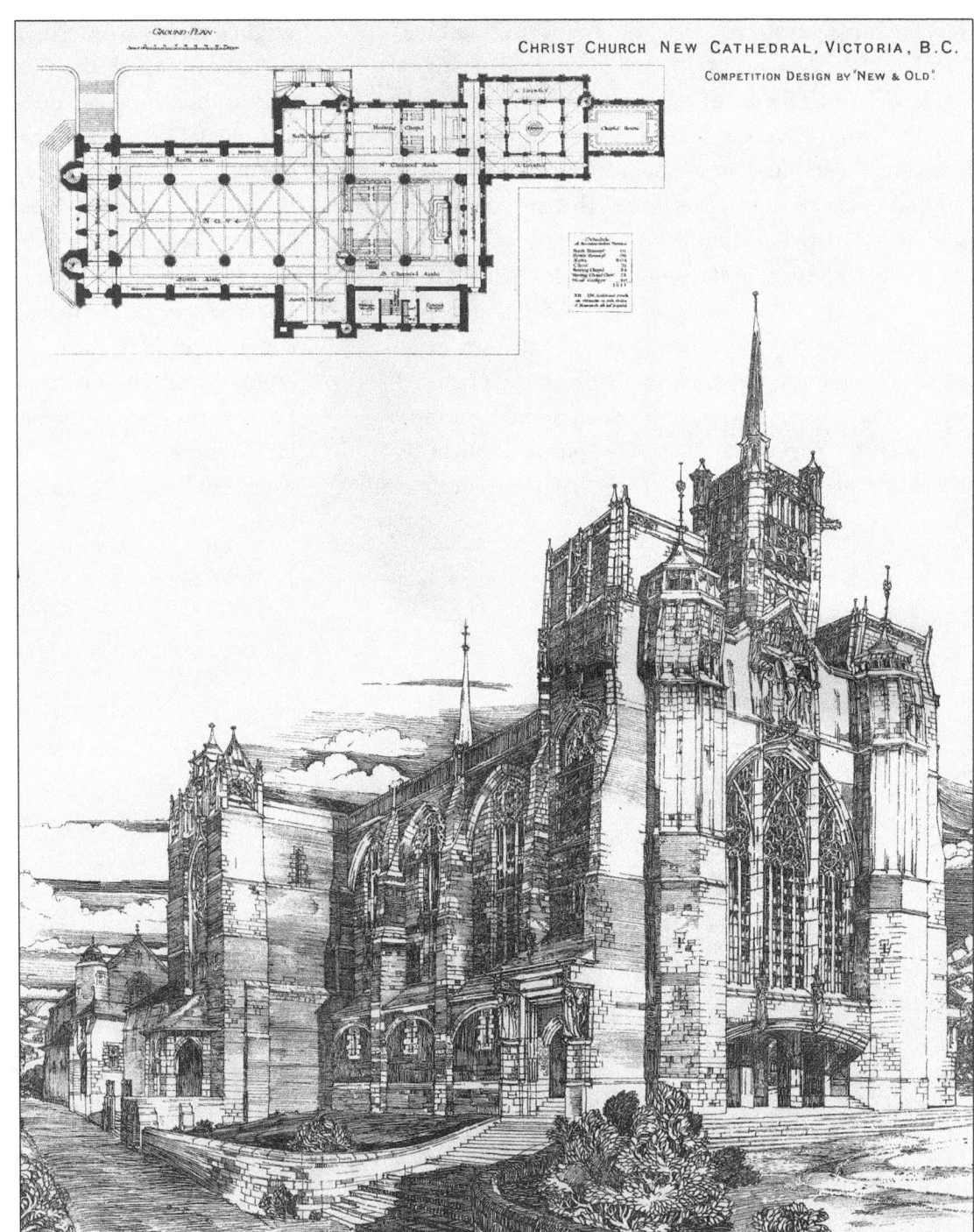

Fig. 22-2. The competition design, plan, and rendering by "New and Old." Published in *The Building News* (London), May 27, 1892. [RIBA Library Books and Periodicals Collection.]

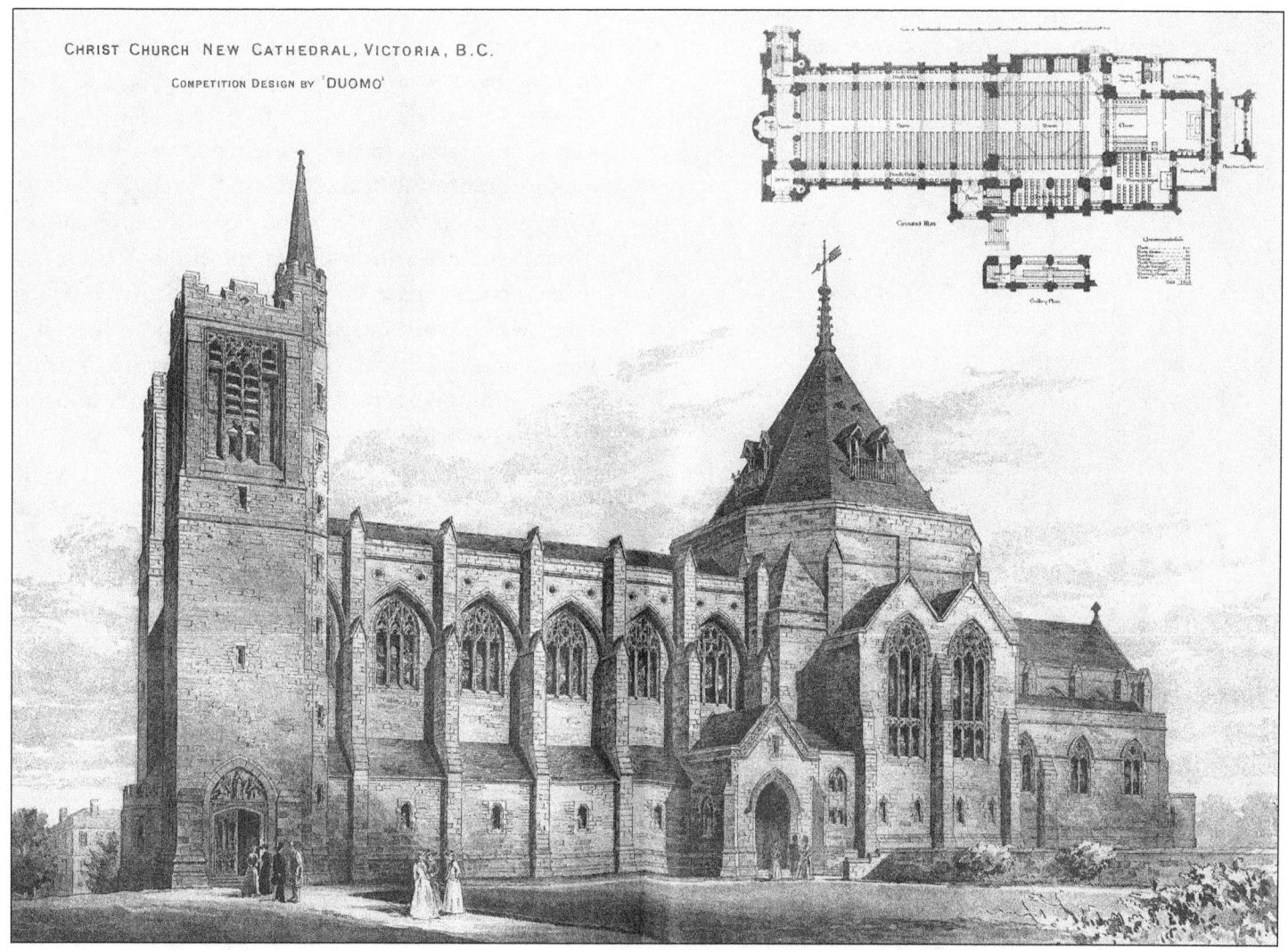

Fig. 22-3. The competition design, plan, and rendering by "Duomo." Published in *The Building News* (London), June 3, 1892. [RIBA Library Books and Periodicals Collection.]

For the next thirty years, lack of money, changing priorities for spending what they had, and indecision regarding the site dogged the project. The site of the second cathedral, on the north side of Burdett Avenue between Blanshard and Quadra Streets, and known as Cathedral Hill, had a sentimental hold on many in the diocese. It had always been the cathedral site, but it was too small to accommodate all the much-needed ancillary buildings, such as the bishop's palace, the deanery, the synod hall, etc. Consideration was given to moving one block east onto the Bishop's Close (site of the present cathedral), or to a site on Rockland Avenue, near Craigdarroch Castle. The matter was settled by yet another eminent British ecclesiastical architect, William Douglas Caroe, who was in the city at the time and was "overwhelmingly" in favour of the Bishop's Close site; it had enough space for all the diocese's requirements, there was the advantage of allowing the cathedral to be positioned so as to command the view up Courtney Street, and worship could continue in the old cathedral until the new one was consecrated.

Finally, the new plan (Figs. 22-5, 22-6) and the new site were agreed and, in May 1926, there was a groundbreaking ceremony at which Bishop Schofield authorized the "commencement of the new Christ Church Cathedral." Over the years Keith had re-worked the design, in part to allow for a phased building program, and partly because the building committee had asked for changes such as "large towers of square shape rising above the ridge of the roof" at the west end.

The foundations were paid for with money raised in 1890 that had been wisely invested, and the push was on to raise enough to finish the nave. A little over three years later, on September 28, 1929, the nave was consecrated. At the west end only the lower courses of the towers were complete, and at the east end was a stucco-clad wooden wall marking the position of the crossing tower. The Depression and then the Second World War stalled almost all work, and although some work was done on the south-west tower in 1941, the cathedral

Fig. 22-4. The competition design by Evers & Keith's. Published in the *Colonist*, January 1, 1893.

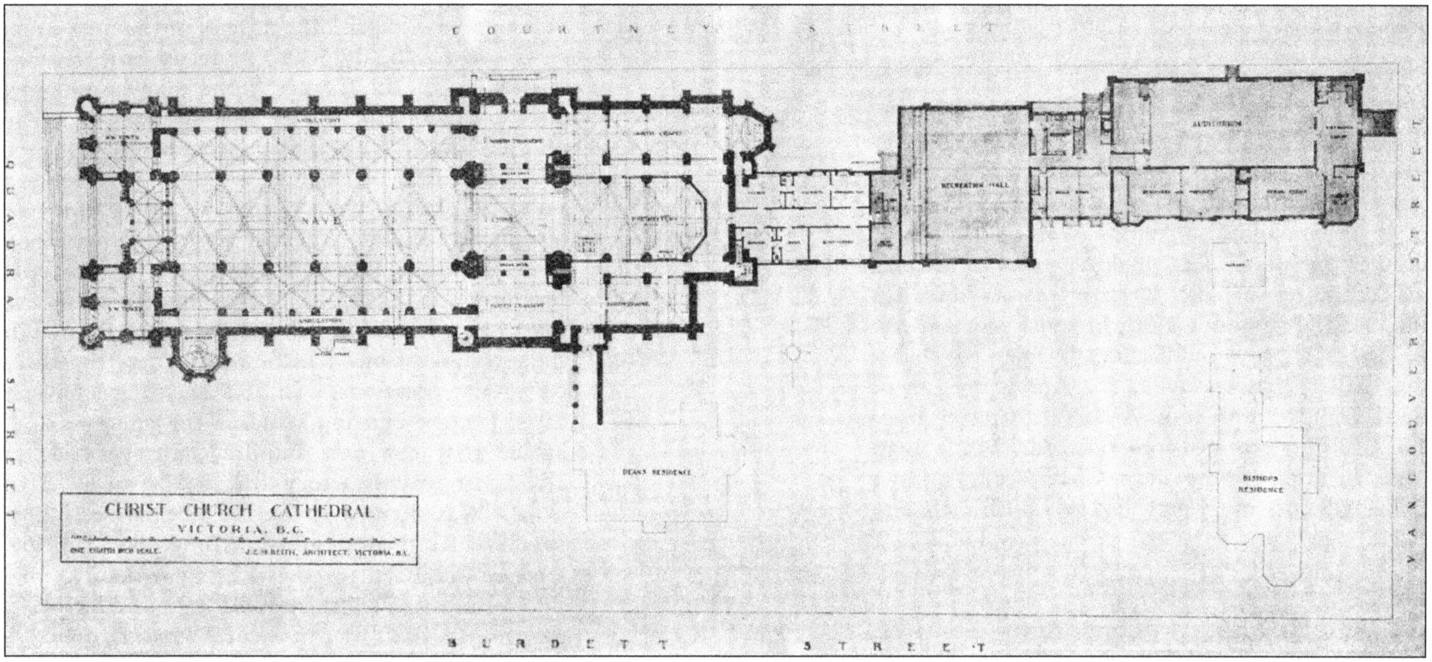

Fig. 22-5. Keith's final plan for the cathedral site, 1926. [Anglican Diocese of British Columbia Archives.]

Fig. 22-6. Keith's final proposal for the cathedral, showing the massive crossing tower and choir beyond. Published in the *Times*, February 10, 1926.

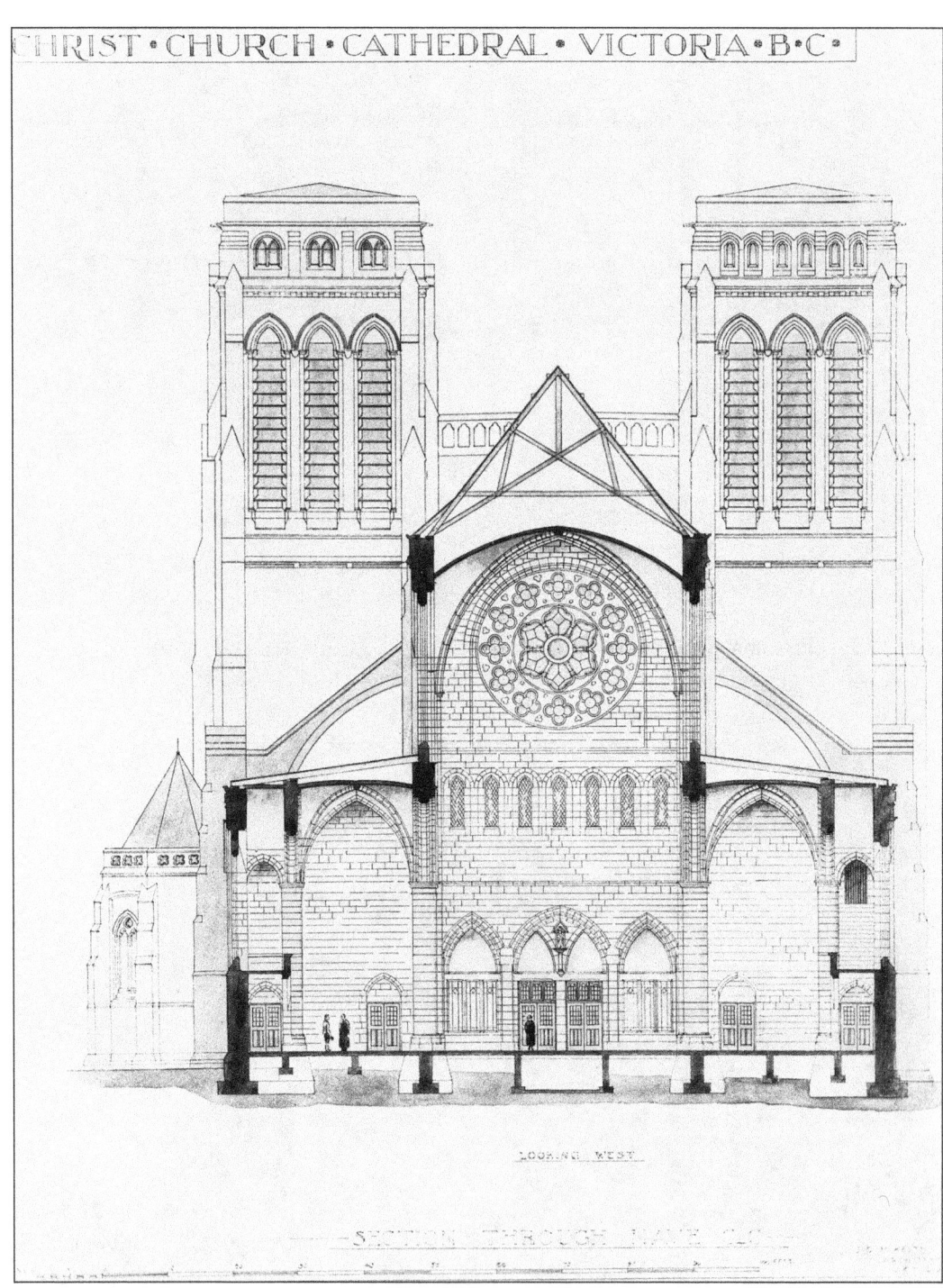

Fig. 22-7. A section through the nave, looking west, showing the planned height of the towers, from Keith's final proposal in 1926. [Anglican Diocese of British Columbia Archives.]

Fig. 22-8. The design for the east end drawn by Cram & Ferguson, 1948. [Anglican Diocese of British Columbia Archives.]

was in much the same built condition that it had been when the nave was consecrated. Optimistically, in 1948 Bishop Sexton announced that plans were being prepared by architect Cram & Ferguson to complete the cathedral with the sanctuary, chapel, and ample vestry space, but these plans would not include the crossing tower, although a spire to mark the crossing might be added later (Fig. 22-7).

Four years passed, but the completion never got underway. Then the synod decided to make strenuous efforts to fund the work. It wanted to be as faithful as funds would allow to Keith's 1926 design (Fig. 22-8), but

Fig. 22-9. A suggested design for the completion of the east end with a spire. [Collection of Simon Wade.]

recognized, as Bishop Sexton had done in 1948, that some reductions to that plan would have to be made. Canon E.P. Laycock was asked to advise, and with his assistance an acceptable plan was devised. This plan also eliminated the crossing tower, and lateral arches were added in place of transepts.

Completion of the west end followed Keith's 1926 plan ... almost. After a concentrated fundraising drive, the towers and the arch between them were finished, although there was just not enough money to take the towers up to their planned height — they are six metres shorter than originally designed and the low pyramidal roofs were not installed. The finished west end was dedicated on July 14, 1957.

That still left the east end, and the building committee's financial woes were compounded by the rising cost of materials coupled with a flagging enthusiasm for donations. Inevitably, the committee was forced to acknowledge that there would never be an east end in the architecturally-correct sense; severe compromises would have to be made. A drawing recently found in the papers of John Wade, architect to the Fabric of the cathedral, shows a modern concept for the east end. Since it was apparent that there would never be enough money for the crossing, and certainly not for a spire, Wade seems to have played with the idea of a spire on the ground. Whether this was a serious proposal or the imaginative doodling of the architect who was well-known for his sense of humour and fun, we shall never know, but we do know it was never built (Fig. 22-9). Another of Wade's suggestions was to give the appearance of a complete cathedral by installing a mirror wall where the crossing should be — this would reflect back the west end, creating the illusion of a full-length cathedral. The wall was to be twenty-three metres wide and eight-and-a-half metres tall, and would "allow reflections of the attractive vaulting, clerestory windows and beautiful rose window of the west wall." This ingenious idea was rejected — not least because no one could envisage how to clean such a vast expanse of glass.

Then Bishop Frame suggested the two-storey solution that we see today. Although Wade was a modernist in his secular work, he felt strongly that Keith's vision should be respected, and immediately recognized that Frame's idea did that, even though it was a substantial reduction of Keith's 1926 design for a crossing and a four bays sanctuary. Built on the foundations of the 1926 crossing tower, this structure contains a chapel in the second storey, with a massive stained glass window on the exterior and a plain glass window on the interior, giving the illusion of depth and a fully realized east end. Of Wade's accepted proposal for the completion of the east end, only the steeples on the four corner towers were not built.

Chapter 23
The Ukrainian Catholic Church of St. Nicholas the Wonderworker

At the corner of Cook Street and Caledonia Avenue stands an unremarkable wooden building, clad in lap siding, and painted white; the Latin cross atop the louvred bell-cote marks it as a church, but it is only closer inspection of the sign attached to the west wall that reveals it to be the Ukrainian Catholic Church. Even closer inspection of the substantial foundation wall at the back of the building reveals ST NICHOLAS THE WONDERWORKER impressed in the concrete. What is not apparent from the exterior is that the wooden structure rests on a basement that is engineered for a much heavier building, and it's finished with a superbly crafted ceiling of three-by-six-inch fir decking supported on massive beams.

The building began life, in 1890, as St. Barnabas Anglican Church. It sat at the back of the lot, to the north of the present building, and served its congregation for sixty years, until it was decided to sell the property and build a new church. It was purchased in 1949 by the Ukrainian Catholic congregation in Victoria. The building's Anglican form — porch, nave, and chancel — did not fully satisfy the liturgical requirements of the Ukrainian Catholics, but they made it work until the late 1980s when a confluence of conditions gave the congregation the opportunity and enthusiasm to make some changes.

The millennial anniversary of Ukrainian Christianity was in 1988, declared the state religion in 988 by the Grand Duke of Kiev, Volodymyr I the Great (980–1015). The late 1980s were momentous years for Ukrainians world-wide as the Communist regime in their homeland began to falter and unravel. In 1991 the people of Ukraine voted overwhelmingly for independence — Canada was the first of the G7 nations to recognize the new nation.

Graduate architect Alexander Teliszewsky moved to Victoria and joined the congregation of St. Nicholas the Wonderworker. With an important anniversary to celebrate, the resurgence of national pride in their nation's independence, and an architect with a passion for contextual expression and structural integrity, St. Nicholas parish decided to celebrate a new era by building a new church. A church that would reflect and respect the Ukrainian heritage and culture, that was fitting for the Ukrainian Catholic liturgy, and recognized its existence in British Columbia.

The cultural and religious heritage of Western Ukraine, specifically the Carpathian Mountains, was chosen as the inspiration for the new St. Nicholas. The region is home to two separate groups, the Boyko and the Lemko, and each has developed its own distinctive form of church architecture. The Boyko translated the cruciform Greek plan from masonry into wood, and the Lemko created a style in which there are three domes, each marking the three liturgically significant areas of the church, ranged in a line from west to east (Fig. 23-1). As in western Canada, the predominant building material in the Carpathians is wood.

Teliszewsky blended these two traditional styles and added references to West Coast architecture, creating what he dubbed "West Coast Byzantine." His scheme clearly expresses the customary Lemko tripartite arrangement — narthex, nave, and sanctuary — with domes, varying in size relative to the liturgical importance of the interior space, each topped with a different style of cross (Figs. 23-2, 23-3). On the main dome a geometric pattern of coloured shingles is drawn from examples in Ukraine, and probably based on traditional embroidery patterns (Fig. 22-4). This Lemko-style plan was modified with Boyko influences to accommodate the tight site. From local architecture he took inspiration from Francis Rattenbury, whose chateau-style roof of the Empress Hotel is emblematic of Victoria; from Samuel Maclure, whose Arts and Crafts homes feature robust eaves brackets; and from the island's First Peoples he took the low-pitched roof of the long house (Fig. 23-5).

Fig. 23-1. A model of the proposed Ukrainian Catholic Church of St. Nicholas the Wonderworker. Note the model does not show the decorative shingle patterns that were planned for the roof. [Alexander Teliszewsky.]

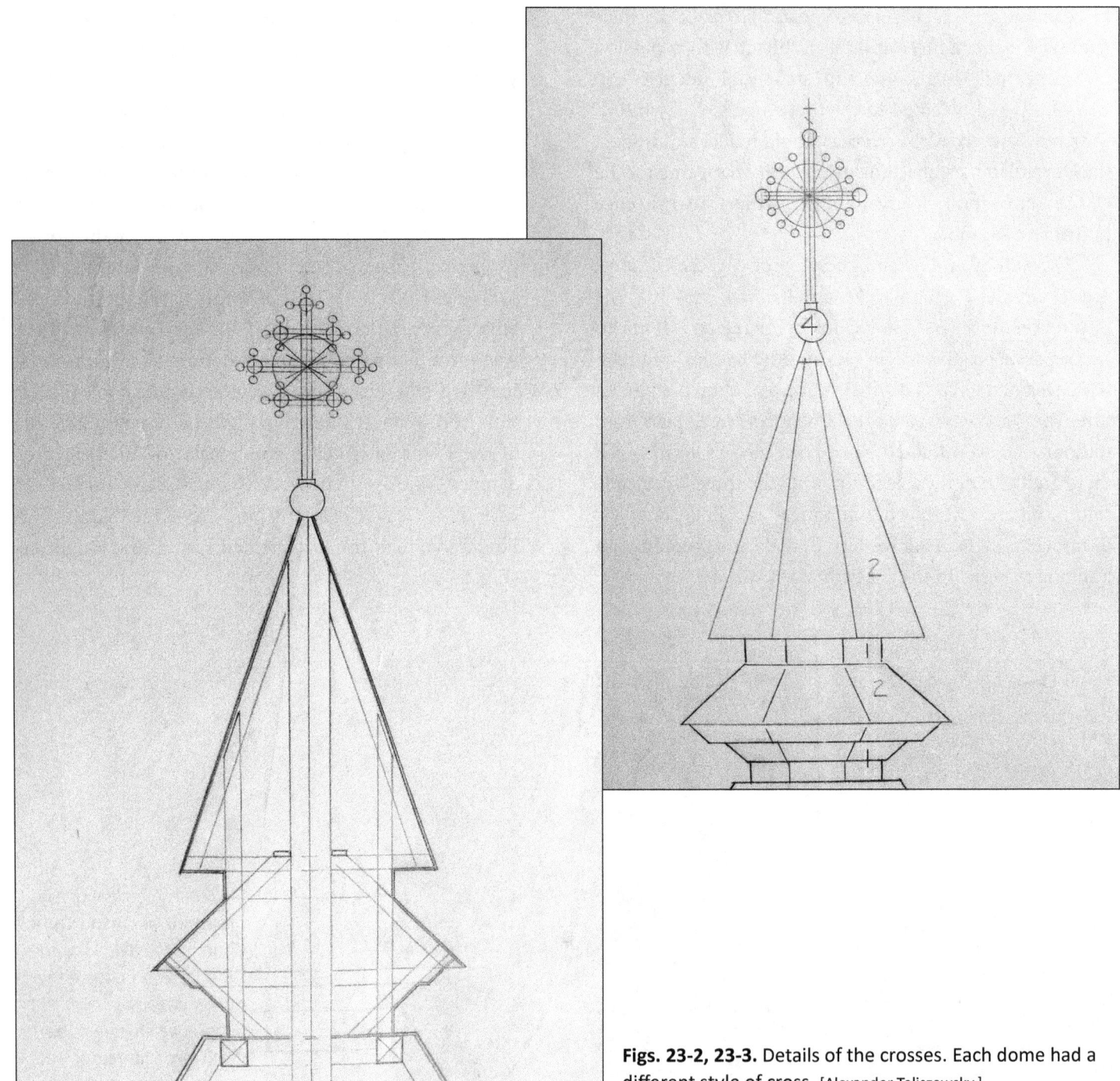

Figs. 23-2, 23-3. Details of the crosses. Each dome had a different style of cross. [Alexander Teliszewsky.]

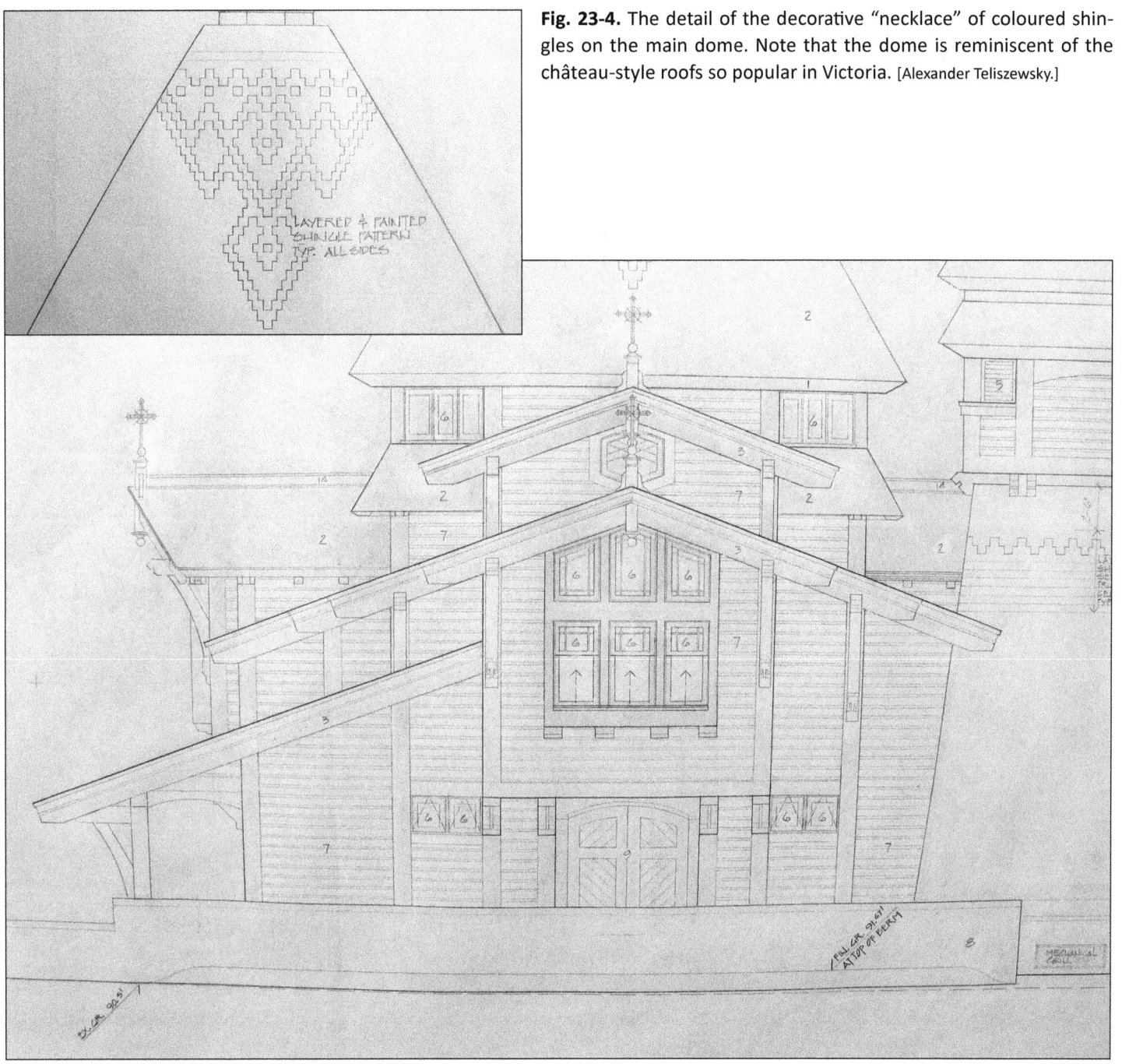

Fig. 23-4. The detail of the decorative "necklace" of coloured shingles on the main dome. Note that the dome is reminiscent of the château-style roofs so popular in Victoria. [Alexander Teliszewsky.]

Fig. 23-5. A part of the Cook Street elevation showing the sturdy eaves brackets and low-pitched roofs. [Alexander Teliszewsky.]

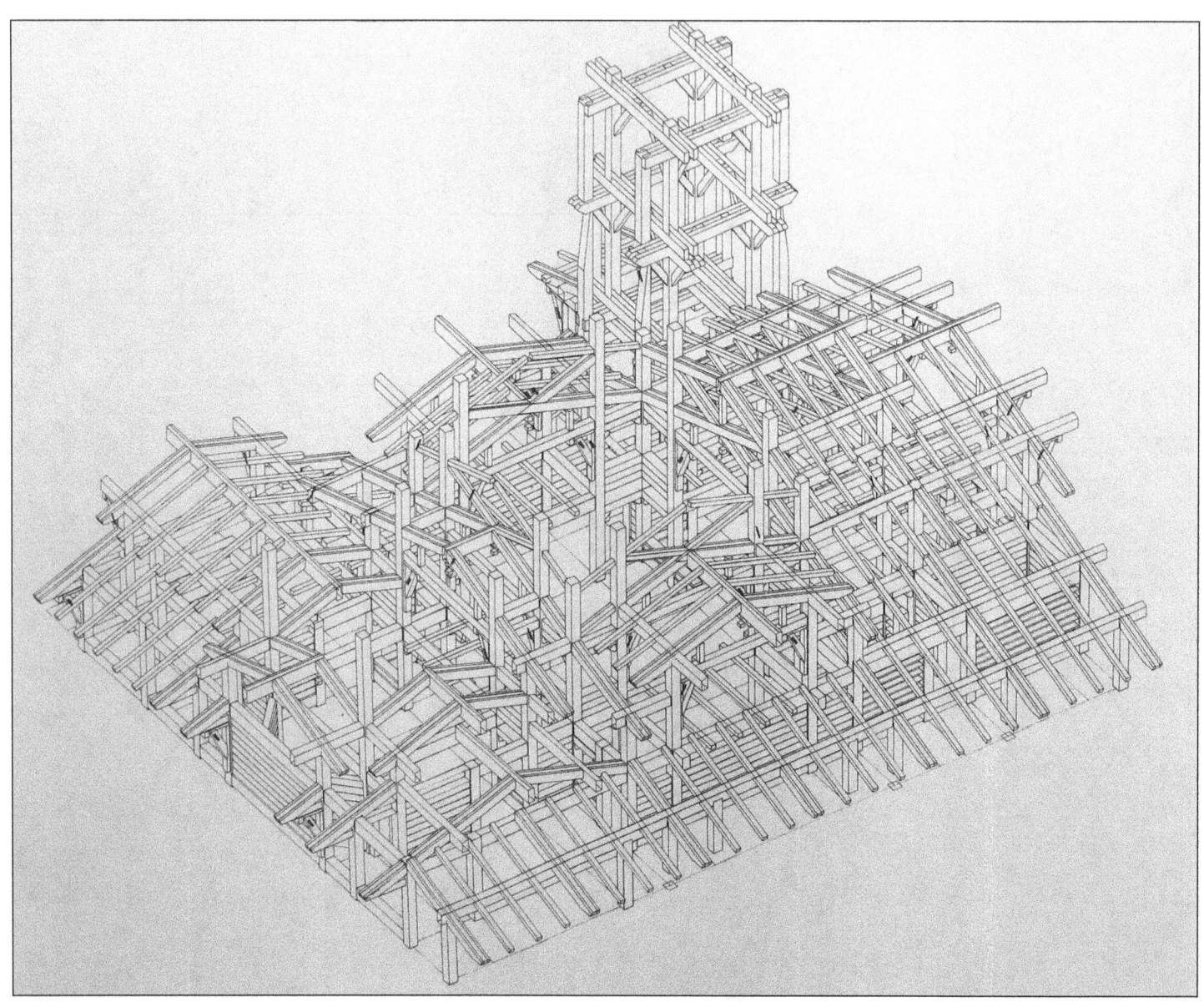

Fig. 23-6. An axonometric projection of the structural timbers. [Tedd Benson, Bensonwood; Ukrainian Catholic Church of St. Nicholas the Wonderworker.]

Building materials and method were, again, influenced by both Carpathian and west-coast traditions. In keeping with these traditions the church was to be of post-and-beam construction, with a heavy timber frame, and shingled roof and walls; no steel or concrete would be used. But early in the design process this rejection of steel and concrete came into conflict with the recently updated building code for Victoria, which had stringent criteria for earthquake and wind-load conditions. Local structural engineers were not convinced that such a large all-wood structure would meet the city's criteria, so Teliszewsky went to Tedd Benson Woodworking in New Hampshire, probably North America's foremost expert in timber framing. Benson prepared a full set of plans for all structural timbers (Fig. 23-6). There was much discussion and many computer simulations, but the experts were finally convinced that the planned framing would meet the building code when they were shown photographs of the interior bracing used in St. Nicholas Orthodox Church in Syniava, Kiev Region, built in 1731 and still standing.

The plan was that the church would be built in front of the old St. Barnabas, so that services could continue while building was in progress. The financial aspects had been decided, and the congregation would only build when they had the money — it would be a slow process. The building committee had approved the design, the bishop was enthusiastic about the project, the city had issued a building permit, and fundraising had filled the coffers with enough to afford to build the basement and buy the sixteen-inch diameter Douglas fir logs for the building's frame. The old-growth timber was harvested in the Carmanah and was too large for the local mill, so had to be taken to one in Royston, which usually mills logs for temples in the far east. As work progressed on the basement, the sawn logs were sent to a workshop in the bush near Coombs, just south of Qualicum Beach. There Werner Richter, with twenty year's experience of timber framing, was shaping some 1,650 pieces of boxed-heart lumber into the structural members of the church's frame. Richter thought it "the most complex post-and-beam structure currently under way in North America." For him it was the "project of a lifetime."

Work continued for three years. The basement was completed and roofed over with tar paper until the frame was ready — it was expected that it would take only six weeks to erect the frame once all the members arrived on site. But the fiscal prudence of the congregation may have been its undoing. The building work had progressed at glacial speed, and during this time the supportive bishop died. Finally a new bishop was installed, and he had concerns about the project; claiming that he thought it too ambitious, he dismissed the building committee. At the church's annual general meeting the bishop gave notice that all the money in the building fund and the land on which the church and rectory stood belonged to the eparchy, and he was taking control. One cannot help but wonder whether it was the possibility that St. Nicholas the Wonderworker would be more splendid than the cathedral of the eparchy at New Westminster that played any role in the decision.

It was a painful time for the congregation; indeed many left in despair. The lumber was returned to Victoria and later sold — some is now visible in the open roof of the Canoe Brew Pub and restaurant on Swift Street. But what to do with the basement? For two more years it remained covered, until eventually it was decided to make old St. Barnabas, now over a century old, structurally sound, and modified to fit onto the new basement. The old building was moved, the plans went into the archives, and the words of the Governor General, Ukrainian-Canadian the Right Honourable Ramon John Hnatyshyn, "… not only are you participating in an exciting and creative endeavour but you are above all, providing a spiritual home consistent with the antecedents of your region," took on a hollow ring.

It was also a painful outcome for other churches in Victoria that had put money into the building fund for what was expected to be a community church for Byzantine Catholics in the city and the island.

COMMERCIAL AND RESIDENTIAL PROJECTS

Chapter 24

Tourist Attractions

THE ARRIVAL OF THE RAILWAY IN Vancouver was not all bad news for Victoria; for the first time there was an easy way to get to the city from east of the Rockies. Victoria and Vancouver both realized that the railway could be used to lure potential settlers and investors to come west; those majestic mountains were more than just stunning scenery, they were a source of minerals. The ocean was teeming with fish, so it only needed some investment to put those fish in cans and send them around the world. And the stately stands of ancient timber could provide a limitless amount of lumber. All that was needed was promotion to get the tourists here, to convince them of the vast array of opportunities, and to persuade them to stay. Herbert Cuthbert, founder of the Tourist Association in 1902, described tourist travel as "the modern colonizer" and was convinced that once they came — "as night follows day" — so would industry. The Tourist Association began a series of advertising campaigns, championing the city as the finest residential city in America, as well as offering facts and figures about the city's business, and boasting that there were "No Blizzards" and "No Malaria."

Attracting potential settlers and investors had been the spirit behind the proposal to showcase the island's products and opportunities in the replica Parthenon in Beacon Hill Park. This was rejected under the terms of the park's trust, but three years later another group of city boosters tried again. This time the building would be a replica of the Hudson's Bay Company bastion that stood at the north-east corner of Fort Victoria (Fig. 24-1). The leading businessmen promoting this "civic enterprise" hoped that it might be built on city-owned land at the back of the Empress Hotel. The building was to be filled with Vancouver Island products: raw materials such as wood, minerals, and whale bone, and the manufactured goods they produced; grains, fruits, and flowers;

and large photographs of the scenic beauty of the island, its roads, farms, and orchards; as well as "inside views of Victoria's manufacturing plants." And an "18-foot diameter spruce timber" would be on display, showing not only the massive dimensions of the island's timber, but with a map of the island painted on it, showing the farms, trees, roads, orchards, etc. The idea of such a permanent exhibition of the island's wealth was nothing new, according to the plan's promoters, but what would make it stand out would be the building, a replica commemorating Fort Camosun — an early name for Fort Victoria — which could not fail to attract tourists.

Fig. 24-1. A proposed replica of a Fort Victoria bastion that architect Jesse Warren published in the *Year Book of the British Columbia Society of Architects*, Vancouver Chapter. [Courtesy AIBC.]

Although architecturally this and the replica of the Parthenon, proposed three years earlier, were poles apart, both schemes were motivated by the same imperative – the promotion of Victoria and the island. Promoters of both schemes were at pains to point out the great benefit to the city and the island, tourists would be awed and may decide to invest and settle, students and teachers would find much to learn; it would be a "never ending advertisement to the city."

The architect of the building was Jesse M. Warren, who had arrived in the city the previous year, and in the year of this scheme (1912) was joined by his brother George — a tireless city promoter. Jesse too was a keen city booster, in an address to the Victoria Rotary Club, of which he was a founding member, his topic was "Why Victoria is destined to become the New York of the Pacific," in which he envisaged the benefits in trade and industry that would come to the city with the opening of the Panama Canal. Unlike his brother, George, who stayed in Victoria and was active in tourist promotion until the 1960s, Jesse left town in 1916 to continue his architectural career in Seattle, disillusioned, perhaps, by the city's failure to get behind schemes such as this and promote the city and the island.

Cuthbert advocated cleaning up and beautifying the city — one of his earliest projects was the reclamation of the James Bay mud flats — but George Warren was convinced that the city needed an image and needed to promote its difference from the rest of North America, its Englishness. He approved of slogans such as "Outpost of Empire" and "a little bit of old England." He wanted gasoline marketed as petrol, the police to continue wearing "Bobby" helmets, and he encouraged efforts to make a frontier town look like an English village — all rather ironic as he had been born in San Francisco, and never set foot in England.

Following the Great Depression, Victoria's economy was in a parlous state; referring to the years since the city had lost its status to Vancouver, David Leeming, Victoria's newly elected mayor (1931–36) and president of the Vancouver Island Publicity Board (VIPB), said that after "the economic losses suffered by the City in the last forty years … the only hope of the City was to extend its tourist trade." But Leeming was not proposing a renewed effort to attract settlers and investors in industry. He, and others in the VIPB, wanted visitors to come to the city, enjoy themselves, be entertained, and spend money — tourism was no longer to attract business, it was the business. Ironically, some ardent boosters went so far as to discourage any industry that might cause pollution and thereby jeopardize the city's "tourist allure."

It was time to attract visitors by offering them exciting entertainment, the most up-to-date attractions, something most would not find at home. In the 1950s tall towers were all the rage. The rapid growth and popularity of commercial television broadcasting in the 1950s gave rise to the construction of tall transmission towers to optimize the signal's reception area. The first of these towers to be built in concrete was in Stuttgart, Germany. It began broadcasting in 1956, and is widely regarded as the prototype for very tall free-standing towers world-wide. As well as transmission facilities the Stuttgart tower has two observation decks and a restaurant, making it an instant tourist attraction.

In Seattle, the Stuttgart tower was the inspiration for the Space Needle, landmark of the 1962 Seattle World's Fair and symbol of the city and the future. This tower is not for television transmission, but rather just a tourist attraction with shops, a revolving restaurant, an observation deck, and a banqueting room. In 1966, Canada was gearing up to celebrate the centennial of confederation and the Dominion of Canada in 1967, and what better way to celebrate than by building an observation deck in the centre of Victoria? Sweeping bird's-eye views of the gracious Inner Harbour, the city, the gardens of Rockland, and the majestic scenery would be a "major tourist attraction."

Skydeck Victoria Ltd. proposed to build this attraction on the south side of the Inner Harbour. The company's proposal noted that it was to be a centennial project, but stressed that the funding for this venture was to come from private sources and no grants would be applied for. The concrete and steel tower was to be one-hundred-metres tall with glass-sided elevators on the outside and an internal staircase for emergencies. At the top would be two observation decks, the lower one enclosed and containing the inevitable gift shop and a coffee shop; a notable omission from the plans was the provision of washroom facilities at this level. The upper deck would be open. The base would house more refreshment opportunities, this time with a washroom, as well as offices and storage. The proposal stressed that particular attention would be paid to "attractive landscaping," and there would be ample parking (Fig. 24-2).

A site on the Inner Harbour, with its splendid assemblage of heritage buildings, the centre of tourist activities, was considered an absolute requirement for attracting visitors, and the company hoped to buy four lots on the waterfront side of Belleville Street between Oswego and Pendray Streets, that were owned by the city. Indeed, the views would be stupendous: south over the parliament building, where the gilded copper statue of George Vancouver atop the dome stands at a height of thirty-nine metres, to the Olympic mountains in Washington state; east to the Empress Hotel, the lush residential area of Rockland, Beacon Hill

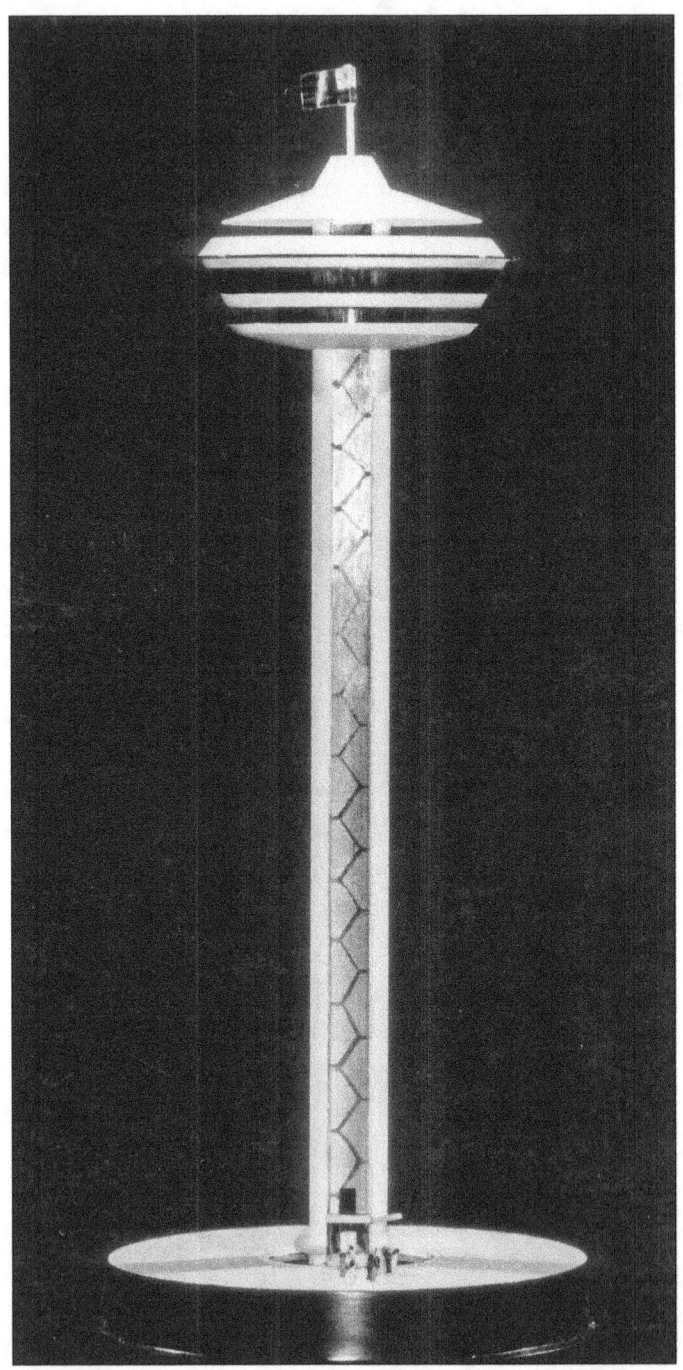

Fig. 24-2. The proposed Skydeck. [CVA, CRS 232.]

Park, and beyond to the Coast Mountains on the mainland, and, on a clear day, the ice-clad volcanic cone of the still-active Mount Baker in the North Cascades of Washington State. To the north would be a bird's-eye view of the city's Victorian buildings, alleys, and courtyards, Chinatown, and the industrial Upper Harbour; to the west the gentle wooded Sooke Hills.

With all these views, it seems that the Skydeck would have been a significant addition to the tourist amusements in Victoria, although whether it would have been a significant addition to the ambiance of the Inner Harbour is another matter. Funding problems derailed the project making that discussion irrelevant.

Another project offering spectacular views was an observation ramp leaping out into space from the top of Mount Tolmie (Fig. 24-3). At 120 metres high, the summit of Mount Tolmie offers sweeping panoramas north to the Saanich Peninsula and south-west to the Sooke Hills, but the view due south to the city is partly obscured; this platform, extending out to the west, would have expanded that view. The proposal was a scheme of the tourist trade group of the Victoria Chamber of Commerce who wanted to develop the tourist appeal of the park and asked architect Rod Clack to draw the plan. The deck was to be eighteen metres long and six wide, and would be built along aeronautical lines which would, according to Clack, protect sightseers from the wind.

The cost for the ramp, parking lot, and landscaping was estimated at $25,000 and the project, which also included widening the roads to the summit, was enthusiastically endorsed by group, which proposed to take it to Saanich parks and beaches committee for approval. The scheme did not go ahead, the roads to the summit are still narrow and winding, and the scenic beauty has to be admired over the fence alongside the pavement. Clack's ramp would certainly have been a tourist attraction, although the cost of road widening, in terms of damage to the Garry Oak meadows, may have been too high a price to pay.

Fig. 24-3. The proposed viewing platform for the summit of Mount Tolmie, from a concept drawing by Rod Clack. [Anna M. Todd, scrapbook, Saanich Archives.]

Chapter 25

Shopping Centres

In the 1950s the population shift to the suburbs coupled with the increasing use of the personal transportation encouraged the creation of shopping centres on the outskirts of town. Such centres provided ample free parking and access to a variety of shops and stores all under one roof, usually with additional amenities for one-stop shopping. In 1954 American entrepreneur Buford J. Seals proposed to build Buford's Trading Post on two blocks bounded by Government Street, Pembroke Street, Douglas Street, and Queens Avenue. Seals, who was a wild west enthusiast, had made a fortune selling army surplus in Seattle, where he had built a western-themed gas station called Premium Tex, with an office building shaped like a ten-gallon hat and washrooms in buildings shaped like cowboy boots — the smaller one for the women — locally known as the Hat'n'Boots.

His proposal for Victoria (Fig. 25-1) was to be modelled on a trading post, much like the fort that was the city's founding building; it was to be clad in "simulated cedar logging" with "true-to-type bastions atop the walls." Initially the plan was for fifty-eight stores, but this figure was raised to sixty-four within a matter of weeks, evidently applications came flooding in from all over the island, the mainland, and as far away as the prairies. The centre was to be run by Buford Development Incorporated, which would manage bulk purchases of such items as cash registers and fixtures thus reducing individual stores' overheads. Local merchants would rent the outlets, the amount of rent being based on their sales figures; and, as the administration would know each store's daily sales figures, it could concentrate advertising, which was provided by the management, on outlets where sales were lagging.

The trading post was to have every amenity, a parking lot for six hundred cars on the northern block, a roof-top restaurant, a bank, and a post office. A nursery and doctor's clinic at the corner of Pembroke and Government Streets would allow mothers to "leave their children in capable hands and start their shopping immediately." And, of course, there was to be a conveniently-located Hat'n'Boots. The *Colonist* reported that Seals was building a market in Seattle to go with his Premium Mex gas station, and one in Surrey, British Columbia. Seals himself claimed that Buford markets were the product of years of intensive research and incorporated ideas from successful markets in the U.S. But his Pioneer Market in Seattle was unsuccessful, although the Hat'n'Boots survived and have been restored and may now be seen, but not used, in Oxbow Park in Georgetown, Seattle. It seems that Seals was better at promotion than the nuts and bolts of business. His trading post in Victoria was not built, which was probably for the best — wild-west conveniences hardly seem the city's style.

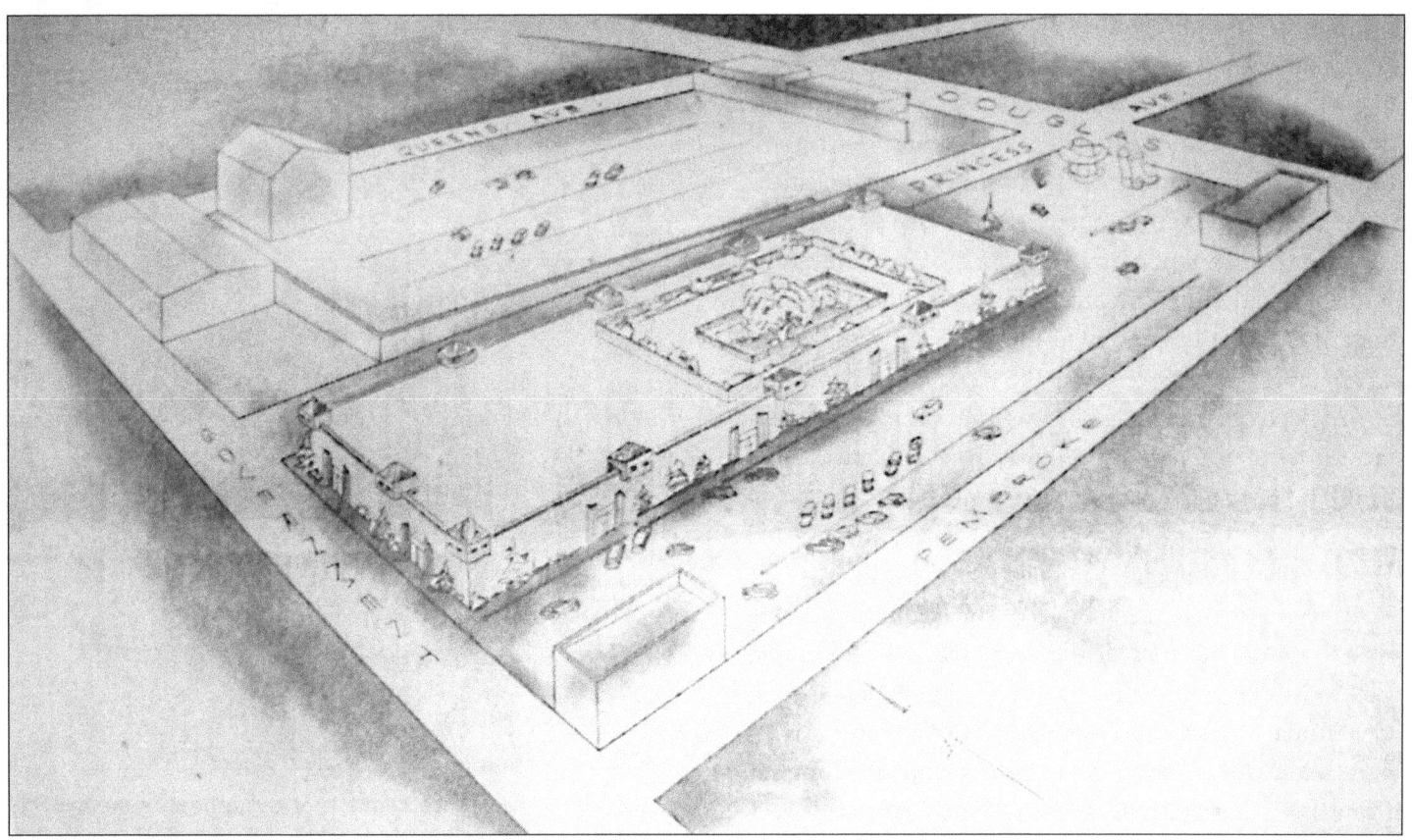

Fig. 25-1. A sketch of the proposed Buford Trading Post, to be located on the two blocks bounded by Government, Pembroke, and Douglas Streets, and Queens Avenue. Note the Hat'n'Boot near the corner of Princess Avenue and Douglas Street. Published in the *Colonist*, April 8, 1954.

A decade later there was a large shopping centre at the north end of the city, called the Town and Country Mall, with ample parking. Conveniently located at a bend in the Trans-Canada Highway, it was ready to snare shoppers coming into town from the north and west. With amendments to the National Housing Act in 1964, funding became available for urban renewal projects other than housing, and the Capital Region Planning Board, in its 1965 overall plan for the city, proposed that a new regional department store in a downtown location would serve a number of purposes. The Johnson Retail Redevelopment would provide a tremendous boost to downtown's service and retail business, which was then stagnating; it seemed likely that no more large department stores would locate downtown, it was too difficult and too expensive to assemble enough land, and potential customers were not making it past the shopping opportunities on the outskirts.

The block bounded by Pandora Avenue, and Store, Johnson, and Government Streets — where Market Square is today — presented the ideal opportunity for a profitable business venture. The block was dilapidated and in need of renovation and was one of the least expensive pieces of property in the downtown core. It was close to the other department stores, Eaton's being just down the street, in what is now the Bay Centre, and the old Hudson's Bay Company store was an easy stroll across the inviting and newly-created Centennial Square. Parking was to be on the roof of the proposed new store, and this would be augmented by the city's new parkades in Centennial Square and Yates Street. But the most crucial benefit was the location, less than four hundred metres from the intersection of the new West Victoria freeway and the Johnson Street Bridge, ideally suited to whisk shoppers passed the entrapments of the suburban malls and into this new shopping experience (Fig. 25-2).

The grand freeway plans of the mid-sixties were never realized, and neither was the Johnson Retail Development, at least not in the form the planners' envisaged. In the 1970s the Bawlf brothers, Sam, a developer,

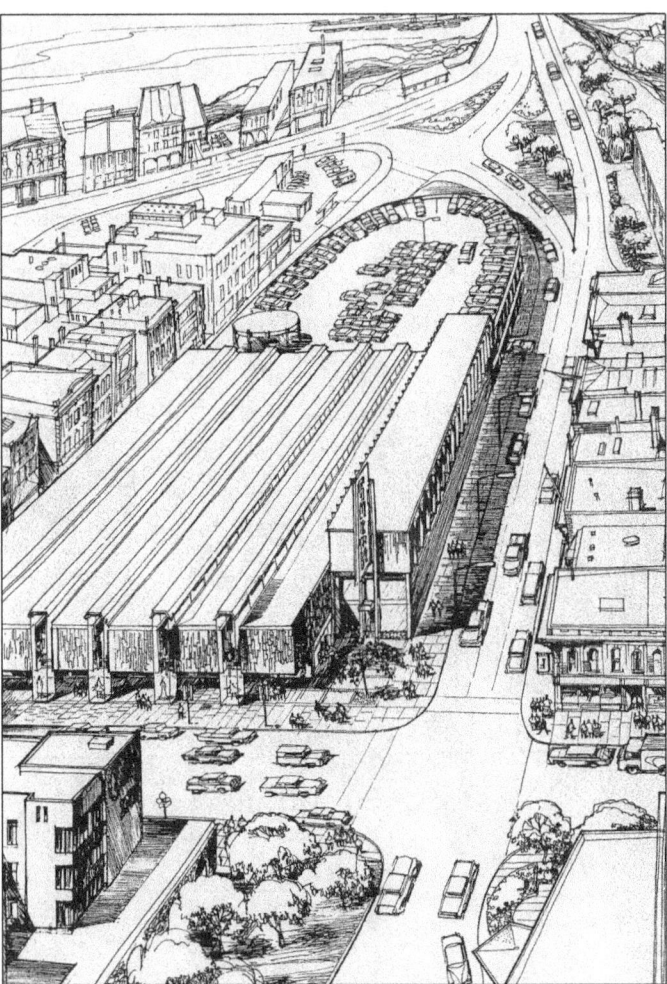

Fig. 25-2. The artist's concept of the redevelopment of the block surrounded by Johnson, Government, and Store Streets, and Pandora Avenue. Pandora Avenue is at the right-hand side, leading to connection with the West Victoria freeway, now the site of Market Square. [CVA, CD 120.]

Fig. 25-3. A rendering of the proposed shopping centre and apartment complex at Simcoe and Menzies Streets. Published in the *Times*, March 18, 1968.

and Nick, an architect, created Market Square. They saved and rehabilitated the late nineteenth-century buildings on the perimeter of the block, and developed the sunken interior, once the path of the Johnson Street ravine, into a performance and exhibition space surrounded by an eclectic mix of intimate retail outlets

The Bay Village scheme (Fig. 25-3) was announced in March 1968. It was to be a shopping centre and a high-rise apartment building at the junction of Simcoe and Menzies Streets in the James Bay neighbourhood. At the time the councillors, and particularly Mayor Hugh Stephen, were convinced that the city needed greater density, and high-rise living was the way to achieve the critical mass of population needed for the city to prosper; and James Bay was the main target for this density increase. The village, designed by Wade, Stockdill, Armour, and Blewitt, was to be built around an existing supermarket that would be enlarged and surrounded by a complex of smaller shops; the seventeen-storey apartment block would contain luxury units.

Hailed as "the greatest thing that ever happened to James Bay," this $3 million project soon became "the greatest thing that never happened to James Bay." One of its architects, John Wade, explained that the project had to be abandoned when the financing "went sour" due to increasing interest rates. But he noted that this might not have happened had the city's approval process been speedier; adding that projects go from committee to committee and back again in a process that may take up to a year, when it could, and should, be done in three months. The city, he said "loses many fine projects simply because it takes too long to approve them."

Chapter 26

HOTELS

IN THE LATE 1880S VICTORIA WAS IN NEED of first-class hotels. Even though the City of Vancouver was the terminus for the transcontinental railway, it was hardly a throbbing metropolis with all the associated amenities. So when business men came to the west coast, they wanted to stay in the comparatively sophisticated city of Victoria. Two hotels were planned: the Driard, which was built at the corner of Fort and Broad Streets, although it has now been unbuilt and a pastiche of its facade incorporated in that of the Bay Centre; and the Canada Western, which was planned for the corner of Wharf and Government Streets, facing the harbour (Fig. 26-1).

The Canada Western Hotel Company commissioned the architectural firm of Wright & Sanders to design its new hotel. This firm had once practised in Victoria, designing such buildings as the synagogue, Temple Emanu-El, and Angela College on Burdett Avenue, but had decamped to San Francisco for greater opportunities in 1866. The firm still kept in touch with old friends and clients in Victoria, many of whom were influential men. Perhaps they were chosen for their prestige, although it was a choice that did not sit well with local architects. Also, the location of the firm's office in San Francisco may have introduced delays. The choice of site was perhaps unfortunate, facing the stinking James Bay mud flats. Although there was talk of draining or dredging them, this had not happened at the time the hotel was planned.

The site had been excavated by January 1891, but the company was running short of funds and was in the process of issuing more shares, but this took time, and the project faltered. The smallpox epidemic that began in May 1892 closed the port and depressed business, and by the end of the year the company was negotiating with the federal government for the sale of the land for construction of a new post office. The citizens and councillors objected, saying that the site was too far from the business district, but their protests fell on deaf ears and the new post office went up in 1896.

Within a decade rumours were flying that the CPR was planning to build a tourist hotel, which indeed it did, right on top of the mudflats which, in what has been described as the "most important civic project in Victoria's history," had been dammed and filled in. So keen was the city to have the hotel that it gave the CPR over two hectares of the reclaimed land, free water for fifteen years, and tax immunity for the same length of time; it also constrained the CPR from using the site for any purpose other than a hotel for a period of fifty years. On January 20, 1958, the fiftieth anniversary of the hotel, the CPR was at last free to do what it wanted with the land and the building — it could sell it, close the hotel, or even demolish it.

There seemed to be no pressing need to close the hotel. Business prospects looked good: it was the province's centennial year and then the World's Fair in Seattle in 1962, both of which would bring visitors to the city and, the CPR hoped, the Empress. Even so, the company decided to pave over the gardens at the rear and reap some financial reward from parking fees. Three years

Fig. 26-1. A rendering of the proposed Canada Western Hotel published in *Victoria Illustrated*. [Courtesy David Watson.]

later the company built a bus station on the south-east corner of the parking lot and leased it to Vancouver Island Coach Lines. Then the CPR became more aggressive in its revenue-generating schemes. It planned to build a twelve-storey luxury apartment building on the south lawn, fronting onto Belleville Street and admirably located for members of the legislative assembly. The bus station was to expand and take over the rose garden, the parking lot was to be increased, a gas station built at the corner of Douglas and Humboldt Streets, and a shopping arcade would occupy the corner of Government and Humboldt Streets (Fig 26-2).

There would be either five or nine shops, depending on interest, and they would be "tastefully constructed" and no more than five-metres tall, with "old world" leaded windows and small domes on the roofs. What the CPR had in mind, according to the hotel's manager, Cyril Chapman, were specialty shops selling antiques and items that would be appropriate for the tone of the Empress, and he was at pains to emphasize that, although a few bushes would have to be removed, the trees would remain (Fig. 26-3).

This was all too much for both the citizens and councillors, and the latter enacted by-laws increasing the setback from the lot line to thirty metres, and limiting building height to twenty-one metres, effectively stopping the plans for the apartment building and the shopping mall. All was not rosy in the hotel's accounts, and the CPR recognized that what most people wanted was the inexpensive, no-frills service of motels rather than the pricey sophistication of places like the Empress. It decided to convert the wing on Humboldt Street to a motel — no porters, no room service — which was an instant success, although it lowered the refined tone of the Empress. One newspaper was appalled to report that "women in shorts and slacks are now a familiar sight in the stately lobby."

The motel may have been popular, but that did not make it profitable, and in 1965 the $1 per year lease for the land under the Crystal Garden would come to an end and could not be renewed, adding yet more financial strain on the finances of the CPR's Empress complex. The building was in poor shape, needing twice the money to repair as it was worth, so the company handed the keys to city and walked away, one problem solved. But the financial troubles were not solved. The company's manager of hotels proposed to demolish all but the Humboldt wing and construct a new building with a lobby, dining room, lounge, and convention centre. Others preferred an alternative solution that also retained the Humboldt wing, but demolished only the south wing, which had been added in 1912, and the conservatory. The original block of the hotel would retain only its lower two storeys, the upper floors would be torn down. The lower would have

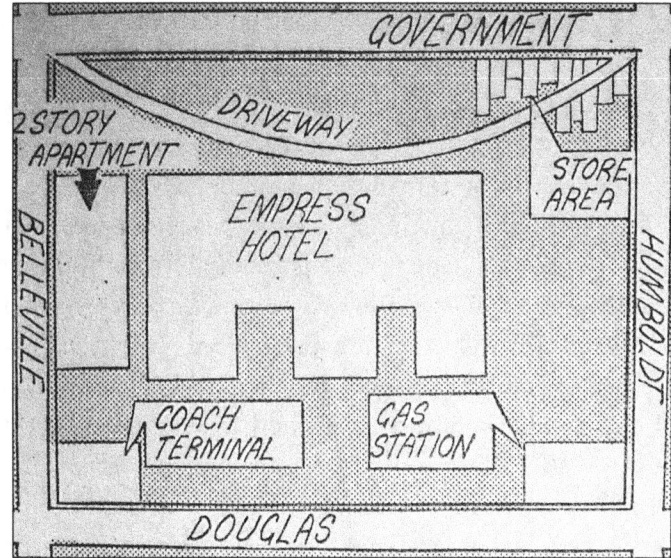

Fig. 26-2. A plan for the redevelopment of Empress Hotel land. Published in *The Province* (Vancouver), August 11, 1962.

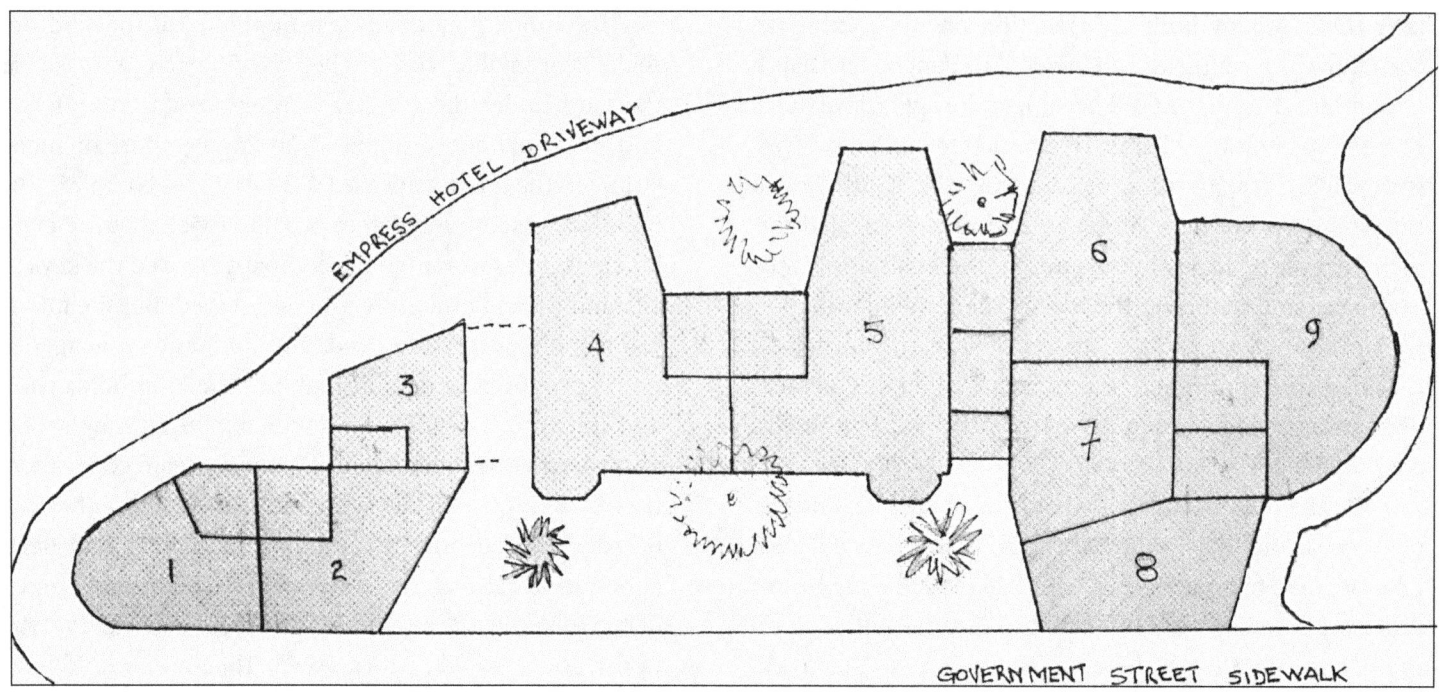

Fig. 26-3. A plan for the shopping arcade on the front lawn of the Empress Hotel, based on a sketch published in the *Times*, November 2, 1962.

a cocktail bar and other public rooms, while the upper would have a modern convention centre.

Before the hotel management decided which of these plans to implement, an engineering report advised that the Humboldt wing was not as structurally sound as they had believed. In fact, the original building, which had settled nearly eighty centimetres in places, had been subjected to constant scrutiny and was now considered to be in a stable condition. Now both the options seemed unworkable. Then rumours began to circulate that the CPR executives, who were meeting in Victoria to decide the hotel's fate, were talking about tearing down the entire structure and building either a "modern, functional highrise hotel" or a "modern motor-hotel of special design."

The Empress Hotel was, one executive told the city council, expensive to operate, not functional, and losing the company a lot of money, but this "splendid relic of the Edwardian era" was loved by the city, by travellers from all across the continent, and by "more than a few members of the CPR board." In June 1966, the CPR announced that it was undertaking a $4 million refurbishment program for the Empress Hotel — none of the company's various schemes would be implemented.

Chapter 27
Business Buildings

Mozart House

When music lover and real estate agent Eric Charman was planning a new commercial building on Broughton Street, he wanted to call it Mozart House as he proposed to play the composer's music in the elevators, and, with over six hundred works in the repertoire, he felt confident that there would be a year's worth of music with no repeats. Architect Alan Lowe designed a nine storey brick office building with an undulating five-storey glass curtain wall to the west, and that had the shape of a "grand piano with a glass curtain shaping its sides" when seen from above, which gave the appearance of cascading onto the second-storey patio. Charman thought it would become a downtown landmark, and "instant heritage," but Charman's business plans changed and he abandoned the idea, for the time being (Fig. 27-1).

Years later, when negotiating leases on a block of retail stores he owned on the north side of Yates Street, Charman was appalled to find that oil had been leaking into the basement from an adjoining property. The stores had to be demolished in order to permit land remediation. Architectural firm Williams D'Ambrosio designed a seven-storey residential and commercial building with one level of underground parking, shops and two lobbies at street level, and four floors of office space topped with two floors of residential accommodation (Fig. 27-2). But the cleanup took, according to Charman, ten years, and resulted in a hole that came to be known as "the Yates Street fishing pond," and eventually this version of the Mozart project was abandoned.

By October 2004 Charman had hired Denford Construction Management to handle the "latest homage to the 18th-century composer." The flow of oil onto the site was "almost nil" and Chris Denford was confident that building work could begin in February. By this time Charman's plans for the Mozart House went well beyond playing Mozart's music in the elevators. The building was to have a place for concerts in a central courtyard, next to the foyer, which would open out to the sidewalk, adding to the ambiance of Yates Street. With the Odeon and Capital 6 cinemas in close proximity, he hoped the 700 block of Yates Street would become the theatre and performance district. Even the proposed building had allusions to music. Designed by Jim Aalders of CEI Architecture, it had tall vertical windows, reminiscent of piano keys, on the west side; the glazing bars on the windows of the main facade were arranged to give the impression of the black and white keys of a piano; and both the roof line and the lights on the colonnade at ground level were shaped like the tails of an eighth note (Figs. 27-3, 27-4).

Fig. 27-1. The proposed Mozart House on Broughton Street. [Project Architect — Alan Lowe, Campbell Moore Group.]

Fig. 27-2. The Mozart House proposal on Yates Street, 2001. [Williams D'Ambrosio Architects.]

Figs. 27-3, 27-4. The second Mozart House proposal on Yates Street. Note the musical allusions in the window arrangement, the roof-line, and the lights on the main facade, 2005. [CEI Architecture.]

The scheme placed emphasis on the renovation of Millie's Alley, a crooked path between Yates and Johnson Streets, which was to be widened with the demolition of a building at its south-western end — a component of the proposal which found favour with the city's planners. After some fine-tuning of the design, the scheme was given the green light by the city council in June 2005. However, by the end of the year Charman pulled the plug and was going to sell the property; since winning approval for the project his health had been poor and he decided to forgo the "stress of construction."

OLD IMPERIAL OIL STATION:
LE CLUB BALISAGE

The Visitor Centre at the corner of Wharf and Government Streets was built by Imperial Oil in 1931. It was a gas station, with pumps on the forecourt at ground level, and service bays for 120 vehicles on the lower two storeys.

Fig. 27-5. The *Le Club Balisage* scheme for the rehabilitation of the Imperial Oil gas station and garage, now the Visitor Centre. [Chris Gower.]

Atop the building, a tower over twenty-four metres tall was capped with a ten-million-candlepower Sperry beacon. The beacon was to guide the increasing volume of sea-plane traffic that was expected to use the harbour. Built during a time of great enthusiasm for all things modern, especially air travel, the building is in the latest style — Art Deco. The gas pumps originally had a large canopy of red pantiles, a reflection of the enthusiasm for the Spanish Colonial Revival style found in California, home of another of the era's crazes, the movies. Would such a "modern" building have been built today, right in the heart of the Free Classic icons of the parliament buildings and the Empress Hotel?

By 1980, the building was unused, but it had, by then, become a much admired local landmark, so some alternative use had to be found — demolition was not an option. Its adaptive rehabilitation was the subject of a study in a heritage conservation course at the university, and one proposal was to convert it into a jazz night club. Student Chris Gower devised a scheme that would return its paint colour to the original off-white, restore the red pantiles and the Art Deco details, and re-activate the beacon. Downstairs, a portion of the second floor would be cut out to create a two-storey nightclub/theatre restaurant, with an upper balcony overlooking a jazz performance stage below. Although some Art Deco elements still remained in the building, the plan was to accentuate these with Art Deco-style stained glass and stage backdrop.

As a counterpoint to the tower, a public observatory would jut out into the harbour and be accessed by an elevated walkway (Fig. 27-5). With the beacon reactivated, it was suggested that a suitable name would be *Le Club Balisage* — a reference to the beacon's role in lighting the path for sea-plane traffic.

Fig. 27-6. An artist's concept of the Pagoda Restaurant at Fisherman's Wharf, superimposed on an aerial photograph. Published in the *Times*, December 18, 1964.

The Pagoda Restaurant

In 1964 a syndicate of local businessmen proposed to build an "inner harbour landmark" — a seven-storey restaurant on Fisherman's Wharf. It was to include an observation deck and six floors of dining rooms, with a banquet room seating six hundred. It is hard to imagine how such a vast amount of dining space could be a sound business proposition, although the "pagoda-type" architectural style and the observation deck would doubtless have enticed visitors (Fig. 27-6).

The Mystery Building

Victoria city planner Steve Barber found a copy of this architectural rendering in his files. He has no idea where the image came from or what scheme it was, and the only information on the drawing is the date: 1968 (Fig. 27-7). There was an announcement in that year, made by the Nordal Group, which proposed to build

Fig. 27-7. Mystery Tower. [Steve Barber.]

a thirty-four storey hotel and conference centre. It was to cost $10 million, and had been designed by architect John Wade. The Nordal family were in the transportation business and owned land where the Harbour Centre Mall is now, between Langley, Broughton, Courtney, and Government Streets, and this drawing puts the building roughly in that location.

So we can probably say that this is a drawing of the proposed Nordal Hotel, although one local architect suggested it was a spoof, done by a colleague of his acquaintance with a particularly mischievous sense of humour, and in response to the city council's conviction, at the time, that high-rises were inevitable and to be encouraged. Indeed, a feasibility report on downtown renewal suggested that the block between Broughton and Courtney Streets might be an ideal location for hotels and a convention centre. Whatever the truth may be, it is tantalizing to ponder that this might have towered over downtown Victoria.

Afterword

At the beginning of this exploration of Victoria's unbuilt buildings and transportation projects, it was suggested that the demands of tourism and the tourist and the strength of the heritage lobby between them played the most significant role in what went onto the drawing board, and what stayed there. Having examined these stories, some of which reach epic proportions, it has become apparent that politics and politicians have also played a part.

Victoria is a relatively small city, but it is the capital of the province. With little industry, and no major corporations headquartered there, the city's income is not sufficient to undertake such projects as were proposed, for example, for the Wharf Street Waterfront, and for Belleville Street ferry terminals. It must rely on contributions from the province or the federal governments — funding that is rarely forthcoming.

Provincial politicians, most of whom are from the mainland — ten from Vancouver — have scant affection for the city; they rush into town on Monday and out again on Friday afternoon, but only when the legislature is sitting. The city has never produced a provincial premier and, in general, the MLAs it does return are not from the majority party. Some premiers have made no bones about their disdain for the place.

It's a small wonder then that the land around the harbour, with the exception of the Empress Hotel and the parliament buildings, is mostly parking lot; that there is no purpose-built provincial art gallery or performing arts centre; and the legislative precinct, while attractive from the harbour side, is backed by a jumble of empty land and isolated Victorian houses.

Until there is a provincial government that places value on its capital city, it seems that it is doomed to have a long list of unbuilts.

Sources

Abbreviations
Colonist: This represents the various titles of the *British Colonist* (Victoria, BC) from its inception in 1858 until its merger with the *Victoria Daily Times*, and creation of the *Times Colonist* (Victoria BC) in September 1980.
CVA: The City of Victoria Archives.
Times: The *Victoria Daily Times* (Victoria, BC).

Chapter 1: City Hall
"$2,100,000 Building Offered Under New City Hall Deal." *Colonist*, October 14, 1960, p. 17.
"Accident in Council Chamber." *Colonist*, February 26, 1907, p. 16.
"Belmont Block Purchase for City Hall Suggested." *Colonist*, March 25, 1947, p. 1.
"Cathedral Hill Becomes Civic Precinct." *Colonist*, December 13, 1960.
"Central Park Best Site Holds Building Inspector J. W. Oosterink." *Colonist*, February 26, 1947, p. 23.
"City Hall Draws Offer." *Colonist*, January 21, 1947.
"City Hall Plans." *Times*, October 15, 1960, editorial.
"City Hall Sale, Plans To Build Termed 'Foolish' by Gadsen." *Colonist*, February 11, 1947, p. 17.
"City Hall Sale Proposal Before Voters on May 1." *Colonist*, April 19, 1947, p. 1.
"Civic Centre Scheme." *Colonist*, December 5, 1913, p. 5.
"Council Accepts $32,500 Tender to Modernize Offices at City Hall." *Colonist*, May 10, 1950.
"Council Accepts City Hall Tender." *Colonist*, February 4, 1947, p. 1.
"Council Engages in Lengthy Debate Over 'Unnamed Local Interests.'" *Colonist*, February 4, 1947, p. 3.
Council Minutes, transcription, CVA, Buildings, Public — City Hall.
"Council to Call Tenders on City Hall Property." *Colonist*, December 1, 1946, p. 1.
"Deal for City Hall Site Appears Officially Dead." *Colonist*, July 6, 1948.
"Drip! Drip! Drip!" *Colonist*, August 17, 1949.
"Early Study Set on Civic Centre." *Times*, October 29, 1957, p. 15.
"The Emergence of Modernism." www.maltwood.uvic.ca/Architecture/ma/design_story.
"Fire Trap." *Colonist*, January 17, 1908, p. 4.
"For Centenary: City Hall in 1962." *Colonist*, November 27, 1960.
Johnson, Dana H. "For Generations to Come: The Town Hall as a Symbol of Community" in Marc de Caraffe, et al., *Town*

Halls of Canada: A Collection of Essays on Pre-1930 Town Hall Buildings. Ottawa: National Historic Parks and Sites Branch, Environment Canada, Parks, 1987.

"Legal Bill Goes to City on 'Dead Issue' Project." *Colonist*, October 26, 1948.

"Main Problem Facing Town Planners Selection of Site for New City Hall." *Colonist*, February 9, 1947, p. 23.

"Mayor's Plan for New Civic Centre." *Colonist*, October 19, 1910, p. 11.

"Mayor's Scheme to Go Over to Next Council." *Colonist*, December 14, 1913, p 7.

Mills, Ted, Janet Wright. "Victoria City Hall." Historic Sites and Monuments Board of Canada Screening Paper, 1977, p. 293.

"Mr. Teague's Plans for the New Market Hall Accepted." *Colonist*, January 1, 1891, p. 5.

"Municipal Council: City Hall." *Colonist*, July 1, 1875, p. 3.

"Municipal Council: New City Hall." *Colonist*, August 30, 1877, p. 3.

"New $400,000 City Hall May Go Up on Blanshard." *Colonist*, February 1, 1947.

"New City Hall Building?" *Colonist*, June 10, 1947.

"New City Hall in Proposals Before Council." *Colonist*, January 7, 1946.

"Offer Received for City Hall Property," *Colonist*, December 1, 1946, p. 3.

"Premiated Design for the New City Hall, Victoria B.C." *Canadian Illustrated News* (Montreal), December 25, 1875, p. 413.

"Proposed Site for New City Hall on Pandora Avenue." *Colonist*, February 2, 1947, p. 3.

"Scurrah Will Hear Land Reserve Plan." *Colonist*, December 9, 1960.

"Site Next to Arena Choice for City Hall." *Colonist*, September 6, 1947, p. 1.

"Special Committee to Study City Hall Repairs." *Colonist*, February 16, 1947.

"Store — City Hall Plan Lacking in Dignity." *Times*, October 26, 1960.

"There'll Be Competition to Provide New City Hall." *Colonist*, October 14, 1960.

Thomas, Christopher, Kim Reinhardt. "*Victoria Moderna* (1945–1970): of Civic Myth and Difference in Modern Architecture." *Journal of the Society for the Study of Architecture in Canada*, Vol. 26, ns. 3, 4 (2001), p. 9.

"To Architects and Builders." *Colonist*, July 13, 1875, p. 2.

"Turns Down New City Hall Scheme." *Colonist*, October 26, 1910, p. 11.

"Vote Put Off Until June On City Hall-Hotel Site." *Colonist*, November 11, 1947, p. 3.

Chapter 2: Centennial Square

Bell, Jeff. "Nine-Storey Option Favoured for Tower." *Times Colonist*, October 16, 1998, p. B1.

_____. "Where You Live — Pounding for Arena a Hot Topic." *Times Colonist*, April 11, 1996, p. 1.

Minvielle, Paul. "Editorial — Will New Square Also Win an Award?" *Times Colonist*, July 11, 1996, p. 1.

Rowlands, Bob. "SO, WHATS NEW? — In the 60s, an Alderman Wanted to Use Whips On." *Times Colonist*, April 20, 1996, p. 1.

"Tower Would Not Fit with Centennial Square." *Times Colonist*, October 4, 1998, p. 13.

A Townscape Rediscovered, a film of the project, CVA.

Ward, Robin. "Revamped Victoria Square Is Refreshingly Modernist." *The Vancouver Sun*, July 27, 1996, p. D7.

Wilson, Carla. "Centennial Makeover on the Way — As the Square Gets a Bit Tattered." *Times Colonist*, November 20, 1995, p. 1.

_____. "Centennial Square Plans Draw Plenty of Comment." *Times Colonist*, October 1, 1998, p. D2.

Chapter 3: Cathedral Hill

"Early Study Set On Civic Centre." *Times*, October 29, 1957, p. 15.

"A Plan for the Capital Region of British Columbia." Capital Region Planning Board of British Columbia, 1959. CVA, CD 9.

"Report on a Civic Centre for Victoria." Capital Region Planning Board of British Columbia, 1957. CVA, CD 275.

Chapter 4: Legislative Precinct

British Columbia Legislative Assembly. *Official Report of the Debates of the Legislative Assembly*, 31 (April 12, 1976) at 837 (Mr. Barber). Online: Debates of the Legislative Assembly (Hansard). www.leg.bc.ca/hansard/31st1st/31p_01s_760412a.htm.

"Legislative Precinct Design Concept and Development Plan," Victoria: City of Victoria, 1981. CVA, CD 73.

"Notice to Architects." *Colonist*, June 17, 1892.

Paul Merrick Architects, "Victoria Accord: Legislative Precinct." Victoria: City of Victoria, 1994. CVA, CD 549, 550.

"A Precinct for Victoria: Recommendations for Development Policies." British Columbia, Department of Public Works, 1975. CVA, CD 74.

Segger, Martin. *The British Columbia Parliament Buildings.* Vancouver: Arcon, 1979.

Wilson, Carla. "James Bay Residents Fear Accord-Fuelled Traffic." *Times Colonist*, March 4, 1994, p. 1.

_____. "Municipal Elections." *Times Colonist*, November 16, 1993, p. 1.

_____. "Province: Accord Isn't Dead, It's Just Sleeping." *Times Colonist*, September 16, 1995, p. 1.

Chapter 5: Convention Centres

"At a Cost of $2.4 Million." *Times*, April 24, 1969.

Bradley, George C. "President's Report." *Greater Vancouver Tourist Association Annual Report 1956.*

"Can it Be Done Without Going to Voters?" *Colonist*, August 28, 1962.

Canadian Register of Historic Places. CPR Steamship Terminal. www.historicplaces.ca/en/rep-reg/place-lieu.aspx?id=3928&pid=0.

"Civic Leader Frank Carson Dies." *Colonist*, April 16, 2008, p. A3.

"Convention Centre: City Hall Files Latest Proposals." *Times*, March 14, 1968.

"Convention Centre Idea 'Unsound Unacceptable.'" *Colonist*, May 12, 1970.

"Convention Centre No Longer City Hall Conversation Piece: City-CPR Plan Dead as Dodo?" *Colonist*, June 8, 1969.

"Convention Centre Report." City of Victoria, 1967. CVA, CD 23.

"Convention Centre Urged For Reid, Cement Sites." *Times*, June 5, 1974.

"Convention Centre Vote Unanimous." *Colonist*, January 31, 1979.

"CPR Stresses Savings in Convention Plan." *Times*, April 24, 1969.

"Crystal Will Make Us … A Leading Convention City: 45 Years Later It's The Same Theme, Same Group." *Times*, November 2, 1968.

Dawson, Michael. *Selling British Columbia: Tourism and Consumer Culture, 1890–1970.* Vancouver: UBC Press, 2004.

"Decision on Centre Awaits City Vote: Wide Community Use Likely." *Colonist*, November 5, 1968.

"Frampton Scolded By Mayor." *Times*, July 28, 1967, p. 19.

Greene, Ronald. Personal communication.

Hancock Nicolson Brook, Michael Geller & Associates. "Wharf Street Waterfront: Issues & Design Brief." Prepared for the City of Victoria and the Provincial Capital Commission, 1989. CVA, CD 135.

"Heavy Community Use Indicated for Centre." *Colonist*, December 5, 1968.

"Is '79 Finally the Year for Convention Centre?" *Times*, December 21, 1978.

"'Mad Hatter' Idea Blasted." *Times*, April 3, 1973.

"Mayor, Two Aldermen Favor Vote on Centre." *Colonist*, November 26, 1968.

"Mayor Promises Vote on Convention Hall." *Times*, November 25, 1968.

"Mayor Supports Plan for Convention Ship." *Times*, October 22, 1969.

"Now it's Ottawa's Turn, Brewin Says." *Colonist*, November 29, 1985.

"Old Hydro Site: $7 Million Project Aired." *Colonist*, October 17, 1972.

"'Until CPR Withdraws': Convention Hall Still Alive, Says Mayor." *Colonist*, July 19, 1969.

"Uptown Site Better: Company Ready with Centre Plan." *Colonist*, March 14, 1969.

Victoria Conference Centre collection.

"Victoria Gives Green Light to $2,500,000 Hall Deal." *Colonist*, August 23, 1968, p. 17.

"Wharf Centre Given Nod By City Planners." *Colonist*, November 1, 1978.

"Wharf Street Main Contender: Convention Centre Guidelines Set." *Colonist*, April 24, 1968.

"Work Starts on Centre," *Times*, November 23, 1979.

Chapter 6: City Beautification

"$1 Million Parking Bylaw Before City Voters Dec. 11." *Times*, November 27, 1958, p. 1.

Barman, Jean. *The West Beyond the West: A History of British Columbia.* Toronto: University of Toronto Press, 1998.

British Columbia, "Papers in Connection with Crown Lands in British Columbia and the Title of the Hudson's Bay Company" in *Report of the Chief Commissioner of Lands and Works for the Province of British Columbia for the year ending 31st December, 1881,* Victoria: Government Printer, 1881. Bound in 1881–1890 Lands and Works Reports, British Columbia, Legislative Library, BC L128.

Capital Region Planning Board of British Columbia. "Urban Renewal Study for Victoria." 1961. CVA, CD 146.

"Council Asked to Speed Off-Street Parking Bylaw." *Times*, November 13, 1958, p. 17.

"Engineer Optimistic Over Parking Garage Prospects." *Times*, November 25, 1958, p. 19.

"First Three of Nine New Parking Projects." *Times*, November 5, 1958, p. 30.

"From This to That." *Times*, November 7, 1958, p. 17.

Lai, Chuen-yan David. *Chinatowns: Towns within Cities in Canada*. Vancouver: University of British Columbia Press, 1988.

"Less Traffic Congestion if Parking Plan Followed." *Times*, November 21, 1958, p. 32.

Mackie, Richard. "Joseph Despard Pemberton." Dictionary of Canadian Biography Online, www.biographi.ca/009004-119.01-e.php?&id_nbr=6361.

Madoff, Pamela. "Heed Planner's Vision for Square." *Times Colonist*, December 24, 2007, p. A11.

"Merchants Back Mall Plan." *Times*, November 12, 1958, p. 18.

"No Opposition from Key Land Owners: Engineer Optimistic Over Parking Garage Prospects." *Times*, November 25, 1958, p. 19.

Tobin, B. A. "Time to Give Nature a Hand: Song of Improvement: Bless the Mall, Bless the Mall." *Times*, November 7, 1958, p. 4.

A Townscape Rediscovered. Film of the creation of Centennial Square and the proposed pedestrian malls, 1966. CVA.

Chapter 7: Beacon Hill Park

"Beacon Hill Tree House Gets No Council Support." *Colonist*, June 1, 1966.

Dawson, Michael. *Selling British Columbia: Tourism and Consumer Culture, 1890–1970*. Vancouver: UBC Press, 2004.

"James Bay Land Use and Transportation Plan." City of Victoria, 1967. CVA, CD 68.

"Last Resort." *Colonist*, March 24, 1965.

"Mr. McGaffey's Suggestion …" *Colonist*, July 7, 1909, p. 4.

"Park Policy." *Colonist*, June 2, 1966.

"Parthenon Idea Is Endorsed: Local Architect to Draw Up Plan of Proposed Rustic Structure." *Colonist*, July 8, 1909, p. 7.

"Parthenon on Beacon Hill." *Colonist*, July 6, 1909, p.7.

"Propose Novel Indian Village: Would Preserve Ancient Arts in Ornamental Concrete for Posterity." *Colonist*, August 26, 1933, pp. 1–2.

"Proposed Replica of the Parthenon for Beacon Hill." *Colonist*, July 11, 1909, p. 1.

Ringuette, Janis. "Beacon Hill Park History," 1842–2009. www.beaconhillparkhistory.org.

"A Spirited Offer." *Colonist*, July 15, p. 4.

"Tree House Up in Air." *Colonist*, May 26, 1966, p. 19.

"Will Exhibit Timbers." *Colonist*, July 6, 1909, p. 6.

Chapter 8: The Gorge Waterway

"'Buy Private Land': Strong Fight Organized Against Park." *Times*, March 17, 1962, p. 21.

"A Castle on Gorge." *Colonist*, October 11, 1962.

"Clubhouse and Layout of Grounds at Gorge Athletic Park." *Times*, May 14, 1927, p. 1.

Day, John. "What of the Gorge?" *Colonist*, October 9, 1938, pp. 1, 3.

"Decide On Appeal in Water Case." *Colonist*, July 31, 1906, p. 2.

"Gorge Park: Edgelow Claims Support." *Times*, March 20, 1962, p. 13.

Forbes, Elizabeth. "Gorge Planning." *Times*, January 26, 1972, p. 28.

Madley, Lewis G. *James Bay Athletic Association: The First 100 Years*. Victoria: James Bay Centennial Book Committee, 1986.

"Medieval Amusement Park Wins Committee Backing." *Times*, March 14, 1962, pp. 1, 6.

Minaker, Dennis. *The Gorge of Summers Gone*. Victoria: Dennis Minaker, 1998.

"New Boathouse J.B.A.A. Will Erect at the Gorge." *Colonist*, May 15, 1927.

"Proposed Development of Gorge Park for Commercial Purposes." Capital Region Planning Board of BC, April 5, 1962. Saanich Archives, Clerk's file no. 5, Box 187.

"Rezoning Application Coming for 'Sherwood Forest' Acres." *Times*, March 20, 1962, p. 3.

Smith, Lloyd, Richard M. Faulks. *The Challenge of the Gorge*. Self-published, Victoria: 1965.

"Union of Victoria and Esquimalt Harbors by Means of a Canal." *Daily Victoria Gazette*, August 1858.

"Week at City Hall." *Colonist*, August 5, 1906, p. 5.

White, J. "Why Sacrifice a Park." *Times*, March 30, 1962. p. 4.

Wills, Archie "The Gorge May Regain Its Old Glory." *BC Magazine*, March 2, 1957.

Chapter 9: Universities

Di Castri, John A. "Administration Building, University of Victoria." University of Victoria, Special Collections, Di Castri Fonds, 4.17.

Hatley Castle. Canadian Register of Historic Places. *www.historic-places.ca/en/rep-reg/place-lieu.aspx?id=15749&pid=0*.
John Di Castri Fonds. University of Victoria, Special Collections.
"Long Range Development Plan, University of Victoria." Revised edition, Vancouver, B.C.: Erickson Massey Architects, 1969. University of Victoria Archives.
Erickson Massey Architects. "Long Range Development Plan, University of Victoria." Vancouver: Erickson/Massey, 1969. University of Victoria, Archives, LE3 V392L6 1969.
"Progress Report on Master Development Plan, University of Victoria." Vancouver, B.C.: Erickson Massey Architects, 1968. University of Victoria Archives.
Segger, Martin. Personal communication.
Smith, Peter L., Martin J. Segger. *The Development of the Gordon Head Campus*. Victoria: University of Victoria, 1988.

Chapter 10: The Art Gallery of Greater Victoria
"Art Is a Good Investment." *Times Colonist*, January 27, 2003, A6.
Bovey, Patricia. Personal communication.
British Columbia Legislative Assembly. *Official Report of the Debates of the Legislative Assembly*, 37 (November 4, 2002) at 4243 (J. Bray). Online: Debates of the Legislative Assembly (Hansard). *www.leg.bc.ca/hansard/37th3rd/h21104a.htm*.
Chamberlain, Adrian. "Art Gallery Eyes Funding for Satellite Venue." *Times Colonist*, January 14, 2003, p. C6.
_____. "Gallery Workers Forced to Cope with Cramped, Soggy Conditions." *Times Colonist*, March 15, 2001, p. D1.
_____. "Victoria Art Gallery Looks for Way Out of Funding Crunch." *Times Colonist*, July 8, 1981, p. 1.
Cleverley, Bill. "Activists Fight to Preserve Downtown Park: Cridge Park Rescue Group Focuses on Future of Lawn Bowling, Green Space." *Times Colonist*, August 23, 2008, p. A3.
_____. "Cridge Park, Lawn Bowling to Stay Green: In a 7–2 Vote, Victoria Councillors Side with Neighbours, Preserve Park Space." *Times Colonist*, January 9, 2009, p. A1.
_____. "Hopes Dampened for New Art Gallery." *Times Colonist*, March 2, 2001, p. C2.
Crean, Susan, ed., *Opposite Contraries: The Unknown Journals of Emily Carr and Other Writings*. Vancouver: Douglas & McIntyre, 2003.
Curtis, Malcolm. "Gallery, Condos Pitched for Motel Site." *Times Colonist*, April 8, 2004, p. A1.
Dakers, Diane. "Dream Team: It Doesn't Look Like Much. In Fact it's Not — It's a Parking Lot. But a Group of Local Entrepreneurs Hopes to Overcome Great Odds to Turn the Site, Known as the Y lot, Into a Top-Notch Arts Facility." *Times Colonist*, August 19, 2000, p. E5.
_____. "Hotel Project Threatens to End Proposed Arts Centre on Y-lot." *Times Colonist*, September 1, 2000, p. D5.
_____. "Royal Study Calls for More Study." *Times Colonist*, August 23, 2000, p. B7.
Gibson, Jim. "Art Gallery Turns Down Proposal for Satellite Location Downtown." *Times Colonist*, November 30, 2007, p. A1.
Harnett, Cindy. "Art Gallery Relocation Could Scuttle Multiplex Plan." *Times Colonist*, February 23, 2001, p. C1.
_____. "Delay Threatens Y-lot Hotel Project." *Times Colonist*, September 8, 2000, p. C2.
_____. "Downtown Hotel Nod Draws Cheers in the Arts." *Times Colonist*, October 6, 2000, p. D3.
_____. "Model to Help Clarify Y-lot Fate." *Times Colonist*, September 25, 2000, p. C1.
Heibel, Yule. "AGGV Downtown: Will it Fly?" *Focus* (Victoria), June 2007, p. 52.
Heiman, Carolyn. "Checkout Time for Crystal Court: Condo Tower Proposed for Site of Affordable Downtown Motel." *Times Colonist*, November 20, 2007, p. A3.
_____. "City Wants to Build on Lawn Bowling Green Park: Art Gallery, Kids' Museum, Offices Proposed for Downtown Block." *Times Colonist*, March 7, 2008, p. A1.
John Neilson & Associates, Architects and Planners. "Future Visions: Phase One: Strategic Planning for the New Art Gallery." August 1991.
Knox, Jack. "Domino Game Shakes City Core: Alan Lowe Sees 'Huge Opportunities' with the Library and Bay Among Key Pieces in Play." *Times Colonist*, November 30, 2002, p. A1.
Litwin, Grania. "Gallery Seeks Advice on Move to Core." *Times Colonist*, July 2, 2008, p. C10.
"Motel Gives Way to Condo Proposal." *Times Colonist*, November 20, 2007, p.A1.
Neilson, John, and Jane (Gehring). Interview.
Neilson, John. "Design Concept for the Proposed New Art Gallery of Greater Victoria." Collection of John Neilson, 1996.
Nesbitt, Carl. "Art Gallery Deserves a New, Larger Home." *Times Colonist*, April 8, 2001, p. A7.
Schleicher, Edythe Hembroff. *Emily Carr: The Untold Story*. Saanichton, BC: Hancock House Publishers, 1978.

"St. Ann Study." Second report, British Columbia Buildings Corporation, Paul Merrick Architects Limited, circa 1992.

Terrell, David. "Arts Centre Needed." *Times Colonist*, September 26, 2000, p. A13.

A Townscape Rediscovered, video recording, CVA.

Tupper, Jon. "Art Gallery Happy with Current Home." *Times Colonist*, March 18, 2011, p. A13.

Woodland, Robert G., Manager of Legislative Service, City of Victoria, to Don Kasianchuk, President of the Board, AGGV, April 15, 1998. AGGV Archives.

"Work Together for the Arts, Too." *Times Colonist*, September 18, 2000, p. A8.

"Working Together to Clean Up Victoria Harbour." Transport Canada press release, May 19, 2004. www.tc.gc.ca/eng/media-room/releases-pac-2004-04-p002e-3287.htm.

Chapter 11: Theatres

Barkerville, National Historic Site of Canada. www.historicplaces.ca/en/rep-reg/place-lieu.aspx?id=14309&pid=0.

Boyce, Conrad. Personal communication.

Gower, Chris. Personal communication.

Luxton, Donald and Associates, Jennifer Nell Barr. *Saanich Heritage Structures*. Victoria, B.C.: Corporation of the District of Saanich, circa 2008.

"A Personal Letter from Barry Morse." Saanich Archives.

"Prospectus Globe Playhouse and Bankside Elizabethan Village." Saanich Archives, vertical files, Shakespeare.

Williams, Terence. Personal communication.

Chapter 12: Victoria Harbour

Acres Western Limited. "Victoria Inner Harbour Renewal Scheme, Market Analysis and Economic Feasibility: A Preliminary Investigation." Vancouver: May 1968. CVA, CD 62.

Arthur Erickson Architects. "Inner Harbour Study." Prepared for the City of Victoria, 1973. CVA, CD 65.

"The Case of Sorby v. the City." *Colonist*, January 5, 1895, p. 5.

Clack, Roderick. "Victoria Inner Harbour Development Recommendations." Prepared for British Columbia Environment and Land Use Committee. Ottawa: National Capital "Downtown — Inner Harbour: Application to Prepare an Urban Renewal Scheme." City of Victoria, July 1967. CVA, CD 61.

Gower, Chris. Personal Communication.

"Inner Harbour Renewal." City of Victoria, April 1971. CVA, CD 64.

"Inner Harbour Study." City of Victoria, 1983. CVA CD 67.

Kalman, Harold. "Thomas Sorby." in Donald Luxton, ed. *Building the West: Early Architects of British Columbia*. Vancouver: Talonbooks, 2003, pp. 125–127.

"Legislative Assembly: Improving the Harbour." *Colonist*, May 18, 1859, p. 3.

"The Mud Flat." *Colonist*, August 11, 1863, p. 2.

"Outline of Harbour Scheme Mr. Sorby Has Been Sent to Ottawa to Explain." *Colonist*, June 4, 1899, p. 9.

Reksten, Terry. *The Fairmont Empress: The First Hundred Years*. Vancouver: Douglas & McIntyre, 1997; 2008.

"Ship Point Amphitheatre." de Hoog D'Ambrosio Rowe Architects, 1993. CVA, CD 329.

"Technical Manual Victoria 1994." Victoria Commonwealth Games Society, circa 1989. CVA, CD 21.

"To Improve James Bay Flats." *Colonist*, December 9, 1900, p. 12.

"Victoria: The Celebration City." City of Victoria, 1994 Commonwealth Games Bid Committee, 1987. CVA, CD 276.

"Victoria Canada 1994." Commonwealth Games Association of Canada, circa 1988. CVA, CD 19.

"Victoria Inner Harbour Renewal: Interim Report." City of Victoria Planning Department, November 1969. CVA CD 63.

"Victoria Viaduct: With Which it Is Proposed to Replace Rickety James Bay Bridge." *Colonist*, August 30, 1892, p. 3.

Williams, Terence. Personal communication.

Wilson, Carla. "Amphitheatre Proposition Dies Unofficial Death." *Times Colonist*, December 11, 1993, p. 1.

———. "City Touting Amphitheatre on Inner Harbor." *Times Colonist*, Nov 6, 1993, p. 1.

Chapter 13: Wharf Street Waterfront

"'Abused' Developer Reid Drops Inner Harbor Plan." *Times*, October 14, 1970.

"'After-Shave Bottle' Building Hit." *Times*, April 16, 1969.

"Aldermen Irked by Chamber Charges That Council Stalling Reid Project." *Times*, April 13, 1971.

"BC Freezes Inner Harbor Developments." *Victoria Express*, April 11, 1974.

"BC To Buy Site — Pollen: New Reid Move 'Just a Feeling.'" *Victoria Express*, April 20, 1974.

"Behind the Waterfront." *Times*, October 4, 1972.

British Columbia Legislative Assembly. *Official Report of the Debates of the Legislative Assembly*, 36 (May 31, 1999) at 12948 (Hon. M. Sihota). Online: Debates of the Legislative Assembly (Hansard) www.leg.bc.ca/hansard/36th3rd/h0531p9.htm.

"Centre Doomed?" *Victoria Express*, February 5, 1974.

"City Did Designing Says Reid." *Times*, January 5, 1971.

"City Kills Reid Centre Plan." *Times*, June 27, 1971.

Clack, Roderick. "Centre Will Spoil Victoria." *Colonist*, September 15, 1970.

"Convention Centre Urged for Reid, Cement Sites." *Times*, June 5, 1974.

Development Proposals, Reid Centre, CVA.

Dakers, Diane. "Fund-Raisers Set Stage for Arts Crusade." *Times Colonist*, May 3, 2001, p. A1.

"Deciding Our Character." *Times*, March 1971.

"Did Sandy Reid Unload Property?" *Victoria Express*, April 13, 1974.

Down, Susan. "Arts Community Awaits Word on Centre." *Times Colonist*, December 31, 2001, p. C4.

_____. "Victoria State of the Arts." *Times Colonist*, February 16, 2003, p. D1.

Downtown Victoria 2020. DV2020 Conference Group. http://dv2020.ca/about.html.

"Ferry Terminal of the Future May Be Established at this Parking Lot." *Times*, January 14, 1964.

Forbes, Elizabeth. "Harbour Doesn't Need a 'Highrise Jungle.'" *Times*, September 9, 1970.

"A Fresh Start." *Colonist*, July 28, 1971.

"Gastown-Type Plan 'Stymied' by Bylaw." *Times*, May 11, 1973.

"Good-Bye Mr. Reid." *Times*, November 12, 1971.

"Government Buys Reid Property for $1.7 Million." *The Victorian*, May 22, 1974.

"Haddock Opposes Reid Plan." *Times*, September 21, 1971.

Hancock Nicolson Brook, Michael Geller & Associates. "Wharf Street Waterfront: Issues & Design Brief." Victoria: City of Victoria and the Provincial Capital Commission, January 1989. CVA, CD 135.

"Harbor 'No' Vote by Haddock Riles Aldermen." *Colonist*, November 11, 1970.

"Harbor Referendum." *Colonist*, November 20, 1970.

"Harbour Developer Attacks Highrise." Clipping, June 22, 1971.

"Harbour Development Under Way." *Times Colonist*, April 15, 1988.

"Hearing on Reid Project Must Await Ottawa Ruling." September 11, 1970. CVA, Development Proposals, Reid Centre, clippings file.

Hotson Bakker and the Campbell Moore Group. "The Wharf Street Waterfront Project: Site Design Brief." Victoria: City of Victoria and the Provincial Capital Commission, January 1989. CVA, CD 139.

"Hydro Tanks Blocking Wharf Street Project." *Times*, March 20, 1970.

"Is The Reid Project the Start of an English Bay Jungle?" *Times*, August 20, 1971.

"It Takes 2 to Negotiate." *Times*, May 5, 1969.

"Jeers Greet Council Okay of Reid Plan." *Times*, September 10, 1971.

"Key Wharf Project Under Way by Summer." *Times*, January 7, 1970.

"Let Me Proceed or Buy Me Out." *Times*, October 27, 1971.

"A Man Sitting on Two Chairs Who Changes His Yea to Nay." *Times*, October 2, 1971.

"Mayor Opposes Poll on Harbor." *Times*, December 10, 1970.

"Mayor Won't Let Reid Interest Go." *Times*, November 26, 1970.

"Money Problems for Reid." August 23, 1971. CVA, Development Proposals, Reid Centre, clippings file.

"Monument to What?" *Times*, August 27, 1971.

"'Moral Obligation' Cements Reid Site: Province's Bungling Rapped." *Victoria Express*, April 6, 1974.

"New Plans Coming From Reid." *Colonist*, December 16, 1970.

"New Reid Centre Chapter Shrouded in Uncertainty." *Colonist*, November 23, 1972.

"Pollen, Reid Tangle." *Times*, September 20, 1970.

"Pollen Gets Support to Buy Out Developer." *Times*, September 1, 1970.

"Pollen Gives Up Fight Against Reid Center." *Free Press*, April 5, 1974.

"Progress of Reid Plan." *Times*, October 31, 1971.

"Province Out and Reid, Too." *Victoria Express*, April 4, 1974.

"Quick Rejection for Reid Plan." *Times*, November 6, 1971.

"The Real Issue — Need for a Master Plan." *Times*, September 9, 1971.

"Referendum Not Rejected on Reid Development." September 13, 1971. CVA, Development Proposals, Reid Centre, clippings file.

"Referendum Set On Purchase of Harbor Land." *Times*, November 30, 1970.

"Reid Centre." *Free Press*, March 2, 1974.

"Reid, Haddock Set Wharf Street Talks." *Colonist*, January 7, 1970.

"Reid Centre: Hotel Complex Target 1974." *Colonist*, February 3, 1973.

"Reid Centre: Willing to Go For People: Developer Cheered, Jeered." *Colonist*, February 26, 1971.

"The Reid Centre — Bye Bye Baby." *Times*, September 22, 1971.

"The Reid Centre — Time to Begin." *Times*, September 15, 1971.

"Reid Centre Finally Gets Green Light." *The Victorian*, April 5, 1974.

"Reid Centre Heading to a Secret Climax." *Victoria Express*, March 7, 1974.

"Reid Centre Not For Sale." Advertisement in the *Times*, November 24, 1972.

"Reid Centre Plans Finally Scrapped." *Colonist*, October 15, 1970.

"Reid Denies Sale." *Times*, November 23, 1972.

"Reid Going Ahead With 'Disaster.'" *The Victorian*, March 8, 1974.

"Reid Harbor Plan Ousted." *Colonist*, July 28, 1971.

"Reid Harbor Pullout Has City Wondering." *Times*, October 15, 1970.

"Reid Huddles With Haddock." *Colonist*, November 26, 1970.

"Reid Open To Any Alternate Schemes." *Colonist*, September 20, 1970.

"Reid Plan Looks Inevitable." *Times*, February 27, 1971.

"Reid Project Not Yet Dead." *Times*, September 18, 1970.

"Reid Property in Government Hands." *The Victorian*, April 12, 1974.

"Reid Property Now up for Grabs." *The Victorian*, February 15, 1974.

"Reid Revamps Harbor Plans." *Times*, December 16, 1970.

"Reid Selling to B.C." *Victoria Express*, April 25, 1974.

"Reid to Face Critics." *Colonist*, September 4, 1971.

"Reid Wants OK Now." *Times*, June 26, 1971.

"Savage Says Poll Favours Reid Plan." August 28, 1971. CVA, Development Proposals, Reid Centre, clippings file.

"Scrap Reid Development." *Times*, August 30, 1971.

"Shelve it Until Next Year." *Times*, November 17, 1971.

"Sierra Blasts Reid Verdict: City More Concerned with Moral Obligation to Developer Than to the Citizens of Victoria." *Victoria Express*, April 9, 1974.

"Stop Stalling Reid Plan Chamber tells Council." *Times*, March 27, 1971.

"Sudsy Tower Scorned." *Times*, April 16, 1969.

"Those Who 'Don't Love City' Against Him: Reid Would Risk Vote." *Times*, February 26, 1971.

"Three Mayoral Hopefuls Slam Reid for Harbour Scheme." *Times*, November 10, 1971.

"Through a High-Rise Darkly." *Times*, August 20, 1971.

"Timidity of 'Planning Pros' Hurts Every Citizen." *Times*, September 4, 1971.

"Victoria Landmark Torn Down." *Vancouver News Herald*, April 15, 1946.

"Victoria's Inner Harbour Today." *Times*, October 2, 1971. A Statement by Reid Properties Ltd.

Waller, F. M., city clerk, to the mayor, Courtney Haddock, enclosing a copy of a letter from Reid to the newspapers, September 2, 1970.

"Want Project To Go Ahead: Reid May Adopt Phased Plan." *Times*, March 17, 1970.

"Waterfront Progress 'Inn' Step." *Times*, November 5, 1973.

"Waterfront Site Sale Confirmed." *Victoria Express*, May 23, 1974.

"Way Clearing for Reid Project: Summer Wharf Start." *Colonist*, January 11, 1970.

Webster, Brian. "The Development and Planning of the Inner Harbour Area of Victoria, British Columbia." MA thesis, University of Victoria, 1984.

"Wharf Parley Shortly." *Colonist*, December 18, 1970.

"Wharf Street Development Running Out of Time." *Times*, August 19, 1970.

"Wharf Street Waterfront, Special Panel Review: Advice and Recommendations." Victoria: City of Victoria, May 9, 1989. CVA, CD 137.

"What Will Be Done — and When: Inner Harbor Future Not Yet Known." *Colonist*, January 4, 1972.

"Who's Been Stung by Harbor Freeze?" *Victoria Express*, April 13, 1974.

"Who's Taking Over Who?" *The Victorian*, April 8, 1974.

Wilson, Carla. "Amphitheatre Proposition Dies Unofficial Death." *Times Colonist*, December 11, 1993, p. 1.

———. "City Touting Amphitheatre on Inner Harbor." *Times Colonist*, November 6, 1993, p. 1.

"Word Soon on Second New Hotel: Nordal Group Modifies Big Waterfront Project." March 12, 1969. CVA, Development Proposals, Reid Centre, clippings file.

Chapter 14: Old Songhees Reserve

Arthur Erickson Architects. "Songhees: Development Theme Study." 1982. CVA, CD 103.

City of Victoria. "Songhees Policy Plan and Design Guidelines for the Songhees Area of Victoria West." 1991. CVA, CD 106.

Gibson, Jim. "JIM GIBSON." *Times Colonist*, February 20, 1994, p. 1.

Gidney, Norman. "Prophets Shape City Future." *Times Colonist*, January 9, 1995, p 1.

Keddie, Grant. *Songhees Pictorial: A History of the Songhees People as Seen by Outsiders, 1790–1912*. Victoria: Royal BC Museum, 2003.

Knox, Jack. "Songhees Design Rule Changes Get Airing." *Times Colonist*, December 30, 1994, p. 1.

Meissner, Dirk. "Railway Museum Derailed by Native Land Claim." *Times Colonist*, September 29, 1994. p. 1.

Moss, Paul. "Editorial." *Times Colonist*, February 12, 1994, p. 1.

Urbanics Consultants Ltd. "Songhees Festival Retail Market Study." 1984. CVA, CD 195.

Victoria Waterfront Enhancement Society. "Songhees Living Historic Village: A Redevelopment Concept for Victoria's South Songhees." 1984. CVA, CD 193.

Wilson, Carla. "City Puts Moratorium on Songhees After Backing Two Housing Projects." *Times Colonist*, February 20, 1994, p. 1.

———. "Council to Eyeball Proposal for Songhees Hotel-Condo." *Times Colonist*, July 29, 1994. p.1.

———. "Councillor Wants Hard Look at Songhees." *Times Colonist*, February 17, 1994, p. 1.

———. "Gingerbread Came from City Hall." *Times Colonist*, February 17, 1994, p. 1.

———. "Public Hearings Scheduled on Revisions for Songhees." *Times Colonist*, October 20, 1994, p. 1.

———. "Songhees." *Times Colonist*, February 9, 1994, p.1.

———. "Songhees vs. False Creek." *Times Colonist*, February 17, 1994, p. 1.

Chapter 15: Belleville Street Waterfront

Adams, John. "James Bay Neighbourhood History." Victoria Heritage Foundation, 2005. www.victoriaheritagefoundation.ca/jamesbayhistory.html.

"Belleville Terminal Plan a Good Start: Aging Ferry Facility Long Overdue for Renewal, but Loss of Coho Vehicle Service a Concern." *Times Colonist*, August 14, 2007, p.A10.

"Belleville Terminal's Future." *Times Colonist*, February 10, 2009, p. A10.

"Belleville Upgrade Deserves Funding." *Times Colonist*, January 2, 2008, p. A14.

British Columbia Legislative Assembly. *Official Report of the Debates of the Legislative Assembly*, 30 (April 21, 1975) at 1536 (Mr. H. A. Curtis). Online: Debates of the Legislative Assembly (Hansard). www.leg.bc.ca/hansard/30th5th/30p_05s_750421p.htm.

British Columbia Legislative Assembly. *Official Report of the Debates of the Legislative Assembly*, 31 (March 30, 1976) at 360 (Mr. Bawlf). Online: Debates of the Legislative Assembly (Hansard). www.leg.bc.ca/hansard/31st1st/31p_01s_760330z.htm.

Cleverley, Bill. "Economic Woes Sideline Landmark: Condominium Project Developers Withdraw Application for Rezoning." *Times Colonist*, October 17, 2008, p. B1.

———. "Landmark Could Spur Harbour Plan." *Times Colonist*, November 24, 2011, p. A1.

Curtis, Malcolm. "$1-Million Shot for Terminal Reno Plan." *Times Colonist*, December 13, 2004, p. B1.

———. "Decision Due by Month's End on Belleville Street Terminal." *Times Colonist*, November 6, 1993, p. 1.

———. "Election Call Put an End to Redevelopment Plan." *Times Colonist*, March 6, 2006, p. A2.

———. "Erickson Redraws Victoria Harbour." *Times Colonist*, September 25, 2004, p. A1.

———. "Gathering Explores Ways to Breathe Life into Waterfront." *Times Colonist*, November 20, 2003, p. C1.

———. "Province Orders Studies on Belleville Terminal Area." *Times Colonist*, March 29, 2006, p. B2.

———. "Terminal Illness." *Times Colonist*, March 6, 2006, p. A1.

Gidney, Norman. "Politicians Sail Across Harbor to Open $1.3-Million Terminal." *Times Colonist*, July 9, 1994, p. 1.

Hancock Nicolson Brook, Michael Geller & Associates. "Wharf Street Waterfront: Issues & Design Brief." Prepared for the City of Victoria and the Provincial Capital Commission, 1989. CVA, CD 135.

Harnett, Cindy. "Conference Centre to get Federal Boost: Ottawa Pledges to Help with Expansion and to Support Belleville Terminal Upgrade." *Times Colonist*, December 29, 2007, p. A1.

Heiman, Carolyn. "Coho Welcome Mat Would Cost $20 Million; Ferry Operation has Huge Parking Requirements, Blocks

View of the Harbour, Chairman Says." *Times Colonist*, August 14, 2007, p. A2.

_____. "Task Force Looks at Ways to Revamp Tired Terminal." *Times Colonist*, March 9, 2007, p. B3.

_____. "Victoria's $100-Million Harbourfront Dream: Blueprint Excludes Coho Vehicle Ferry." *Times Colonist*, August 14, 2007, p. A1.

_____. "Victoria's Gateway Deserves Attention from Governments." *Times Colonist*, August 30, 2007, p. B1.

Hume, Jim. "Decades-Old Harbour Plan Still Fresh: Wharf Street Proposal." *Times Colonist*, September 9, 2007, p. D9.

Persson, R. "Pyramid Threatens City's Heart." *Times Colonist*, October 15, 2008, p. A17.

Stonebanks, Roger. "Victoria Clipper Moving Home to New Inner Harbor Terminal." *Times Colonist*, June 29, 1994, p. 1.

"Time for a New Welcome Mat." *Times Colonist*, April 1, 2006, p. A12.

"Time for Vision for Waterfront." *Times Colonist*, November 24, 2011, p. A12.

Wilson, Carla. "CPR Building Could Live Again as Ferry Terminal: Harbour Authority's Vision Starts with Slate of Shops and Offices." *Times Colonist*, October 29, 2011, p. A1.

_____. "Province: Accord Isn't dead, It's Just Sleeping." *Times Colonist*, September 16, 1995, p. 1.

_____. "Work on Belleville Terminal Slated for March." *Times Colonist*, February 17, 1994, p. 1.

Chapter 16: Oak Bay and Sidney Harbours

Crane, McGregor & Boggs. "Are You Thinking of Building a House and Making a Home in Victoria?" Advertisement for Oak Harbor, *Colonist*, May 10, 1891, p. 6.

"Duly Incorporated: The Articles Filed of the Oak Bay Land & Improvement Company." *Colonist*, March 29, 1891, p. 5.

Gower, Chris. Interview.

Oak Bay, British Columbia: In Photographs. Victoria, B.C.: Corporation of the District of Oak Bay, 2006.

Chapter 17: CPR Terminal

"B.C.'s Deadly Ripple Rock Blown Up." *http://archives.cbc.ca/on_this_day/04/05*.

Grant, George Monro. *Ocean to Ocean, Sandford Fleming's Expedition Through Canada in 1872*. London: Sampson Low, Marston, Low, & Searle, 1873, chapter 12.

"History (of the CPR)." *www.vpl.ca/cpr/history.html*.

Lamb, W. Kaye. "Alfred Penderell Waddington." *Dictionary of Canadian Biography Online*.

MacLachlan, Donald F. *The Esquimalt & Nanaimo Railway, The Dunsmuir Years: 1884–1905*. Victoria: B. C. Railway Historical Association, circa 1986.

Ormsby, Margaret A. *British Columbia: A History*. Vancouver: Macmillan of Canada, 1958.

"Ripple Rock." *www.crmuseum.ca/exhibits/ripplerock.html*.

Tolmie, William Fraser to W. Armit, secretary HBC, December 19, 1870, BCA, MS-0557, William Fraser Tolmie Fonds, Box 2, Letterbook Typescript, pp. 116–125; what Tolmie referred to as Valdez Island is the two islands: Sonora and Quadra.

Chapter 18: Freeways

British Columbia Legislative Assembly. *Official Report of the Debates of the Legislative Assembly*, 35 (March 23, 1993) at 4744 (Hon. M. Sihota). Online: Debates of the Legislative Assembly (Hansard). *www.leg.bc.ca/hansard/35th2nd/h0323am.htm*.

"Overall Plan for the City of Victoria." Victoria, B.C.: Capital Region Planning Board of British Columbia, 1965. CVA, CD 120.

Traffic Research Corporation. "Capital Region of British Columbia Transportation Study." March 1965. CVA, CD 10.

"Transportation Report on the Present Status of Transportation Planning in the City of Victoria." City of Victoria, Traffic Engineering and Transportation Planning Department, 1970. CVA, CD 309.

Chapter 19: Gordon Head Memorial Air Park

"Administrative History of the Gordon Head Airport Proposal." Saanich Archives.

"AIRPARK WARNING RED." *Times*, December 17, 1948.

"Says Flower Men Ready to Acquire Their Own Planes." *Times*, April 23, 1946.

Smith, Peter L. and Martin Segger. *The Development of the Gordon Head Campus*. Victoria: University of Victoria, 1988.

White, Elwood and Peter L. Smith. *Wings Across the Water: Victoria's Flying Heritage 1871–1971*. Madeira Park, B.C.: Harbour Publishing, 2005.

Chapter 20: Gorge Inland Waterway

Downtown Victoria 2020. DV2020 Conference Group. *http://dv2020.ca/about.html*.

Gower, Chris. Interview.

"Union of Victoria and Esquimalt Harbors by Means of a Canal." *Daily Victoria Gazette*, August 1858.

Chapter 21: St. Ann's Academy
"The Academy Gardens." Proposal to the Provincial Capital Commission. The Academy Gardens Corporation, February 29, 1988.
Barr, Matthew John. "The Impact of Politics and Interest Groups on Heritage Development in Victoria, BC: The Case of St. Ann's Academy." MBA essay, University of Victoria, 1993.
British Columbia Legislative Assembly. *Official Report of the Debates of the Legislative Assembly*, 29 (February 17, 1970) at 447 (Mr. Tisdalle). Online: Debates of the Legislative Assembly (Hansard). www.leg.bc.ca/hansard/29th1st/29p_01s_700217p.htm.
British Columbia Legislative Assembly. *Official Report of the Debates of the Legislative Assembly*, 34 (June 7, 1988) at 4915 (Mr. Blencoe). Online: Debates of the Legislative Assembly (Hansard). www.leg.bc.ca/hansard/34th2nd/34p_02s_880607p.htm.
British Columbia Legislative Assembly. *Official Report of the Debates of the Legislative Assembly*, 36 (May 31, 1999) at 12948 (Hon. M. Sihota). Online: Debates of the Legislative Assembly (Hansard). www.leg.bc.ca/hansard/36th3rd/h0531p9.htm.
Daniel, Peter J. "St. Ann's Commitment." *Times Colonist*, August 14, 1991.
"Intriguing Options for Old St. Ann's." *Times Colonist*, June 25, 1988.
King, Michaeleen. Archivist, Sisters of St. Ann Archives (SSAA), Victoria. Interview.
Lavoie, Judith. "St. Ann's National Treasure." *Times Colonist*, August 25, 1988, p. B1.
Marie-Jean-de-Pathmos, Sister, S.S.A., *A History of the Sisters of St. Anne*. New York: Vantage Press, 1961.
Matters, John. "Jubilee and St. Joseph's Accepting Term Plan." *Colonist*, May 15, 1968, p. 36.
Raab, Sister Frieda. Interview.
Skelly, Richard. "St. Ann's Future Brightens." *Times Colonist*, 1991.
"St. Ann Study." First report, British Columbia Buildings Corporation, Paul Merrick Architects Limited, circa 1992.
"St. Ann Study." Second report, British Columbia Buildings Corporation, Paul Merrick Architects Limited, circa 1992.
"St. Ann's Academy Snow Job?" *Fairfield Observer*, September 1988.
"St. Ann's Decision Difficult to Judge Says Irked Brewin." *Times Colonist*, April 2, 1988.
"Three Conservation Reports on St. Ann's Academy." University of Victoria, March 1992.
"Tourist-Lure Plans for St. Ann's Thrown Out." *Times Colonist*, September 17, 1991, pp. A1, A2.
"Un-Convent-Ional Path for Staid St. Ann's." *Times Colonist*, April 4, 1988.

Chapter 22: Christ Church Cathedral
"Architect's Dream Come True." The Province, February 22, 1980.
Barlow, David. *An Architectural History of the Buildings of Christ Church Cathedral, Victoria BC*. Victoria: The Archives of the Anglican Diocese of British Columbia, July 2009.
"Christ Church Cathedral Competition, Victoria. B.C." *Canadian Architect and Builder* (London), May 20, 1892.
"A Competition was Instituted Last Year for Designs for Episcopal Cathedral to Be Erected in Victoria, B.C." *Canadian Architect and Builder*, Vol. 5, issue 6 (June 1892), p. 56.
"Fire Inquest." *Colonist*, October 9, 1869, p. 3.
"John Charles Malcolm Keith." Dictionary of Scottish Architects. www.scottisharchitects.org.uk/architect_full.php?id=201852.
"The New Cathedral." *Colonist*, October 20, 1872, p. 3.
Plumpton, Sara. "The Building of Christ Church Cathedral." Typescript in the possession of David Barlow.
"Proposed New Christ Church Cathedral." *Times*, February 10, 1926, p. 16.
"Synod Told $250,000 Needed for First Unit of Cathedral." *Times*, February 10, 1926, p. 9.
"Total Destruction of Christ Church Cathedral by Fire." *Colonist*, October 2, 1869, p. 3.
Ward, Robin and Donald Luxton. "J. C. M. Keith" in Donald Luxton, ed., *Building the West: The Early Architects of British Columbia*. Vancouver: Talonbooks, 2003.

Chapter 23: The Ukrainian Catholic Church of St. Nicholas the Wonderworker
Archive of the Ukrainian Catholic Church of St. Nicholas the Wonderworker.
Gidney, Norman. "Timber for God — Logs Dry in Coombs for City Church." *Colonist*, September 25, 1995, p. 1.
Hewryk, Titus D. *Masterpieces in Wood: Houses of Worship in Ukraine*. New York: Ukrainian Museum, 1987.

Kelty, Fr. Brian, Mary Kelty, and Alexander Teliszewsky. Interviews.
"Ukrainian Churches in Canada." www.ukrainianchurchesofcanada.ca.
Yekelchyk, Serhy. *Ukraine: Birth of a Modern Nation.* New York: Oxford University Press, 2007.

Chapter 24: Tourist Attractions
Barr, Jennifer Nell. "Jesse Milton Warren." In Donald Luxton, ed. *Building the West: The Early Architects of British Columbia.* Vancouver: Talonbooks, 2003, p. 398.
Dawson, Michael. *Selling British Columbia: Tourism and Consumer Culture, 1890–1970.* Vancouver: UBC Press, 2004.
"Mr. Hayward's Platform: Upbuilding and Development of Victoria Its First and Foremost Plank." *Colonist,* January 7, 1907, p. 7.
Reksten, Terry. *More English than the English: A Very Social History of Victoria.* Victoria: Orca Book Publishers, 1997.
"Skydeck Victoria Ltd." CVA, CRS 232.
"The Tourist Association: Bureau of Information Ready for Business: Formal Opening Tuesday." *Colonist,* April 6, 1902, p. 2.
Ward, Robin. *Victoria & Its Remarkable Buildings.* Madeira Park, BC: Harbour Publishing, 1996.

Chapter 25: Shopping Centres
"Builders' Bubbles: Whatever Became of Imaginaction? Bay Village? Belmont Towers? Etc." *Colonist,* June 24, 1970, p.21.
"Construction Is Scheduled to Start this Year." *Times,* March 18, 1968.
"Hat'n'Boots." www.roadsideamerica.com/story/2235.
"Overall Plan for Victoria." Capital Region Planning Board, 1965. CVA, CD120.
"Trading Post Plans Expanded, Construction to Start May 31." *Colonist,* April 22, 1954.
"Vast Super-Market Planned for Victoria: Project Will Cost $1,500,000." *Colonist,* April 8, 1954.

Chapter 26: Hotels
"Board of Trade Council: Proposed Location of the New Dominion Public Buildings." *Colonist,* April 12, 1893, p. 3.
"Canada Western: A Glimpse at the Plans of Victoria's New Hotel — Palace." *Colonist,* June 11, 1890, p. 5.
"Canada Western Hotel." *Colonist,* January 30, 1892, p. 5.
"Canada Western Hotel Co." *Colonist,* February 11, 1892, p. 5.
"Civic Business: Objections to the New Post Office Site." *Colonist,* April 25, 1893, p. 8.
"Empress Lawns to Become Park." *Times,* July 25, 1963, p. 17.
Mortimer, G. E. "Multi-Million Scheme For Empress Area?" *Colonist,* August 12, 1962, p. 17.
"The New Hotel." *Colonist,* January 15, 1891, p. 5.
"Proposed Canada Western Hotel." *Colonist,* January 1, 1892, p. 5.
Reksten, Terry. *The Fairmont Empress: The First 100 Years.* Vancouver: Douglas & McIntyre, 2008.
Shackleford, Ted. "City Ponders Swapping Pool for Lawn." *Colonist,* July 26, 1963, p. 13.
"Shop Arcade Project Studied for Empress." *Times,* November 2, 1962, p. 13.
Street, Ian. "New Regulations: CPR Plans in Peril." *Colonist,* November 1, 1962, p. 21.
Victoria Illustrated. Victoria, B.C.: Ellis & Co, Corporation of the City of Victoria, 1891.
"Victoria's Big Hotel: The Canada Western Hotel Scheme to be Adopted and Carried Out." *Colonist,* September 12, 1891, p. 2.
"Victoria's Empress Hotel May Get Changes." *The Province* (Vancouver, BC), August 11, 1962, p. 18.

Chapter 27: Business Buildings
Barber, Steve. Interview.
Charman, Eric. Personal communication.
Cleverley, Bill. "Dispute Over Admiral Inn Replacement: Local Residents Unhappy with Size and Setback of Proposed Project." *Times Colonist,* June 22, 2011, p. 1.
_____. "Economic Woes Sideline Landmark: Condominium Project Developers Withdraw Application for Rezoning." *Times Colonist,* October 17, 2008, p. 1.
Curtis, Malcolm. "Developer Shelves Plan for Yates Street Project." *Times Colonist,* December 13, 2005, p. B1.
_____. "Hole to Be Filled, Charman Vows." *Times Colonist,* October 30, 2004. p. B1.
_____. "'Landmark' Scheme Proposed for Charman Property on Yates." *Times Colonist,* February 18, 2005, p. B2.
_____. "Stress Takes Toll on Key Projects: A Building Boom's Unfinished Business." *Times Colonist,* June 18, 2006, p. D6.
_____. "Tribute to Mozart Wins Public Hearing: Windows Added to 12-Storey Building's Blank Wall." *Times Colonist,* May 27, 2005, p. B2.

Gallagher Tim. "The Art of Development: Victoria's Mozart Building Promises to Hit All the Right Notes." *British Columbia Report*, May 7, 1990.

Gower, Chris. Interview.

Lawson, J W. "Nice Building, Bad Name." *Times Colonist*, June 20, 2008, p. 13.

Litwin, Grania. "The Charman Life, Ever so Grand" *Times Colonist*, March 18, 2007, p. B4.

Mason, Chris. "Tribute to Mozart Gets Green Light: Charman Sees the Start of a Downtown Revival." *Times Colonist*, June 12, 2005, p. B1.

"Mozart House to Have Artistic Touch." *Times Colonist*, May 28, 2005, p. B4.

Persson, R G. "Pyramid Threatens City's Heart." *Times Colonist*, October 15, 2008, p. 17.

"Proposed Pyramid Too Tall for Site." *Times Colonist*, October 16, 2008. p. 5.

Rupp, Carl-Jan, HCMA. Interview.

"Seven-Storey Pagoda-Type Restaurant." *Times*, December 18, 1964, p. 21.

VanDyke, Pieta. "Heritage Buildings Worth Protecting." *Times Colonist*, August 23, 2008, p. 15.

"What Will Be Done — and When: Inner Harbor Future Not Yet Known." *Colonist*, January 4, 1972.

Wilson, Carla. "BUILDING PROMISES ... Tearing Down Dreams." *Times Colonist*, February 16, 1997, p. 1.

"Word Soon on Second New Hotel: Nordal Group Modifies Big Waterfront Project." March 12, 1969. CVA, Development Proposals, Reid Centre, clippings file.

Index

Aalders, Jim, 210
Academy Close, 36, 169, 173
Academy Gardens, 170–73
Amphitheatres, 82, 97–98, 108, 119, 121–22, 139
Anderson, David, MP, 89, 136
Anderson, Malcolm, 66
Art Gallery of Greater Victoria, 83–93, 174
Arthur Erickson Architects, 105–08, 110, 111, 124, 126, 132, 133
Associated Architects (Bill Lipsey, Stanley Cox, Philip Chang, John Gauld), 49, 50
Auditoriums, 19–20, 23, 33, 46, 84, 89, 173

B.G. Marr and Associates, 41, 43
Bankside Elizabethan Village, 94–97
Barber, Steve, 215
Barrett, David, 116–17, 133
Bastion Square, 15, 24, 56, 65, 86, 109, 114, 116, 117, 118, 122
Bawlf, Nick, 202–04
Bawlf, Sam, 117, 202–04
Bawlf Cooper Associates, 50
Bay Centre, 127, 202, 205
Bay Street, 45, 125, 129, 156

Bay Street Substation, 45, 46
Bay Village, 204
BC Hydro, 86, 89
Beacon Hill Park, 36, 37, 40, 61–66, 83, 156, 173, 195, 198–99
Begbie, Sir Matthew Baillie, 61, 63, 65
Belleville Street, 36, 43, 45–46, 49, 50, 68, 90–92, 109, 132–33, 136, 139, 141, 169, 198, 207, 219
Bennett, Bill, 46, 117
Bennett, W.A.C., 20
Benson, Tedd, 191
Bentall, G., 21
Bing Thom Architects, 122
Blair, John, 62
Blanshard Street, 16, 18, 30, 32, 36, 41, 53, 54, 58, 86, 90, 91, 153–54, 156, 180
Blencoe, Robin, 171–72
Blomfield, Sir Arthur, 177
Bovey, Patricia, 83, 89
Boyce, Conrad, 96–97
British Columbia Airways Limited, 158
British Columbia Buildings Corporation (BCBC), 170, 173
British Columbia Electric Railway Company, 142

Broad Street, 15, 18, 56–57, 125–26, 205
Broughton Street, 30–33, 53, 209, 210, 217
Buford's Trading Post, 200, 201
Burdett Avenue, 18, 30, 180, 205
Bute Inlet, 149–51

Caledonia Avenue, 186
Canada Western Hotel, 205, 206
Canadian Architect and Builder, 35
Canadian National Railway (CNR), 45, 154, 156
Canadian North Pacific Railway, 124
Canadian Pacific Lawn Bowling Club, 92
Canadian Pacific Railway (CPR), 41–43, 45, 46, 104, 105, 124, 132–33, 149–51, 206–08
Canadian Register of Historic Places, 46
Capital Improvement District Commission, 69
Capital Region District (CRD), 24–25
Capital Region Planning Board (CRPB), 20, 30, 33, 70, 202
Caroe, William Douglas, 180
Carpathian Mountains, Ukraine, 187, 191
Carr, Emily, 63, 83
Carson, Frank, 48, 50
Cathedral Hill, 18, 19, 20–21, 23, 30–33, 180
CEI Architecture, 210
Centennial Committee, 71
Centennial Park, 135
Centennial Square, 16, 23, 24–29, 40, 53, 56, 89–90, 152, 202
Chambers Street, 16, 53
Chapman, Cyril, 207
Charman, Eric, 43, 209, 214
Chinatown, 25, 57–58, 199
Christ Church Cathedral, 16, 30, 97, 131, 176–85
Christie, Thomas, 114–15
Church of Our Lord, 174
City Hall, 15–23, 24, 25, 30, 31, 33, 43–44, 53, 62, 116–17
City Lights, 97–98
City Parks Committee, 70
Civic Heritage Trust, 89
Clack, Roderick, 19, 20, 24, 53, 56, 115, 199
Commonwealth Games, 109, 111, 120, 121
Concerned Citizens Association, 173
Concert Properties, 90
Convention Centre Report, 40, 46

Cook Street, 16, 53, 133, 153, 186, 189
Cooper, Mel, 46
Cormier, Michael, 136
Courtney Street, 30, 180, 217
CPR Steamship Terminal, 38, 46, 133, 135, 139
Craigdarroch Castle, 20, 180
Cram & Ferguson, 183, 184
Cresswell, Henry R., 62
Cridge Park, 92, 174
Cridge Park Rescue Group, 93
Crystal Court Motel, 90
Crystal Garden, 40–43, 46, 50, 68, 92, 171, 207
Curtis, Hugh, 46, 50
Cuthbert, Herbert, 104, 195, 197

D'Ambrosio urbanism + architecture, 123, 139
Daniel, Peter, 171, 173
De Cosmos, Amor, 150
de Hoog D'Ambrosio Rowe, 25, 29, 121
Demers, Bishop Modeste, 167
Denford Construction Management, 209
Di Castri, John A., 74–77, 133–35
Dick & Wickson, 34, 35
Dominion Construction, 20–21
Douglas, James, 51, 67, 72, 101, 132, 161
Douglas Street, 18, 25, 26, 36, 40–43, 49, 50, 53–54, 86, 92, 154, 200, 201, 207
Downtown Victoria Community Alliance, 122–23, 161
Driard Hotel, 125, 205
Dunsmuir, James, 81

Edgelow, Geoffrey, 69
Elworthy, Harold, 44
Empress Hotel, 41–44, 46, 50, 68, 69, 105, 108–10, 114, 115, 117, 124, 130, 132, 139, 144, 187, 195, 198, 206, 207–08, 214, 215
Erickson, Arthur, 78, 105–07, 108–10, 124, 133–34, 136
Erickson Massey Architects, 78–81
Esquimalt, 40, 67, 69, 96, 149, 150, 151, 154, 161
Esquimalt & Nanaimo Railway (E&N), 124, 125, 154, 156, 163
Esquimalt Harbour, 69, 124, 161, 163–64
Evers & Keith, 177, 180

Index

Fairfield Road, 86
Faulks, Richard, 71
Ferrey, Benjamin, 176, 177
Ferrey, Edmund, 177
Finlayson Building (Hartwig Court), 114, 117, 118, 109
Finnerty Farm, 158
Finnerty Road, 160
Fisgard Street, 25, 40, 57
Fisherman's Wharf, 215
Fleming, Sandford, 149, 151
Fortin, Dean, 93
Frame, Bishop, 185
Freeways, 23, 65, 71, 151, 152–57, 202
Fuller, Thomas, 34

Gadsen, B.J., 18
George, Percy, 18
Gibson, William Wallace, 158
Globe Theatre (Playhouse), 94–97
Gordon Head, 73
Gordon Head Memorial Air Park, 73, 158–60
Gorge, 65, 67–72, 161
Gorge Inland Waterway, 161–64
Gorge Waterway, 67–72, 161
Gorge Waterway Improvement Association, 69
Government Street, 23, 25, 36, 38, 39, 40, 45, 53, 56–58, 65, 66, 86, 87, 90, 91, 102, 109, 200–02, 205, 207, 214, 217
Gowans, Alan, 12
Gower, Chris, 143, 161, 163, 215
Granville, 150, 151
Granville Island, 117, 125
Greene, Morris, 44

Haddock, Courtney J., 114, 116, 117
Hallmark Heritage Society, 12, 173
Hamilton, Austin, 90
Harbour Centre Mall, 217
Harris Green Park, 16
Hartwig Court, *see* Finlayson Building
Hat'n'Boots, 200, 201
Hatley Castle, 81
Hatley Park, 81, 164
Hayward, Charles, 104

Helmcken, Dr. John Sebastian, 63
Helmcken House, 167
Heritage Advisory Committee, 58
Heywood Avenue, 66, 169
Hill, Ken, 173
Hills, George, 176
Hillside Avenue, 153
Hnatyshyn, Right Honourable Ramon John, 192
Hockey, Bill, 171
Hooper & Watkins, 167, 168
Hotel Sidney, 144, 145
House of All Sorts, 63, 83
Hudson's Bay Company (HBC), 11, 51, 52, 53, 67, 101, 113, 114, 124, 150, 161, 195, 202
Hughes, Alan, 96
Hughes Condon Marler Architects, 139
Humboldt Street, 36, 40, 43, 50, 85, 86, 167, 168, 169, 171, 207
Humboldt Valley, 86
Hume, Jim, 43

Imaginaction, 44
Imperial Oil Station, 214–15
Inner Harbour, 34, 45, 69, 70, 108, 109, 111, 112, 116–17, 119–20, 124, 133, 134, 136, 141, 198–99, 215
Island Highway, 69, 153, 163

James, P.L., 46
James Bay, 39, 52, 53, 64, 65, 66, 83, 98, 101, 102, 103, 108, 109, 132, 133, 134, 139, 152, 154, 156, 175, 197, 204, 205
James Bay Athletic Association, 68
James K.M. Cheng Architects, 90
John A. Neilson & Associates, 50, 86
Johnson Retail Redevelopment, 202
Johnson Street, 16, 40, 53, 56, 101, 109, 124, 202, 204, 214
Johnson Street Bridge, 18, 109, 110, 116, 125, 132, 156, 202

Kaleidoscope Theatre, 98, 173
Keenleyside, Hugh, 96
Keith, J.C.M., 16, 97, 176, 177, 180, 181, 182, 184, 185
Kingston Street, 39

Landmark ("Pyramid"), 139, 141
Langley Street, 86, 217

Lansdowne Field, 158
Lansdowne Road, 73, 78, 158
Lantzius, John, 171
Laurel Point, 104, 108, 109, 119, 132, 133, 154, 155, 156
Laycock, Canon E.P., 185
Le Club Balisage, 214–15
Leeming, David, 197
Legislative Precinct, 34–39, 219
Lewis, Richard, 101
Light Rail Transit, 39, 156
Lime Bay, 125
Lord Chamberlain's Players, 94
Lowe, Alan, 25, 39, 90, 93, 209

Macdonald, Sir John A., 150
Mace Homes and Investment Ltd., 45
MacLaurin Building, 74, 75, 78
Maclure, Samuel, 187
Madoff, Mark, 173
Madoff, Pamela, 90
Malahat Building, 86, 109, 114, 117–18, 122
Mallandaine, Edward Jr., 34, 35
Maltwood Estate, 94, 96
Marathon Realty, 133–34
Maritime Museum, 15, 86, 118
Market Building (Hall), 16, 18
Market Square, 23, 202, 204
Marwell Construction Company, 20, 21
Massey, Geoffrey, 78
McGaffey, E., 63
McKenzie Avenue, 154, 159
McKinnon, Alan, 46
McKinnon, N.J.R., 44
McPherson Theatre, 24, 25, 53, 89
Memorial Arena, 18, 40, 90
Menzies Street, 36, 38, 39, 132, 133, 203, 204
Merrick, Paul, 46, 86, 117, 139, 173, 174
Michaud, Father Joseph, 167
Michigan Street, 36, 37, 38, 39, 64, 65, 66, 156
Morley, Alfred J., 16, 18
Morse, Barry, 94–95, 96, 97
Moss Street, 83, 90, 93, 229
Mount Tolmie, 199
Mozart House, 209–14

National Housing Act, 202
Neighbourhood Improvement Program, 58
Neilson, John A., 97
Nordal Hotel, 215, 217
Norris, Fred, 169

Oak Bay Land and Improvement Company (Limited), 142
Ocean Cement, 40, 114–18, 133
Ogden Point, 113, 141, 154
O'Grady, Terrence, 116
Olafson, Harold, 45
Old Songhees Reserve, 69, 109, 111, 119, 124–31, 132, 140, 156
Oosterink, J.W., 18, 19
Oswego Street, 139, 198
Overall Plan for Victoria, 1965, 23, 65, 152, 154, 202

Pacific Nations Place, 129, 130
Pacific Opera Victoria, 121–22
Pagoda Restaurant, 215
Pandora Avenue, 16, 18, 41, 53, 202
Parliament Buildings, 34–36, 50, 68, 102, 104, 105, 108, 109, 110, 116, 119, 120, 122, 124, 132, 198, 215, 219
Parthenon, 40, 62, 63, 195, 197
Patricia Bay, 152, 160
Patricia Bay Freeway, 153, 154
Paul Merrick Architects, 39, 122, 136, 173
Pemberton, Joseph Despard, 52–53
Pembroke Street, 87, 200, 201
Pendray, William J., 102, 132
Pendray House, 132, 141
Pendray Street, 132, 135, 139
Penwell Street, 50, 86
Performing Arts Centre, 85, 86, 89, 120, 121, 130, 219
Pioneer Square, 30, 31
P.L. James Building, 86
Police Buildings, 15, 24–25, 197
Pollen, Peter, 45, 48, 96, 114, 116, 133
Portage Inlet, 67, 69, 71, 72, 161–63
Provincial Capital Commission (PCC), 46, 86, 117, 133, 136, 170–71, 173
Provincial Government Buildings, *see* Parliament Buildings

Q Lot, 39
Quadra Street, 16, 18, 30, 53, 65, 152, 153, 180

R. Gordon Knight and Associates, 69
Rattenbury, Francis Mawson, 34, 36, 46, 68, 104, 105, 121, 132, 187
Reid, J.A. (Sandy), 114–18, 132
Reid Centre, 46–48, 86, 109–10, 116–18, 122, 123, 133
Richmond Street, 158
Richter, Werner, 191
Ringuette, Janis, 65
Ripple Rock, 150
Rock Bay, 52, 86–87, 89, 104
Rockland Avenue, 180, 198
Roger Hughes Architects, 25
Royal British Columbia Museum, 50, 132, 167, 171
Royal Oak Drive, 94, 152
Royal Roads Military College, 81
Royal Roads University, 81–82
Royal Theatre, 30, 31, 89

Saanich, 18, 69, 73, 151, 152, 157, 160, 168–69, 199
Saanich Road, 94, 152, 160
Schofield, Bishop, 180
Scurrah, Percy, 20
Seals, Buford J., 200–01
Selkirk Trestle, 67, 154
Selkirk Water, 69, 156
Sexton, Bishop, 184–85
Shelbourne Street, 158
Sherwood Forest Playland, 65, 70–71
Ship Point, 101, 108, 117, 119, 120–22, 133
Siddall, Robert W., 20, 21, 73, 74
Sidney, 104, 142–45, 152
Sierra Club, 66
Sihota, Moe, 156
Simcoe Street, 83, 203, 204
Simon Fraser University, 78
Skydeck, 198, 199
Smith, H. Badeley, 102
Smith, Lloyd, 71
Songhees Living Historic Village, 125, 127
Songhees Nation, 124, 127, 161
Songhees Reserve, 70, 124
Songhees Point, 108, 129, 154, 155
Sooke, 151, 152, 199
Sorby, Thomas, 34, 35, 103, 104
Space-Age Tree House, 65

Spencer, Sara, 83
St. Ann's Academy, 36, 84, 86, 167–75
St. Ann's Rescue Coalition, 173
St. Barnabas Anglican Church, 186, 191
St. Joseph's Hospital, 168–69
St. Lawrence Street, 66
St. Nicholas the Wonderworker, 186–92
Stephen, Hugh, 43, 45, 204
Stewart, Ian, 41
Store Street, 57, 86, 87, 202
Superior Street, 36, 38, 39, 102
Swartz Bay Ferry Terminal, 113, 152–54
Swift Street, 97, 191

Teague, John, 15, 17, 167
Teliszewsky, Alexander, 186, 187, 191
Thetis Cove, 69, 161, 163
Tiedemann, Hermann Otto, 176
Tillicum Road, 71
Tisdale, Milton, 65, 70
Tolmie, William Fraser, 150
Tolmie Avenue, 153, 154, 156
Toone, Alfred, 40
Tourism, 11, 12, 23, 53, 58, 62, 64, 65, 68, 69–70, 84, 93, 94–95, 104, 123, 124, 133, 141, 144, 156, 164, 171, 195–99, 219
Tourism Victoria, 133, 141
Tourist Association, 53, 62, 104, 195
Town and Country Mall, 156, 202
Trans-Canada Highway, 71, 72, 152, 154, 156, 157, 160, 164, 202
Transport Canada, 89, 114, 133
Turner, David, 39, 121

Ukrainian Churches, 186–92
University of Victoria, 24, 40, 73–81, 94, 96, 112, 120, 127, 130, 166, 173, 215
University Women's Club, 70
Upper Harbour, 69, 156, 199
Uptown, 156

Van Horne, William C., 150
Vancouver, British Columbia, 11, 19, 39, 46, 113, 117, 120, 142, 149, 150, 151, 195, 197, 205
Vancouver Island, 50, 51–52, 63, 133, 149–50, 151, 195, 197
Vancouver Island Coach Lines, 207

Vancouver Island Development League, 62
Vancouver Island Publicity Board (VIPB), 197
Verheyden, Charles, 167
Victoria Accord, 39, 86, 121, 173, 175
Victoria Advisory Planning Commission, 116
Victoria Chamber of Commerce, 46, 116, 117, 158, 199
Victoria College, 73, 160
Victoria Conference Centre, 40, 42, 50
Victoria Conservatory of Music, 173
Victoria Electric Railway & Lighting Company, 97
Victoria Heritage Foundation, 12
Victoria Waterfront Enhancement Society (VWES), 48, 125, 127
View Street, 16, 53, 54, 55, 56
Visitor Centre, 40, 124, 214

Waddington, Alfred, 149
Wade, John, 130, 185, 204, 217
Wade, Stockdill, Armour, and Blewitt, 204
wade williams corporation (later partnership), 98, 109, 134
Wagg & Hambleton, 50, 171
Warren, George, 197
Warren, Jesse M., 196, 197
West Saanich Road, 94, 152
Westbank Corporation, 90–92
Wharf Street, 34, 40, 41, 46, 86, 101, 108, 109, 110, 113–23, 124, 132, 219
Whittaker, Henry, 64
Wilkinson Road, 154, 157
Williams, David, R., 65
Williams D'Ambrosio Architects, 81, 209
Wilson, John, 63
Wilson, Richard Biggerstaff, 23, 24, 56, 73
Windsor Park, 142
Wright, Robert, 89–90, 121
Wright & Sanders, 53, 205
Wurster, Bernardi & Emmons (WBE), 73, 75, 78, 81

Y-Lot, 85, 86, 89–90, 121, 173, 175
Yates Street, 15, 16, 56, 125–26, 202, 209–14

OF RELATED INTEREST

Unbuilt Toronto
A History of the City That Might Have Been
by Mark Osbaldeston
9781550028355
$26.99

Unbuilt Toronto 2
More of the City That Might Have Been
by Mark Osbaldeston
9781554889754
$26.99

Unbuilt Toronto explores never-realized building projects in and around Toronto, from the city's founding to the twenty-first century. Delving into unfulfilled and largely forgotten visions for grand public buildings, landmark skyscrapers, highways, subways, and arts and recreation venues, it outlines such ambitious schemes as St. Alban's Cathedral, the Queen subway line and early city plans that would have resulted in a Paris-by-the-Lake

Readers may lament the loss of some projects (such as the Eaton's College Street tower), be thankful for the disappearance of others (a highway through the Annex), and marvel at the downtown that could have been (with underground roads and walkways in the sky).

Featuring 147 photographs and illustrations, many never before published, *Unbuilt Toronto* casts a different light on a city you thought you knew.

Quill & Quire cited *Unbuilt Toronto* as a book filled with "well-researched, often gripping tales of grand plans," while *Canadian Architect* said that it is "an impressively researched exploration of never-realized architectural and master-planning projects intended for the city." Now *Unbuilt Toronto 2* provides an all-new, fascinating return to the "Toronto that might have been."

Discover the scrapyard statue planned for University Avenue, the flapper-era "CN Tower" that led to a decade of litigation, and an electric light-rail transit network proposed in 1915. What would Toronto look like today if it had hosted the Olympics in 1996 or 1976? And what was the downtown expressway that Frederick Gardiner really wanted?

With over 150 photographs, maps, and illustrations, *Unbuilt Toronto 2* tracks the origins and fates of some of the city's most interesting planning, transit, and architectural "what-ifs."

Available at your favourite bookseller.

DUNDURN
www.dundurn.com

What did you think of this book? Visit www.dundurn.com for reviews, videos, updates, and more!

www.ingramcontent.com/pod-product-compliance
Lightning Source LLC
Chambersburg PA
CBHW082038230426
43670CB00016B/2696